Contents

CW01499419

Whose Game?

Rebecca Joyce Kissane *and*
Sarah Winslow

Whose Game?

Gender and Power in Fantasy Sports

TEMPLE UNIVERSITY PRESS
Philadelphia • Rome • Tokyo

TEMPLE UNIVERSITY PRESS
Philadelphia, Pennsylvania 19122
tupress.temple.edu

Library of Congress Cataloging-in-Publication Data

Names: Kissane, Rebecca Joyce, 1973- author. | Winslow, Sarah, 1978-
  author.
Title: Whose game? : gender and power in fantasy sports / Rebecca Joyce
  Kissane and Sarah Winslow.
Description: Philadelphia : Temple University Press, [2020] | Series:
  Sporting | Includes bibliographical references and index. | Summary:
  "This book uses surveys and interviews with participants in online
  fantasy sports leagues to interrogate what they get out of their play.
  Many men use fantasy sports to perform a sporting masculinity
  unavailable to them through traditional sports participation"—Provided
  by publisher.
Identifiers: LCCN 2019024290 (print) | LCCN 2019024291 (ebook) | ISBN
  9781439918869 (cloth) | ISBN 9781439918876 (paperback) | ISBN
  9781439918883 (pdf)
Subjects: LCSH: Fantasy sports—Sociological aspects. | Mass media and
  sports. | Masculinity in sports. | Communication and technology.
Classification: LCC GV1202.F35 K57 2020 (print) | LCC GV1202.F35 (ebook)
  | DDC 794.9—dc23
LC record available at https://lccn.loc.gov/2019024290
LC ebook record available at https://lccn.loc.gov/2019024291

Acknowledgments

*W*hose Game? benefited from the support and assistance of many people and organizations. First and foremost, we are indebted to those who completed our survey and spoke with us about their fantasy sports experiences; without them, this book wouldn't exist. We received research grants from Lafayette College's Academic Research Committee (ARC) and Clemson University's Department of Sociology, Anthropology, and Criminal Justice Summer Research and Teaching Innovation Program. We are also grateful for the indexing work of PJ Heim, which was also made possible through a grant from Lafayette College's ARC. Undergraduate research assistants, who were funded through Lafayette College's EXCEL Scholars Program, provided invaluable help with various aspects of the project. In particular, we would like to thank Chace Leuba, Emily Kim, and Alexis Grandy who read, edited, and commented on drafts of the manuscript and researched academic literatures for the book; Pricilla Compton and Cory Spera who helped to gather and open code message board data; and Dana Ahern and Laura Dallago who helped transcribe the interviews.

We have published earlier versions of some of the material in this book in *Gender & Society*, *Social Currents*, and *Sage Research Methods Cases*. As such, we are indebted to Joya Misra and Jo Reger, successive editors of *Gender & Society*; Toni Calasanti and Vincent Roscigno, editors of *Social Currents*; Ailsa Dann, associate editor of online library products at Sage Publishing; Carole Maurer, content development supervisor at Sage Publishing; and the anonymous reviewers for all of their insightful commentary and suggestions on each of these pieces. We would also like to thank the session organizers, discussants, fellow panelists, and audience members who offered valuable critique, feedback, and questions on our work at academic conferences (the American Sociological Association and Society for the Study of Social Problems annual meetings in particular) and our colleges (Clemson University Honors College's Thoughts Worth Thinking Series and Lafayette College's Faculty Research Forum and A&S Club Faculty Lecture Series).

Additionally, we are both greatly appreciative of our students, colleagues, and friends. Students and colleagues in the National Scholars Program and Honors College at Clemson provided Sarah with much support, encouragement, and patience; special thanks go to Bill Lasser and Danielle McFarquhar for graciously accommodating Sarah's many writing days. Rebecca is thankful for her anthropology and sociology department colleagues and students, and would like to especially acknowledge Caroline Lee, Dave Shulman, and Andrea Smith who read and commented on drafts, offered advice, and provided encouragement throughout this process. Moreover, we would like to thank Rick Eckstein and Rory McVeigh, mentors to Rebecca and Sarah, respectively, since their undergraduate days, who offered moral support, advice, encouragement, and guidance on the book project and articles related to it. We would also like to extend our thanks to Kathy Edin for her generous sharing of insights into the book writing process. And Rebecca is tremendously grateful for the Pub Quiz crew—Steve Belletto, Michael Feola, Wayne Fishman, Josh Sanborn, Helena Silverstein, Jen Talarico, Simon Tonev, and Andy Vinchur—who provided countless hours of support, diversion, laughter, camaraderie, guidance, and feedback on various aspects of the project.

We must also acknowledge all those at Temple University Press who helped navigate this project from draft chapters and prospectus to a published book. In particular, we would like to thank the anonymous reviewers, the editorial board, the copyeditors, the marketing department, and most importantly, Ryan Mulligan, our editor, for their assistance, advice, and thoughtful comments throughout this process. The book is stronger as a result of the anonymous reviewers and everyone at Temple, and we are indebted to them.

Finally, we are both grateful to our families, without whom this book would not have been possible. Even though they often did not quite understand what we were doing or why we were doing it, our parents, siblings, and Sarah's children (Reeve and Laken) supported us in countless ways. We cannot begin to express how thankful we are to our spouses, David and Stephanie, who helped us when they could, listened when we needed a sounding board, picked up the workload at home when we were buried in the book, entertained us and made us laugh, and loved and supported us throughout this process.

Whose Game?

1

Introduction

Fantasy Sports, Real Sports, and Gender

> I just went to the league site to see a beautiful, beautiful thing.
> TURF KINGS[1] BOUNCED FROM THE PLAYOFFS!! ON THE VERY
> LAST DAY!!!!! SUCK IT, TURF KINGS!!!!!!!!!!!!!!!!!!!!!!!!!!!!!!!!
> *sniffle*
> It's just so . . . goshdarn purdy

T his email, sent to the author from a friend in her fantasy football league while they both worked in their campus offices, encapsulates the fantasy sports experience for many participants. Fantasy sports provide a point of connection for participants who use new media to connect with others—often those they already know—when long workdays and/ or distance make face-to-face interactions challenging. These friends use a shared language of competitive banter to interact around a common interest, and the discussion that ensues subsequently moves on to other topics, including work commitments and an upcoming social event. As college professors, they spend large portions of the workday in front of their computers, which means they can check the status of their fantasy sports leagues and exchange nonwork emails rather invisibly and without consequence. Importantly, what distinguishes this exchange from many other sports-related interactions is that the author is a woman and her friend is a man. They play side by side in the same fantasy sport leagues and relate to each other through their participation, yet they often do so through characteristically masculine (but rather good-natured) banter. Here, the emphasis is on basking in the glory of making it to the playoffs—which both of them did—and celebrating the competitive, collective triumph over another team's falling short.

Whose Game? draws on a rich array of data that focus on the perspectives of individual everyday fantasy sports players to examine these and other dynamics in the U.S. context. In particular, the book positions fantasy sports as a new, more engaged and competitive fandom, which simultaneously represents, bolsters, and threatens traditional fandom. Gender is deeply institutionalized and embedded in interactions here, both among and between men and women, and fantasy sports reflect and reproduce dynamics of race and class inequality as well. Moreover, the gender project that fantasy sports represent bleeds into participants' leisure, work, and family lives, not only providing a means of sports engagement and connection to others but also producing discord, stress, unproductivity, and isolation. We situate these findings in literature and theory on gender, real and fantasy sports, fandom, and digital gaming. Ultimately, *Whose Game?* advances a narrative of privilege in which participants not only construct, perform, are held accountable to, and are impacted by gender but also, at times, contest and potentially transform it.

The Fundamentals of the Game

This book focuses on everyday players participating in traditional fantasy sports leagues in the United States. At least two elements of this require unpacking, as they shape what we do and do not argue about the contours of the fantasy sports experience. First, our focus is on *traditional fantasy sports leagues (TFS)*. These involve everyday individuals'—"managers" in fantasy sports language—building virtual sports teams that include real-life athletes who accumulate points based on their performance in actual sporting events (typically, professional men's football, baseball, ice hockey, or basketball games) over the course of a season. For example, an individual playing in a fantasy professional football league might roster the quarterback of the New Orleans Saints, the running back of the Arizona Cardinals, the kicker of the Baltimore Ravens, the defense of the Denver Broncos, and so on. That manager's team competes in a league, usually consisting of ten to fourteen teams, in which other managers have selected a different assortment of players for their roster slots.

While earlier, homegrown versions of fantasy sports may have existed, sociologist William Gamson created the first documented version, what he called the Baseball Seminar, in 1960.[2] Many elements of Gamson's game linger in modern fantasy sports, including a season-initiating draft prior to the opening day of the real sports[3] season during which managers build their fantasy sports rosters. Although in standard league drafts managers alternate selecting players for their teams, participants in the Baseball Seminar rostered their players through an auction-style draft. In auction drafts, managers alternate nominating an athlete for everyone in the league to bid on; each athlete is then rostered on the team with the highest bid. Baseball Seminar managers' $10 buy-in provided them with a $100,000 budget, reflecting another common element of auction-style draft formats—the amount managers have to spend on players dwindles as they fill their roster slots. Regardless of the draft format, fantasy sports managers may modify their squads as the season progresses by dropping underperforming or injured players, picking up available alternatives off the "waiver wire," and/or trading players with other league managers.

Gamson's league focused on baseball, but a group of individuals connected to the Oakland Raiders extended the format to football shortly after 1960. In both cases—and still true today—managers earn points based on their roster of players' performance in real games. In head-to-head leagues, the season proceeds with the fantasy teams in the league squaring off against one another in weekly matchups. The collective points each team gains through the performance of its athletes—a football team, for instance, may garner one point for every ten rushing yards, six points per touchdown, and so forth—determine who wins or loses the matchup. At the end of the season, those fantasy teams with the best records in the league compete against one another in the playoffs, the conclusion of which results in a winner being crowned.

In 1979, Daniel Okrent fashioned a different version of the game—the rotisserie format, particularly favored in fantasy baseball. Teams in rotisserie leagues accumulate points in various categories over the entire season rather than competing one-on-one with another team weekly. Each fantasy team then receives a ranking for each of the tracked categories (e.g., one could be first in the league for home runs, third in steals, sixth in pitching strikeouts, etc.), which determines the team's overall standing in the league. This system, rather than head-to-head records, identifies which teams make the playoffs and eventually win the league.

A 1981 *Inside Sports* article detailed Okrent's rotisserie league, and with that publicity, participation in fantasy sports began to increase. In 1990, *USA Today* estimated five hundred thousand people were playing. It is estimated that currently more than fifty-nine million people play in the United States and Canada alone—more than six times the number playing in just 2005.[4] Although football and baseball remain the most commonly played sports (first and second in popularity, respectively), auto racing, basketball, golf, ice hockey, and soccer also capture a portion of the fantasy sports market.[5]

Researchers and industry professionals attribute much of the explosion in fantasy sports participation to the rise of the Internet. In fantasy sports' early days, Gamson, Okrent, and others had to labor over box scores; compile and calculate scores by hand; research players by watching or listening to sporting events or reading newspapers or magazines; and draft or alter their teams in person or via direct communication with other league members. Now, the modern fantasy sports players who form the basis of our investigation accomplish all of this through the use of fantasy sports platforms and other online services and resources. Moreover, the rise of new and traditional media allows for a different, more immediate experience for current fantasy sports players. Instead of waiting for the newspaper to calculate their teams' performance, they can watch fantasy-relevant plays as they unfold on the RedZone channel or MLB.TV app and monitor their teams' performances in real time on fantasy sports platforms (e.g., ESPN's Fantasycast or Yahoo's StatTracker). Accordingly, the game is not only more pervasive but also more immediate and engaging than in its early years.

Recently, daily fantasy sports (DFS) have provided participants another outlet for their fantasy sports interests. In DFS, individuals create their rosters daily and typically compete for money against strangers online. These contrast with TFS leagues in which participants play over the course of an entire sports season with a set of other managers, all or a subset of whom they typically know.[6] Although DFS experienced a rapid rise in popularity after their introduction and remain newsworthy due to legal challenges, TFS are the most popular means of fantasy sports participation. Fantasy Sports Trade Association (FSTA)[7] data indicate that 84 percent of fantasy sports players participate in traditional leagues and 63 percent play exclusively in such leagues.[8] Because we are interested in the experiences of typical fantasy sports players and how they unfold over time as they interact with those inside and outside their leagues, *Whose Game?* necessarily focuses on those in TFS leagues. Unlike those who primarily or play only DFS, TFS participants' involvement is sustained over the course of a season (and often many years) and framed against the backdrop of existing social relationships. This book thus meets players where they are, which is largely in TFS leagues.

The second and related issue to keep in mind while reading this book is that we are interested in *everyday fantasy sports players* and what their attitudes, experiences, and interactions can tell us about fantasy sports and how they fit into larger landscapes of sports, fandom, virtual spaces, gender, and social inequality. These players represent a distinct and rather privileged group. The majority are men (71 percent), affluent (more than half have annual household incomes exceeding $75,000), and well educated (50 percent have a college degree or more).[9] They are typically non-Hispanic Whites (approximately 90 percent of players), with those identifying as racial or ethnic minorities rather evenly divided among Hispanic/Latinos, Asians/Pacific Islanders, and Blacks.[10]

Our book builds on a small but growing body of fantasy sports research, much of which explores general motives for playing, consumption, and fandom among participants and their time and financial investments (sometimes linking these investments to other variables such as motivation).[11] This research reveals that individuals are motivated to play for entertainment, social interaction, and competition, or as a diversion from other life matters.[12] Fantasy sports participants, already bigger sports fans on average than nonparticipants, increase and change their consumption of real sports as a result of their involvement in fantasy sports.[13] Accordingly, fantasy sports players invest sizable amounts of time and money into the hobby and sports more generally.[14]

For further context, this literature reveals not only similarities but also differences between TFS and DFS players. TFS and DFS players both play for entertainment and escape purposes, with entertainment being the predominant factor for all groups of players. Competition motivates those who play TFS (regardless of whether they also play DFS) more so than DFS-only players, while gambling and financial reasons motivate DFS players (including those who also play TFS) more so than TFS-only players.[15] DFS-only and DFS/TFS players consume more sports media than TFS-only players,[16] perhaps in part because DFS, by definition, requires frequent interaction with an electronic fantasy sports platform. There is also evidence that DFS is even more male dominated than TFS. In one study, 34 percent of the TFS players were female compared to only 8 percent of the DFS players.[17] It is likely, then, that the dynamics we uncover with regard to consumption and gender may be intensified in DFS, a less integrated context with more emphasis on media consumption and financial investment.

Previous research has focused on the meaning of these individual demographics and behaviors for the fantasy sports industry more broadly. Scholars typically frame players, their motivations, their experiences, and the presence or absence of particular groups in the hobby in terms of market share, potential revenue, and opportunities for expansion. It is perhaps not surprising that fantasy sports research has taken this industry-focused approach. Estimates are that fantasy sports are a $7.22 billion industry, with more than half of revenue arising from TFS.[18] Sunk costs for fantasy sports materials (e.g., draft kits, access to premium fantasy sports websites, magazines, etc.) alone average $46 annually for players eighteen years and older.[19] Moreover, while the industry has been keen to distance itself from gambling—the FSTA had an entire web page explaining why fantasy sport is not gambling[20]—the hobby typically involves a cash buy-in (70 percent of players pay a league fee),[21] with the most successful teams in TFS collecting the "winnings" at the end of the season.[22] Fantasy sports are big business—for professional sports leagues, those hosting fantasy sports leagues, sports media, and corporations that target or otherwise benefit from fantasy sports participants and their activities (e.g., as venues for draft parties).

While the industry is certainly the backdrop against which any analysis of the topic is set, this book is not centrally concerned with what players' experiences and interactions mean for the business of fantasy sports. Instead, we focus on how participants' involvement in fantasy sports is interwoven with their sense of themselves as sports fans and as men and women, how their experiences with fantasy sports reflect and sometimes challenge larger gender structures, and how fantasy sports affect their relationships with others. We advance an argument that fantasy sport is a space that presents opportunities for diverse and varied interactions between and among men and women while also perpetuating inequities that disadvantage those who are not men, White, and upper-middle class.

The Field of Play: Theory and Research

Sports are a masculine and male-dominated institution. The mean entry age for boys into organized sports in the United States is 6.8 years old, about four in ten boys play on a high school sports team,[23] and 61 percent of boys in grades three through twelve claim that sports are a big part of who they are.[24] Two-thirds of men describe themselves as sports fans,[25] and men represent a sizable proportion of those who watch sports on television—in most, but not all, cases comprising the majority.[26] To be sure, girls and women are not absent from this space. They have been participating in and consuming sports since sports' inception in the United States and have been increasingly doing so over the last several decades, in part because of the greater access to sports that the passage of Title IX in 1972 afforded girls and women.[27] Yet their numbers remain lower than those of boys and men. One-third of girls now play high school sports; the same proportion report that sports are a big part of who they are.[28] Despite notable exceptions such as the Williams sisters and the 2015 FIFA Women's World Cup, women athletes and women's sports receive far less coverage than men athletes and men's sports.[29] Fantasy sports, too, are heavily dominated by men, with nearly three-quarters of participants being men.[30]

But this book is concerned with much more than the numerical dominance of men in fantasy sports. Instead, we are interested in illuminating fantasy sports as a gendered arena dominated by men and masculinity and how aspects and consequences of play vary by sex and gender. By considering previous research on gendered bodies and interactions, masculinity and femininity, intersectionality, and gender in institutions including traditional sports, we advance an argument that fantasy sports offer unique opportunities for inclusion and transformation while simultaneously privileging well-educated White men and their experiences.

Understandings of male and female bodies as different or even diametrically opposed frame much public and pop psychology understanding of gender.[31] Such conceptions traditionally define gender as a configuration of practices and traits—they could be emotional, behavioral, or attitudinal—that in the United States have historically been envisioned as tied to the (presumed) binary, biological sex categories of male and female.[32] In reality, of course, there is overwhelming similarity in male and female bodies and more variety exists within sex categories than between them. Moreover, research demonstrates that biological explanations for behavior—for example, the argument that sex differences in hormones are responsible for men's aggression—are insufficient.[33] Yet beliefs abound that men and women are significantly and essentially different from each other and that naturally occurring sex differences provide the "basis for the social pattern of gender."[34]

While scholars have long debated and problematized the link between sex and gender,[35] sociologists hold that gender is a social, not biological, reality.[36] Although early thinking focused on a sex roles approach that tied gender to sex categories and produced a set of dichotomous behavioral and attitudinal expectations, contemporary research and theory moves beyond static definitions of gender as something that adheres solely to individuals. Instead, gender is dynamic, tied to social power, and embedded in social institutions and interactions. Such a framework allows us to see how gender is created and re-created in ways that not only reproduce but also challenge traditional patriarchal power, including in institutions such as sports.

To think about gender in this way is to consider not just how it is reflected in individual bodies or actions but also how it exists at the macro level. One way this manifests is in ideological notions of "ideal" masculinity (and femininity). Raewyn Connell theorized a hierarchal gender order built and sustained through cultural consent and institutional legitimation.[37] At the pinnacle of this gender order is hegemonic masculinity, a term used to refer to configurations of practice of dominance, variously defined as including heterosexuality, strength, and stoicism. Although not necessarily a statistical norm in terms of the behavior of actual men, hegemonic masculinity is ideologically and institutionally dominant. It may not be the way most men *are*, but it is an ideal type signifying the way most men *should be*. It is also fundamentally relational.[38] Hegemonic masculinity is defined as much by what it is as by what it dominates—subordinated and marginalized masculinities (e.g., gay masculinities) and all forms of femininity, including its counterpart emphasized femininity, which revolves around submission and compliance.

Critics argued that Connell's early work reified particular categories of masculinity and femininity, and researchers have since embraced the notion of multiple masculinities, documenting and theorizing a host of masculinities across various countries, localized settings, groups, and contexts.[39] Some, such as Tristan Bridges and C. J. Pascoe, have explored "hybrid masculinities," which blend hegemonic masculinity with some elements of marginalized or subordinated masculinities and even some components of femininity.[40] However, because they still claim legitimacy through their association with hegemonic masculinity, hybrid masculinities may obscure systems of power rather than challenge gender (or other forms of) inequality.

To examine gender at the macro level also involves highlighting its embeddedness in social institutions. Cultural ideologies about gender, masculinity, and femininity (as well as race, class, sexuality, etc.) shape how institutions are structured, including the norms and regulations that govern them. Some institutions, such as the military, involve clear requirements that differentiate men and women (e.g., registering for selective service) while others, such as workplaces, are structured in ways that emphasize gendered expectations (e.g., by offering family leave to women but not to men). In all cases, gendered ideals—often based on real or presumed biological, bodily distinctions—are built into the very workings of organizations, such that these institutions themselves become gendered. The result is that one group—either men or women—is seen as a better "fit" or more deserving of belonging.

While gender is embedded in ideology, culture, and social institutions, it is also constituted and reconstituted in social interaction.[41] Candace West and Don Zimmerman coined the term *doing gender* to refer to gender as a routine and active accomplishment of everyday interaction. Rather than a fixed identity naturally adhering to individuals, gender is a performance wherein we utilize various resources—clothing, behaviors, postures, social settings—to enact the expectations of the sex category within which we would like others to place us. Key to this process is accountability—individuals perform gender with an eye toward how others will interpret their actions, with the goal of being identified as appropriately gendered and thus avoiding negative assessment. While contexts, resources, and means for doing gender vary,[42] gender is omnipresent. We are always accountable to it. And insofar as men are accountable to the ideal of hegemonic masculinity, doing gender for men in a patriarchal society involves, according to sociologist Matthew Ezzell, "signifying dominance."[43] Importantly, gender is not just done in interactions between men and women. Indeed, the recognition of multiple masculinities encourages us to study interactions among men, as these are also key to the simultaneous re-creation of gender *and* dominance.

Interactions are, of course, embedded in social institutions that make available, facilitate, and allow certain gender performances and practices. Institutions and macrolevel structures also frame the way individuals interpret performances and those involved in them. Sociologist Cecilia Ridgeway argues that gender is a primary cultural frame through which we structure and interpret social life—our identities, experiences, interactions, and institutions.[44] Cultural assumptions about how men and women are and what men and women should do—what Ridgeway refers to as gender beliefs— shape our interpretations of ourselves and others and thus form the backdrop for social interaction. Gender beliefs shape interactions insofar as they prime us to expect certain attitudes and behaviors from others; for example, the expectation that women will be collaborative while men will be focused on their own success shapes our expectations of them in group settings. Ridgeway further argues that the effects of gender beliefs on how individual actors are assessed and held accountable to gender will be greater or lesser based on the presumed relevance of gender in a particular institutional setting. In contexts culturally typed as masculine, gender beliefs will strongly favor men, and according to Shelley Correll, Stephen Benard, and In Paik's research, women will be held to higher performance standards in order to gain legitimacy.[45]

Sports as an institution and interactional space are key for the production, reproduction, and maintenance of gender and the embodiment and perpetuation of hegemonic masculinity. In many ways, sports reify the importance of bodily distinctions, remaining one of the few domains in which we widely accept and valorize sex segregation.[46] Presumed physiological differences in male and female bodies legitimize this segregation, and, indeed, the media, the public, and sporting authorities have devoted much time and energy to reinforcing binary sex categories even in the face of biological evidence that defies the reality of such dichotomies.[47] The institutionalization of gender in this domain reinforces such sex segregation. The characteristics we associate with sports—competition, dominance, one-upmanship, toughness, physicality, and aggression—are also those that undergird the social construction of masculinity in U.S. society. It is therefore not surprising that dominant cultural ideologies repeatedly reinforce notions that girls and women must engage in athletics separately from boys and men because they just cannot compete with them—regardless of the type of sporting event (e.g., we even segregate board game competitions).

Furthermore, because sports are gendered masculine at the institutional level, athletics are particularly salient for the performance of manhood.[48] Sports for many boys and men act as requisite gender training, wherein they come to learn appropriate masculine traits and equate sports participation, knowledge, and success with masculinity.[49] Because of the physicality of (most) sports, men and boys deploy their bodies—and are held to expectations that they willingly do so—in the interest of performing appropriate masculinity. Sports effectively provide the resources for doing masculinity, a performance that is very much embodied. By being muscular, physically fit, and willing to use their own bodies as weapons, male athletes receive acclaim and display appropriate masculinity.[50] Conversely, coaches, teammates, or the public may label a male athlete who fails to sacrifice his body for the team and "tough it out" after an injury—who, in other words, does not perform hegemonic masculinity—a "girl" or a "wuss." Such an athlete risks being associated with femininity and subordinated masculinities. Boys, accordingly, learn through sports that they should be aggressive, be mentally and physically strong, and be dominant over others.

The stakes for men and boys are high here—the institutionalization of gender in sports means that gender beliefs are particularly salient. Men thus enter this arena against a backdrop of expectations that their performance will align with traditional masculinity. The gender frame is so powerful that men need not play sports or embody physical ideals to garner masculinity points. As Sara Crawley, Lara Foley, and Constance Shehan detail, men who have not achieved athletic success or currently cannot do so (e.g., due to age or injury) gain "vicarious masculinity" through athletic successes of other men (e.g., pro-athletes) and, for some, reliving their former athletic glory.[51] Although most men do not have the bodies or physical capabilities of male elite athletes, all men gain vicarious masculinity by their existence, as maleness in general (and the male body) becomes associated with athletic prowess. Thus, the nonathletic can achieve vicarious masculinity and "bank on positive accountability to masculinity" "simply by having a male body and knowing all the pertinent sports statistics."[52] Similar dynamics play out in digital gaming. Although they vary significantly in the physicality involved in them and men and women participate with and against each other in virtual domains, digital game culture constructs masculinity and provides a setting whereby men police, perform, and accomplish a manhood revolving around competitiveness, brazen talk, rationality, control, and heterosexuality.[53]

Importantly, sports provide an institutional framework against which close relationships between men—which might otherwise challenge the performance of traditional masculinity—can flourish. [54] Constructions of hegemonic masculinity in the United States are based on heterosexuality, and this intersection of gender and sexuality makes intimate connections among men difficult.[55] Sports, constructed as a masculine domain, can provide "a means of communication and connection" for men[56]—a safe vehicle through which they can both embody hegemonic masculine practices *and* establish close bonds with one another, even if these bonds are contingent on their athletic performance and/or sports literacy.[57] Thus, some boys (consciously or not) are drawn to sports to become part of an "instant family," to connect to their fathers, brothers, and other men in the community, regardless of whether these goals are fully realized.[58] Sports are a place where intimate connections to other men and the performance of masculinity are mutually constitutive rather than conflicting.

Girls and women, whose numerical representation has increased dramatically since the passage of Title IX, nonetheless participate in sports against a backdrop that associates sports with men and masculinity. Traditionally framed as lacking the physical aptitude, knowledge, investment, and/or interest to belong and succeed, institutional structures and individual men construct "women as outsiders."[59] Female athletes are physically set apart from male athletes by sex segregation and conceptually set apart from them through labeling and patronizing behaviors that serve to mark them as *women* athletes rather than just athletes.[60] When participating in sports, whether as athletes or coaches, women find their competency questioned, their access and roles limited, and their successes dismissed. They are also not taken seriously, are constantly surveilled, and are made to feel unwelcome in certain sporting arenas.[61] And the media often render women in sports invisible or sexualize and trivialize them.[62] Women of color, in particular, face marginalization both in their sports and in media coverage of them.[63] Digital games and gaming cultures similarly marginalize or erase women. They are frequently absent as characters in games, and even when portrayed or available, they are often sexualized, presented as the objects of violence, and/or relegated to subservient and inactive roles.[64] Women in gaming find they must abide by gender rules, filling stereotyped gender roles both within and outside the games, and face verbal harassment.[65] Gamergate[66] highlights the extreme, wherein women not only faced symbolic violence but the real threat of physical violence in response to men's fears and anger regarding women's perceived intrusion into a sphere that was until recently deemed men's own.[67]

Even as sports consumers, "women are 'Others' because what it means to be a legitimate sports fan . . . is to be a man, particularly one who conforms to the hegemonic masculinized aspects of sporting cultures."[68] As fans, women are marginalized partly because constructions of femininity are incompatible with the fervent, aggressive, and often misogynistic and homophobic chants integral to fandom.[69] Women's assumed inferiority in sports-related knowledge further weakens their authenticity as fans, as do presumptions that sexual attraction to players or desires to build and maintain relationships with men motivate their fandom.[70] Notably, even when men promote women's sports spectatorship, they do not see women as authorities or "equals in dialogue and participation."[71] As such, even highly experienced and knowledgeable women report men marginalize and exclude them from sports conversations.[72]

Gender beliefs thus frame women as inferior, and institutional structures support and reproduce such cultural beliefs in myriad ways. Increasingly, though, girls and women assert themselves and seek inclusion in athletic contexts, challenging gender stereotypes in varied and even contradictory ways. Some women push against notions that sports are reserved for men by positioning themselves as just like men and suggesting that those with male bodies must not always or only perform masculinity.[73] Others challenge the stereotype that women are less skilled by making it obvious they are women while proving their worthiness in their sport—they do femininity while also doing athleticism.[74] Some women contest the notion that athletic bodies are necessarily male bodies by posing nude or scantily clad to show off their muscular, performance-based bodies.[75] Still others, such as women who participate in roller derby, play with gender while competing in their sports in ways that both highlight and subvert it, simultaneously exhibiting and embracing masculine (e.g., using their bodies as weapons, being aggressive, wearing injuries with pride) and feminine qualities (e.g., wearing sexually provocative uniforms).[76] In these cases, women call into question the binary on which the social construction of masculinity and femininity rests. They do gender in ways that blend elements of femininity and masculinity, effectively challenging how gender is institutionalized in sports. In the process, they potentially gain power—individually and collectively—and make changes to this highly masculinized space.[77] As such, some have argued that sports today are increasingly a "contested terrain" in which the contours of gender in bodies, interactions, and institutions may be pushed, redefined, and confused.[78]

The central question in this book is how these gendered structures and processes play out in fantasy sports and their consequences. As inequality scholars, we have marveled at the dynamics of gender as we played and observed fantasy sports and were disappointed to find little sociological research on the topic. Existing work largely operates from a sports management and marketing perspective and typically considers gender only in terms of statistical differences in reported behavior and attitudes between men and women. Brody Ruihley and Andrew Billings, for example, find that, among players, men are more invested in fantasy sports than women, as they average more years of involvement, participate in more fantasy leagues per year, and report spending more time per week on fantasy sports than women do.[79] Men who play fantasy sports also score higher in their reported sport fanship (e.g., identifying as a "big fan" or finding it important for one's favorite team to win) and their perceived fantasy sports–related knowledge than do women who play.[80] Conversely, Ruihley and Billings find more similarity than difference between men and women in motivations to play fantasy sports, with only two of seven motivations being different for men and women who participate in the hobby (men more frequently reported playing fantasy sports for "enjoyment" and to "pass time").[81]

In one of the few pieces that focuses on gendered dynamics and processes, Nickolas Davis and Margaret Carlisle Duncan find that men "use fantasy sport participation as a means of reaffirming their masculinity" much like they use real sports.[82] The authors argue that fantasy sports provide a way for men to feel in control, experience power and dominance over others, demonstrate their sports knowledge, and bond with one another in a space that is relatively free from the intrusion of women.[83] Likewise, Luke Howie and Perri Campbell in their study of a ten-team fantasy National Basketball Association (NBA) league in Australia report that such leagues are "masculinized 'fantasyscapes' where 'manly' men toy with the limits of heteronormative realities" through their use of team names, engage in "typical locker room banter" and trash-talking in online message boards, and bond and socialize with other men.[84]

Our work builds on this by exploring the ideological and institutional constructions of gender in fantasy sports, the configurations of gender practice embedded in them, and the consequences of the sexed and gendered aspects of the hobby. *Whose Game?* shows how gender manifests in a context that is less physical than real athletic participation but more active than fandom. Here, instead of just spectating and rooting for results as a traditional fan, one is active in guiding the outcome of a virtually played competition. Fantasy sport is also a space in which there is no formal sex or gender segregation. Yet the combatants overwhelmingly make use of male athletes competing in sports occupying the "institutional center" (i.e., football, baseball, and basketball), those which scholars argue are especially important for the perpetuation of hegemonic masculinity and from which women have been largely excluded.[85]

We also tease out how race and class are implicated in this space. Kimberlé Crenshaw first introduced the concept of "intersectionality" to feminist theory in the late 1980s.[86] She argues that a "single-axis analysis," such as focusing on gender alone, fails to capture and erases the actual experience of individuals who are "multiply-burdened," such as Black women.[87] Instead, she and others, such as Patricia Hill Collins, call for intersectional analyses that unlock how patterns of domination are interconnected with concurrent identities (e.g., race, gender, class, and ethnicity) and translate to "intersecting oppressions."

More concretely, what intersectional scholars push us to understand is that women and men (or Blacks and Whites, the affluent and the poor, etc.) are not homogeneous groups who experience the same systems of power in the same ways. Intersectionality recognizes that gender operates differently when and because it is interconnected with other forms of inequality. For example, research on media imagery indicates dominance for White men frequently looks like leadership while for Black men it looks like aggression or danger.[88] Moreover, the aforementioned expansions of hegemonic masculinity available in hybrid masculinities are largely limited to young, White, heterosexual men—precisely those men whose power allows them to embrace nonhegemonic ideals.[89]

Intersectional analyses are critical yet largely absent in research on fantasy sports. Some research has examined sex and gender, although, again, this has largely focused on reporting statistical differences between men and women with limited exploration of gendered processes. There is even less attention to race in fantasy sports research and that which exists frequently approaches the topic of Blacks' nonparticipation from a sports marketing perspective. In one of the few existing investigations, Joris Drayer and Brendan Dwyer found that the dominant reason for nonparticipation among Blacks is their lack of awareness and understanding of fantasy sports.[90] Those with an understanding of fantasy sports reported they did not use the Internet or computers for leisure and interpreted fantasy sports as a waste of time, partly because they are not "real." Some also considered the monetary aspects of the game as a reason not to get involved, as they associated this negatively with gambling. This work frames Black men's nonparticipation in fantasy sports through the lens of a loss of market share and pays little attention to whether and how race may interact with class, gender, or other dimensions of inequality.

While we focus on fantasy sports as a gendered arena, what we do more broadly is describe and unpack a case of intersecting privilege. Recall the demographics of fantasy sports players in the United States, demographics that our sample of players mirror—White, class-privileged men (and to a lesser extent women). These individuals are typically professionally employed and have the resources, time, and workplace environments allowing them to play. Being geographically mobile and having busy work and family lives, these people also may be a group with a particular need to find ways to connect with others, something that fantasy sports, as we will document, afford. Thus, it may be little wonder that not just men but particularly White, middle- and upper-class men dominate the space. Yet we argue that it is not just that these men are numerically dominant and enact dominance here but that fantasy sports as an institution privileges attributes—statistical acumen, time for leisure pursuits, competition, power, dominance—that reflect their particular constellation of race, class, and gender.

The Game Plan

We use a mixed and multimethod approach to make our case regarding the gender and general dynamics of fantasy sports, employing quantitative and qualitative data obtained via an online survey and in-depth interviews with fantasy sports players, ethnographic observations at an annual fantasy sports trade conference, and posts on fantasy sports–related message boards and forums. The bulk of this book's findings emerge from analyses of survey and interview data. The online survey included 396 respondents who self-identify as having played fantasy sports and an additional 57 who answered the survey but indicated never playing. We also analyze forty-seven in-depth interviews with fantasy sports players to gain more detailed information on their views and experiences. More than two-thirds of our players are men, about 95 percent are White, and the majority are upper or middle class (e.g., more than three-quarters have at least a bachelor's degree). More than two-thirds were between twenty-five and forty-four years old at the time of the survey or interview, and the majority were married (see the appendix for additional details).

We supplement these data with information gleaned from our analyses of posts on public, online fantasy sports chat forums and message boards and from ethnographic observations at an FSTA summer conference. The former allows us to examine what sorts of things fantasy sports enthusiasts discuss with one another in the anonymized context of message and chat forums. The latter provides us with information on the big business side of the industry and how industry insiders and power brokers think about participants and frame issues in fantasy sports.

With the exception of our observations during the FSTA summer conference, our data focus on everyday fantasy sports players who participate in traditional fantasy sports leagues. Our sample of players mirror typical TFS participants in the United States—White, relatively affluent, well-educated men and women. They also participate in the most popular fantasy sports in this country, all of which employ only male professional athletes—fantasy (National Football League) football, (Major League Baseball) baseball, (NBA) basketball, and (National Hockey League) ice hockey. Because of this, we provide an account of fantasy sports from their perspective and experiences and not from that of other types of fantasy sports players, such as high-stakes TFS players, DFS participants, those playing more fringe fantasy sports (e.g., Women's National Basketball Association or soccer), or those who are intersectionally oppressed (e.g., Black women). Thus, this book addresses a domain of intersecting advantage, making privilege visible and contributing to the development of a "sociology of the superordinate"[91] as we detail the gender dynamics of a rather ordinary space—fantasy sports—for the typical player.

In what follows, *Whose Game?* demonstrates that fantasy sports are more than just an inconsequential leisure activity. They affect how we consume sports, our rooting interests, and the nature of our engagement with them. They cultivate, solidify, and complicate social networks, workspaces, and families. Moreover, we argue that fantasy sports are a domain culturally typed masculine in which gender beliefs are reflected and reinforced and through which men and boys signal masculine selves—with both negative and positive ramifications for relationships. Importantly, the space is not just gendered but also classed and racialized. Particular types of men—White, professional, highly educated—dominate the space, and the controlling form of masculinity reflects and reinforces their privilege. Yet we also see opportunities for transformation of the gender order. Gender and women's subordination are contested. A version of masculinity that is broader than traditional hegemonic masculinity is enacted, and men connect with one another in ways that both reinforce and challenge gender beliefs. Women also employ the hobby, sometimes strategically, to make inroads with men and gain legitimacy in spaces dominated by men and masculinity.

The book begins (in Chapter 2) by explaining how fantasy sports offer a complex and contested version of sports fandom—one that blends elements of traditional fandom with a new, more individualized and less passive form that gives its participants some modicum of control and accomplishment but that also alters rooting interests and sports consumption. We explain how these processes and related ones, such as roster decisions, are deeply gendered, offering readers their first insights into fantasy sports as a masculine domain and gender project.

Chapter 3 concentrates on how fantasy sports allow men to perform and accomplish what we term *jock statsculinity*. Jock statsculinity combines elements of the masculinity that emerged alongside organized sports in the late nineteenth and early twentieth centuries in the United States—a masculinity akin to the hegemonic ideal type that centers on one-upmanship, competition, athleticism, control, and aggression—with a more nerdy and boyish masculinity that involves escaping responsibilities and being strategic, tech savvy, rational, and adept with statistics. This chapter demonstrates how fantasy sports provide aging, socioeconomically powerful White men the ability to "stay in the game" and do manhood in ways that overlap but diverge from that of both traditional sports and digital gaming.

Chapter 4 centers on issues related to women's participation (or lack thereof) in fantasy sports. We argue that structural barriers and prevailing gender beliefs favoring men and disadvantaging women in sports and society more generally limit women's full inclusion. Those women who play fantasy sports often feel their gender acutely and, at times, confront men who seem hell-bent on pushing against women's intrusion. Men question women's competency and motives, discount their successes, and engage in behaviors that create hostile and intimidating environments. Yet women exercise agency in this space as well, reproducing and resisting traditional conceptualizations of masculinity and femininity, often simultaneously.

Chapter 5 elucidates how the White, geographically mobile, professional men and women who play fantasy sports use their involvement to connect to others and how men and women do so to differing ends, to differing degrees, and in differing ways. We demonstrate how both men and women direct their efforts at bonding and networking through their fantasy sports participation *toward men*. Women, however, seem to use the hobby more strategically than men do. Men rely more heavily on fantasy sports as *the* means to stay in touch and bond with others, particularly men friends and family members.

Although fantasy sports have the potential to provide enjoyment, improve the sports viewing experience, and forge and strengthen relationships, they also come with downsides, including forgoing other activities and social interactions, experiencing negative emotions, and changing the degree and nature of interactions with others in ways that may strain them. These are the themes we explore in Chapter 6, focusing on the implications of time and emotional investments in fantasy sports for work, family, and social relationships and how men suffer more significant negative ramifications related to the hobby.

Finally, Chapter 7 summarizes the main lessons from the book—how fantasy sports offer a new and contradictory form of fandom, how they are deeply gendered but in ways that facilitate new performances of sporting masculinities and femininity, and how they move beyond mere play to influence social relationships, work lives, and families. We also explain where we see the hobby going in the future and review directions for additional research on this complex domain.

2

It's All Just a Game, It's Just a Different Game

Fantasy Sports as Personalized, Competitive, and Contested Fandom

Cole,[1] a married, White, forty-three-year-old man with two children, started playing fantasy sports eight or nine years ago, motivated in part by having been "a sports fan" his "whole life." Like many middle- and upper-class fantasy sports participants, Cole has been geographically mobile throughout his life, shifting his team allegiances as he moved. Because he grew up in New England, his most enduring attachment is to the Boston Red Sox, although he now lives in eastern Pennsylvania, where he has "become a much bigger Phillies fan."

With his fantasy sports participation, Cole has seen both an expansion and a transformation of his sports fandom. He is "far more aware of . . . the major leagues [NFL and MLB] as a whole, rather than just a couple of teams" and gets "greater enjoyment out of watching sports." Whereas before Cole played fantasy sports he might watch and follow only his local teams, now he "absolutely" watches more sports on television. In his words, because fantasy sports give him a "stake" in sporting events in which he had none before, he watches, roots during, and enjoys more games involving various real sports teams. He explains:

> Virtually any game that's on is one that I have some sort of stake in or has people that may be interesting to me in the future [for fantasy sports reasons]. Whereas in the past if a Panthers versus Titans game was on, I could care less, . . . now I still don't care a lot, but there is

something for me to watch in that game, and I certainly gain more enjoyment out of that.

Yet Cole also sees his fantasy sports participation as presenting some challenges to his former sports fandom. When he first started playing, "there were a lot of people that would not draft Yankees on principle, because everyone in the league was Red Sox fans [sic] and . . . did not want to root for the Yankees." Although, he says, "on the margins, I am more likely to draft a Red Sox or Phillie[s player] because you'd rather root for the player and the team at the same time," he has come to accept that winning in fantasy sports may mean rostering and rooting for the "enemy." When his real-life favorite teams cannot win a particular game, are having a miserable season, and/or are out of the running for the playoffs, he will disregard his real team affinities and root for his fantasy players instead. He gives as an example, "I might *even* root for a Yankees pitcher to get a hold, which I would *never ever* have done [before fantasy sports]. [As a Red Sox fan,] it would have been treason!"

While moments exist when his fantasy team and real-life allegiances converge, this is generally not the case. This forces Cole to forgo his traditional fandom in favor of a fantasy sports fandom, one in which participants root for individual athletes to do well not because they play for a particular team but because they will garner points "for them" in this virtual sporting competition. And this ultimately means Cole is not the same sports fan that he once was. He admits:

> I'm not as passionate a supporter of my teams as I used to be. I do feel that actually—that I was a different baseball watcher when I was just a passionate fan of a team. There was something that was very attractive about that, so I'd say that's a downside [to fantasy baseball participation].

Fantasy sports can engender new fan attachments, and Cole acknowledges that his fantasy sports involvement has created some longer-term interest in certain athletes on his fantasy team. He notes, however, that any attentiveness or connection to fantasy players is "not the same as being a Red Sox fan. . . . I don't think it's very durable, though I do have a bit of nostalgia for guys I had in the past when I'm watching a game." Moreover, Cole's connection to some athletes arises, at least in part, from a sense of ownership of the players and concern with what they can do *for him* currently or in the future. He says:

> I guess it's both an emotional and, for lack of a better word, a proprietary interest in players, especially those who are keepers[2] and who

I've had for several years. Those also happen to be the best players. . . .
I don't get too attached to "filler" players, but if the guy has a high
upside or I can get excited about the future, then I get more attached!

The "upside" that Cole mentions is the number of points a player can earn.
Accordingly, athletes are useful—and demand loyalty—because of what they
can do *for him*. He explains that he nearly let the thrill of a single athlete's
contribution to his success cause him to pass up a "good trade offer": "I was
reluctant to trade him away just as I was watching him earn for me every
time he started." But Cole made the deal because, for him, loyalty makes
sense only if it maximizes his bottom line.

Fantasy sports thus provide Cole with a sense of control and ownership
he cannot get from being a traditional fan. Equally important, they provide a more direct sense of success as players' achievements on the field of
play become Cole's achievements in his fantasy leagues. And Cole believes
strongly that his own knowledge, skill, and hard work drive his success.
While he acknowledges that "things of luck" will "help decide the seasons
just like in real sports," overall, he finds that fantasy sports require a lot of
"skill" and "attention" during the draft, in "trolling the waiver wires," and
in making decisions throughout the season. Cole believes that "good" managers take the hobby "seriously" and draw on their formable skills (e.g., in
analyzing players' statistical histories) and therefore have considerable control over their success. Fantasy baseball particularly appeals to him because
the "scope for managing"—for manipulating the roster and daily lineups—is
grander, which maximizes the "satisfaction" from all the "small little moves
you get right" throughout the season. Because he believes "there is a knowledge premium," he works hard to acquire knowledge and analyze athletes.
He does not "think the point of fantasy sports is to make social or personal
judgments on the players" and describes a management style that involves
looking "statistically" at the "histories" of athletes, listening to "a good deal
of baseball radio," and watching games to "see how they play" whenever he
can. Such investments can have a "huge payoff" for his fantasy team and,
ultimately, for Cole.

Cole's account mirrors that of other everyday traditional fantasy sports
participants, particularly those who fit the demographic of the average player—White, middle- or upper-class men. Traditional sports fandom often
brings individuals to the hobby, and in some ways fantasy sports involvement promotes greater knowledge, consumption, and appreciation of real
games and the league, making participants "better fans." But the fandom
and sports experience available in fantasy sports is distinct from traditional
fandom—it is both competitive and highly personalized. As a form of competitive fandom, fantasy sports can disrupt former fan allegiances, rooting
interests, and understandings of the game—a reality that does not sit well

with all participants. Fantasy sports force their participants to grapple with a more personalized fandom that gives them a sense of ownership and control and fosters the formation of individual attachments to real-life athletes. What the athletes can do for the fantasy manager partially or entirely dictates such attachments. In Cole's language, it is about watching an athlete "earn" for him and having a "proprietary interest" in the athletes. And while these managers cannot control the outcomes of fantasy sports matchups to the extent a real-life manager can, many still feel that they are in control and that their skill, effort, and attention to detail—not their traditional team loyalties or concern for off-field conduct—are what matters.

Although Cole does not explicitly say so, integral to this new, personalized, active fandom is a set of gendered and racialized power dynamics. In fact, this is why we selected Cole as the first participant to introduce to our readers. Although fantasy sports are nonphysical and computer-mediated, they are, like real sports, dominated by men and masculinity. The perceived "best" players are competitive, statistically savvy, analytical, knowledgeable about sports, and in control of their "success" in accruing the most points and winning the league. These traits—dominance, aggression, rationality—are all key elements of traditional hegemonic masculinity. Fantasy sports participants exercise power by drafting, playing, and trading the athletes on whom their success is predicated. Moreover, these largely White, middle- and upper-class men manipulate and virtually own athletes who are, for the most part, of color. That fantasy sports participants like Cole leave largely unacknowledged these gendered and racialized elements underscores the myriad ways in which Whiteness and masculinity simultaneously—and in intersecting and conflicting ways—dominate this space.

Fantasy Sports and Fandom

Traditionally, fans engage with sports by watching live events, rooting for desired outcomes, displaying team loyalty, and gaining sports-related knowledge. Once largely limited to individuals as passive consumers of sporting events and information, traditional fandom and the associated consumption of sports media have evolved in recent decades as media sources have expanded and changed, allowing fans to be more connected, active, and involved.[3] With technological advances, sports fans can and do engage with their favorite teams, athletes, and sports any time of day and any day of the week via traditional media (e.g., television and radio) and new media platforms (e.g., social media via mobile devices).[4]

New media platforms, in particular, allow their users more interactivity and agency. Fans who use them are producers, rather than mere consumers, of knowledge; they are active crafters of their fan experience and identity who interface with other fans, athletes, and sports journalists.[5] Fans can use new media to tailor the content they consume (e.g., by using apps that filter information related to their favorite teams) and to monitor scores, live sporting events, and player statistics at work or on the go.[6] Message boards, fan forums, and social media also give fans a platform to detail their experiences and offer their own commentary on sporting events.[7] They enable fans to express themselves and their identity as sports enthusiasts, to "publicly pronounce their loyalties to an ever-expanding audience,"[8] and to garner attention and recognition from others. They can accomplish this via second and third screens from the comfort of their homes as they watch live sporting events on traditional media platforms. All of this creates a more immersive, more engaged fan experience than was possible before the rise of new media.[9]

Fantasy sports seemingly represent a next step in this progression—an extension of active, immersive fandom that expands, changes, and challenges traditional fandom. Some works suggest that the fantasy sports participant represents a sort of superfan—someone who purchases more merchandise, attends more live games, watches more televised games, and spends more time on the Internet and other communication devices than a traditional fan.[10] Sports engagement, however, is not just about quantity. It is also about type, and on this count fantasy sports fandom is distinct from traditional fandom in several ways.

Traditional fandom typically involves allegiance to a favorite team or teams. Fans may have favorite athletes, but they are likely to play for the fans' favorite team(s). In contrast, fantasy sports involve interest in and allegiances to individual athletes and the plays they make, regardless of their true team affiliations. The fantasy sport team's players are dispersed throughout the league, heightening interest in the entire league. Herein lies a paradox of fandom in the age of fantasy sports: participants' interests become simultaneously broader (the whole league rather than an individual team) and narrower (a single play or an athlete rather than an entire game or team).

Fantasy sports participants add a league-wide focus to their existing team fandom as they shift their attention from one or two favorite real teams to other teams or the league more generally.[11] For example, they are more likely than nonparticipants to watch and attend not only the games of their favorite real team but also those of other teams. While professional sports leagues have capitalized on this increased market,[12] some commentators have expressed concern that fantasy sports challenge loyalty to a fan's favorite real team and argue that this is one way fantasy football in particular "has ruined the NFL experience."[13] And, indeed, the expansion of fandom has changed the sports fan experience for fantasy sports participants. Brendan Dwyer's research indicates that although highly involved fantasy football participants profess loyalty to and identify strongly as fans of their favorite real team (even more so than nonfantasy participants), when push comes to shove, they may opt not to watch the team's games if other concurrent games are more important for their fantasy sports team's fate.[14]

As fandom takes a league-wide perspective, it simultaneously narrows in other ways. Participants become interested in plays rather than games, since the outcome of any given possession—a touchdown, home run, goal, and so on—is what earns them points in their fantasy league. As a result, fantasy sports participants may switch their viewing among multiple games airing at the same time, root for sequences of events disconnected from the real game's outcome, lose sight of the real game's victors and losers, and continue watching long after the real game's winner is clear.[15] One need not be confined to watching televised sports or even participating in fantasy sports to experience this transformation of fandom. Fantasy sports have infiltrated live sporting events. Starting in 2011, the NFL ordered teams to display fantasy sports statistics at all home games.[16] Thus, much to the consternation of some traditional fans, fantasy sports shape the fan experience for everyone.[17]

Just as fantasy sports shift the focus to single plays or series of plays, they also direct participants' attention away from real teams to individual athletes. Fantasy sports participants often become attached to the individual players they draft, using possessive terms to refer to them (e.g., "my guy"), developing "player crushes," and displaying player "cyberfidelity."[18] In fact, nearly three-quarters report purchasing memorabilia related to their fantasy teams.[19] At the same time, some evidence exists that the depth of connection to individual players is shallow and short term. Unlike allegiances to real teams, which often endure extensive losing streaks, according to the majority of fantasy sports participants, their attachment to a given player does not continue beyond the season.[20]

This attachment to individual players—simultaneously intense and relatively brief—can and does conflict with traditional fandom for some participants in that the players on their fantasy team and their favorite real team often divide loyalties. Selecting fantasy athletes from their favorite real sports team to align attachments to individual players with team loyalties can lessen this conflict. Participants may also deliberately avoid selecting players on their real favorite team to keep their rooting interests separate. Others engage in what Mujde Yuksel and colleagues call *safe selection*—avoiding individual players for whom they cannot root for reasons ranging from their affiliation with a rival real team to their objectionable off-field behaviors.[21] Whatever the strategy, the freedom—and even necessity—to make such choices illustrates how fantasy sports allow for a more individualized experience than traditional fandom.

Central to the individualization of the fantasy sports experience is a level of agency and control not experienced in traditional fandom. About a decade ago, Erica Halverson and Richard Halverson coined the term *competitive fandom* to describe the type of fandom fantasy baseball promotes, fandom that moves beyond the traditional variety, even in its current more interactive and immersive form.[22] Yuksel and colleagues further argue that a distinct feature of fantasy sports is the co-creation involved. Players participate "in the construction of their personalized experiences"[23] and "take an active role in their fan practice"[24] as they control the rules of the game and reward structures in their leagues, their roster decisions, and their investment in the hobby. Aided by new media technologies that allow them to easily gather data and watch multiple games at once for scouting and tracking purposes, fantasy participants utilize their knowledge and statistical predictions to exert and experience some level of control over the outcomes of competition.[25]

Certainly, though, control here is incomplete. Much like traditional fans, fantasy sports participants cannot determine how real-life players will perform on the field of play or whether they will suffer serious injury that prevents them from playing and hurts their teams.[26] But fantasy sports managers, like their real-life coach or general manager counterparts, make decisions about whom to play from a group of athletes they have chosen and in the context of a set of rules that they are at least partly involved in creating. This affords them a level of agency and control beyond that of traditional sports fans.

Fantasy sports–engendered feelings of control, attachment, and ownership fundamentally change the experience of fandom and sports spectatorship. Traditional fans bask in the reflected glory (BIRG) of their favorite teams' successes, sharing in them and communicating their affiliation with the team (e.g., by wearing team gear) and their victories.[27] They also engage in CORFing (cutting off reflected failure) when their teams do poorly, distancing themselves from them by not communicating their team affiliation, avoiding other fans, and circumventing discussion of the team or the loss.[28] Although Brendan Dwyer, Rebecca Achen, and Joshua Lupinek find similar levels of BIRGing and CORFing with regard to real and fantasy teams,[29] the stakes and benefits of BIRGing and CORFing differ with fantasy sports. Participants are more directly tied to the success or failure of their fantasy sports teams than traditional fans, who are mere spectators. The process of co-creation supports a greater psychological feeling of ownership, and, indeed, research indicates that fantasy sports participants feel a greater sense of pride because they have constructed their teams.[30] Moreover, that the outcomes of fantasy sports matchups are quantifiable, measurable, and agreed on (i.e., a scoreboard demonstrates who is the "better" fan) makes legitimacy in this space more recognizable than in traditional fandom, in which the markers of success (e.g., winning arguments against other fans or owning a lot of sports memorabilia) are less clear and/or potent. As such, Dwyer, Achen, and Lupinek surmise that "perhaps, there is more personal image at stake to project and protect" in fantasy sports than in traditional fandom.[31]

In other words, the glory and failure involved in fantasy sports wins and losses—just like the fantasy sports experience itself—are personalized and not merely reflected.

Fantasy sports thus offer a distinct version of fandom—one that is productive and personalized and has the potential to conflict with traditional fandom. At its foundation is also a gendered and racialized power structure that is both similar to and different from that in traditional fandom and gaming culture. Numerically, White men prevail in fantasy sports. But beyond that, ideologically and structurally, masculinity and Whiteness dominate them in mutually supportive and reinforcing ways. More specifically, key elements of masculinity—control and dominance—intersect with the privilege of Whiteness to produce a set of structural and performative power dynamics that reflect and reinscribe intersecting inequalities in this space.

A growing body of research on traditional fandom has attended to the role of gender in fan identification and behaviors. Although men and women do not differ in the likelihood of their self-identification as sports fans, men consume more sports media and spend more time discussing sports.[32] On a deeper level, the experience of being and identifying as sports fans is gendered. Andrei Markovits and Emily Albertson argue that men's fandom and women's fandom are distinct in the importance they place on affect and knowledge. They argue that women have less sports knowledge and are less invested in this knowledge as a marker or aspect of fandom. Rather, loving teams, players, and sports is more central. Sports and fandom are more social for women. In the words of sociologist Kim Toffoletti, fandom holds "considerable meaning and significance for women—creating a sense of personal and group identity, fostering community, and promoting feelings of enjoyment, connection, well-being and pleasure."[33] Men's fandom, in contrast, which emphasizes knowledge, frames sports and athletic events as competitive pursuits.[34]

Yet to say that fandom is gendered is not just to say that men's and women's individual fan identities and behaviors differ. In fact, the very definition of fandom at the institutional level is modeled on male bodies, Whiteness, and heterosexuality and aligns with traditional conceptions of hegemonic masculinity.[35] The majority of fan studies have focused on men who are fans of sports at the institutional center, describing fan identities and behaviors and setting a bar for legitimate fandom based on a male and masculine norm. Men emphasize knowledge in their fandom, and that knowledge becomes a prerequisite for authentic fandom. Moreover, sports language is, according to Markovits and Albertson, "a language of men. . . . Speaking sports is analogous to speaking 'man,' and by virtue of men having to speak it, the language itself assumes a male quality."[36] While increased acceptance of women may change who we think can be a sports fan, it leaves unchanged the underlying power structure that presumes and perpetuates the dominance of men. Indeed, sports fandom is seen as essential for men and a "choice" for women.[37] Statistical information about women's sports fandom is set in the context of sports that men play and run, and women's presence in these contexts paradoxically supports the dominance of men and masculinity insofar as it increases the viewership and revenue of men's sports.[38]

Set against this backdrop, the marginalization of women sports fans is not surprising. Indeed, insofar as the definition of fandom itself is masculine, illegitimate sports fandom is that which is associated with traditional, heteronormative femininity.[39] That women's loyalty is tested and must be proven is evidence that this is a masculine space, and women's increased presence has done little to change the association of sports with men and masculinity.[40] As a result of men's dominance, men can engage in behaviors, such as inattention during sporting events, that render women inauthentic and illegitimate as fans.[41] Moreover, genuine fans must have both passion and knowledge—the latter being integral to men's relationship to sports and less central to women's fandom.[42] In fact, fandom is so closely aligned with both masculinity and sports knowledge that Markovits and Albertson advocate for an entirely different term to describe women who are knowledgeable sports fans—sportista. What distinguishes a sportista from a fan is that she not only loves sports but also knows them. Because men are, by definition, presumed to do both, they do not need a separate label.

Importantly, race, class, and sexuality intersect with gender in definitions and experiences of fandom. Simply put, women who gain legitimacy as fans typically do so from other positions of privilege. Women who are fans of the Australian Football League, for instance, assert their fandom from positions of power insofar as they are White, middle class, and heterosexual.[43] Katelyn Esmonde, Cheryl Cooky, and David Andrews' interviews with women sports fans reveal a similar dynamic.[44] Being White and middle class shapes these women's acceptance as fans; they not only had the time to engage in behaviors that help establish their legitimacy but also did so from privileged positions that afford them comfort in the space. In short, individuals and groups, such as women, are effectively excluded from authentic fandom unless they engage in particular, narrowly defined fan practices—that is, those associated with hegemonic masculinity—and can leverage their membership in other dominant groups to stake some claim to belonging.

Gaming research provides further insights for understanding the racialized power dynamics in fantasy sports. David Leonard argues that sports video games are rooted in minstrelsy, reinforcing White dominance by allowing White participants to play at being Black.[45] Reflecting an "oppositional binary"[46] of adoration and disdain for Blackness, largely White players celebrate and (virtually) embody the strength and athletic prowess of Black bodies while simultaneously controlling their supposed aggression. Far from being transgressive—as playing the other might allow—Leonard argues, "sports games legitimize stereotypical ideas about black athletic superiority and white intellectual abilities."[47]

Underlying Leonard's argument is the notion that Black bodies become something to be possessed in video games. Thomas Oates applies a similar logic to football fandom, coining the term *vicarious management* to describe the presentation of athletes as "commodities to be consumed selectively and self-consciously by sports fans."[48] By tracing the roots of vicarious management from the White supremacy of the nineteenth century through traditional sports gambling practices, he argues that new media technologies offer novel economic grounding for this commodification of personhood and a resultant fandom positioning athletes as property that can be consumed, manipulated, and, ultimately, discarded. Oates uses a frame of "racialized androcentrism"[49] to elucidate vicarious management, linking the racial dynamics Leonard notes—in which the aggression and physical prowess of Black bodies can be consumed in ways that also control those bodies—to masculine power dynamics. Underrepresented as athletes in sports at the institutional center, privileged White men find the vicarious management embedded in contemporary sports fandom to be a site where they can "try to resecure their stronghold on sport culture."[50]

This all comes to a head in fantasy sports in ways that scholars have not fully explored. Indeed, Oates argues that new media, the foundation on which fantasy sports rest, exponentially increase the possibilities for commodification and manipulation.[51] Unlike traditional fandom, in which fans consume mainly games and memorabilia, fantasy sports involve the consumption of actual athletes—they are purchased in drafts, traded or sold in deals, and discarded in releases to the waiver wire. While video gamers arguably have more control over the bodies they virtually inhabit in that they dictate their movements in the digital field of play, fantasy sports participants have greater ownership through this process of drafting and trading. Who these largely White men players are buying and selling are predominantly men of color, a fact made evident in an August 2017 ESPN sketch in which players—mostly Black—were auctioned off to the highest bidder (almost exclusively White men).[52] The sketch, criticized for its likeness to a slave auction, is a reflection of how gender and race are "central to the acquisition, maintenance, and exposition of power that is paramount in sport, and evidenced within fantasy sports."[53]

In this chapter, we explore the relationship between fantasy sports participation and traditional sports fandom, noting their points of convergence and conflict. We argue that the type of experience fantasy sports offer is one that is highly personalized, in which success purportedly rests in the hands of the participant. Importantly, we assert that this engenders a certain mind-set focusing on skill and control and does so in ways that reflect and reproduce the gendered and racialized dynamics in sports and digital gaming more generally.

Fantasy Sports as an Extension and Transformation of Traditional Fandom

Many men and women reveal that their fantasy participation complements and enhances traditional fandom. Like Cole, they position fantasy sports as "an extension" of traditional sports fandom, asserting they participate because they are "sports fanatic[s]" and "love 'real' sports." Traditional fans feel a sense of unbridled joy when their favorite real team scores or wins a game, and what fantasy sports players describe feeling during games mirrors and potentially enhances this. Archie, a casual fantasy sports player[54] and a Vikings fan, exemplifies this point. He told us he gets "the sports fan rush" through fantasy sports that is similar to "watching a sporting event and your team gets a slam dunk or scores a touchdown on a long pass." He continued, "You go, 'Yeah!' or 'Booyah!'" even if now "I'm going wooo in front of the computer [*laughing*]."

This enhancement of traditional fandom is partly because, as previous research would suggest, fantasy sports extend participants' focus beyond favorite real teams to the league as a whole. Players reveal that fantasy sports make "every team that you have a player on become like your home team." As Mike, a dedicated player who is a die-hard Eagles fan, put it, "I just am pretty much into football, so I'd watch anyway . . . [but fantasy football] makes the games more interesting if you have something to watch individually." This expansion of interest leads fantasy sports players to watch *more* games than they would otherwise. Some participants, like Bob, a hard-core player, merely make general claims that they "definitely watch more sports" than before they played fantasy sports. Others note that they previously had watched only their favorite teams; but as fantasy sports participants, they now watch other teams' games as well, thus adding to their overall spectatorship and fandom of sports. Jamie, a Philadelphia sports fan and dedicated fantasy player, explained:

> You end up watching more of the games because you have more people invested. When we were growing up, and even before fantasy sports, you watched your home team games—the ones that you were rooting for—but you didn't care about that third or fourth or fifth game because you really weren't invested in them. But now, if you've got two or three players in those [games]—two or three players could mean the difference between winning for the week or losing for the

week—you might watch the game to see how they do or you might scout players.

The participant experience in fantasy sports is not just an extension of team-based loyalties to an increasing number of teams or to the league as a whole. As Jamie alludes to above, underlying this league-wide focus is a new, more individualized set of allegiances and interests. Rather than rooting for real-life teams or certain plays only insofar as they support an overall win for a real team, fantasy sports players cheer for individual athletes on their fantasy teams and root for certain scenarios to arise that will maximize their fantasy points. Furthermore, they do so regardless of the impacts these may have on a real game's bottom line. This changes the viewing experience, as Rebecca, a hard-core player who describes herself as "fickle" in her team loyalties, notes:

> You root for your fantasy players, not for real teams . . . like wanting a quarterback to throw an interception at any particular point in the game. . . . Whenever you are watching the sport, you are rooting for some sort of victory, and this is just a different form of victory that you are rooting for. . . . It's not necessarily any weirder or any more bizarre than rooting for some set of strangers on a field called the Phillies that you will never have any real interaction with, wearing their brand in terms of T-shirts or hats or sweats or whatever. It's all just a game; so it's just a different game.

That one is paying attention to and rooting for individual plays and players has the potential to set fantasy sports fandom on a collision course with traditional fandom, at least for fans who are less "fickle" in their loyalties than Rebecca. In this way, fantasy sports fandom not only changes but perhaps also conflicts with traditional fandom. Yet many fantasy sports participants take advantage of the customization the hobby provides to mitigate these potential conflicts. Part of the co-creation involved in fantasy sports is that unlike fans of "real" sports teams, fantasy sports participants exert a greater measure of control over their fan experience.

One way this manifests is in team rostering, and here we find that many of the participants with whom we spoke practice what Yuksel and colleagues term *safe selection*.[55] For some, this means avoiding players on their rival real teams. Anne, a dedicated player who has played fantasy sports for more than five years, explained, "I'm a Giants fan. I live in New York. I will not pick up any Cowboys. It's just a standard rule for me. I can't root for them, and I don't want to have to root for them, I guess. I have just never ever drafted or picked up a Cowboy ever." Likewise, Thraka, a dedicated player who has played for more than eight years, reported:

> I will not draft as a rule, unless I absolutely have to, and I know a lot
> of people will say there's no loyalty in fantasy football, [but] I still
> don't want the Dallas Cowboys' quarterback. . . . If Tom Brady in his
> prime was playing for the Dallas Cowboys, I probably wouldn't draft
> him. Just because every time the Dallas Cowboys get a touchdown, I
> throw up a little in my mouth.

By adopting such selection strategies, managers like Anne and Thraka personalize the fantasy sports experience and reduce the potential conflict between fantasy and nonfantasy rooting interests.

Rostering strategies are but one element of the personalization distinguishing fantasy sports fandom from traditional sports fandom. Inherent in the co-creation available in fantasy sports is that participants have an increased level of power and influence over the contours of their participation. Traditional fans can choose for which team to root, but they have no control over which players their favorite team drafts, releases, plays, or benches. Fantasy sports afford participants the ability to do all of these things. Of course, fantasy managers cannot fully control how many points their teams gain. Athletes get injured, coaches call plays and referees issue penalties that favor some athletes over others, weather affects the playing conditions, and athletes have "fluke" games. But while participants commonly acknowledge that "luck is always, always in play," a plurality think that factors within their control ultimately determine outcomes more so than luck or chance.[56] In these players' estimations, success hinges on the time and effort they invest, their experience, and their aptitude for analyzing and acting rationally upon fantasy sports–relevant information. Steve, a dedicated player who has played for more than five years, exemplifies this thinking. For him, success is largely about being "smart" and keeping up with the news. He explained:

> I think usually you have a good bit of control, because I think if
> you draft well, that sets you up, and then if you are smart about the
> pickups you make during the year, and you're on the ball and you are
> following guys who are injury replacements or just kind of coming
> on out of nowhere, I think you have a lot of control.

With this perceived sense of control, fantasy sports participants can experience positive real game plays as success for and a reflection of *themselves*. Players' managerial choices are what make the events occurring on the field of play significant and rewarding, as they are the ones competing through their virtual manipulation of the real-life athletes. Thus, the co-creation inherent in the engaged, competitive fandom characteristic of fantasy sports promotes a oneness between the fan and the real-life athletes on his or her fantasy team. Indeed, while traditional fans may BIRG of their favorite team's successes, for fantasy sports participants, the glory is not merely reflected. Instead, the achievements of their fantasy sports squads are *their own achievements*.

Importantly, both men and women experience the fantasy sports fan practices and understandings described above. Both groups are often drawn to the hobby because of their love of real sports, and they similarly root and cheer emphatically during games. They also share the sentiment that with their fantasy sports participation, their interest in and consumption of real sports have increased and broadened from a handful of favorite real-life teams to the entire league. Additionally, men and women alike express an increased focus and interest in some of the minutiae of games—the play-by-play doings of individual athletes that have implications for fantasy sports scoring. Furthermore, fantasy sports on the whole offer both men and women co-creation opportunities, giving them additional levels of control and active engagement that traditional fandom cannot provide them.

It is also the case that both men and women fail to acknowledge the class and race dynamics inherent in their feelings of control. It is the privilege of the powerful to exercise control over their own experiences, and we were struck by how little our participants—by and large White and well educated—reflected on or problematized the agency they are afforded in crafting the contours of their fantasy sports experience. Moreover, not a single participant acknowledged that the players being manipulated in fantasy sports are mainly men of color. Yet fantasy sports largely involve White fans' drafting, playing, and releasing such athletes. As such, White participants—both men and women—exercise virtual control and ownership over Black and Latino bodies in this space.

Gendered Co-Creation and Personalized, Competitive Fandom

To say that men and women who play fantasy sports share a number of the same experiences and viewpoints does not mean that fantasy sports fandom and the everyday practices involved are gender neutral. Men feel a greater sense of control over and, by extension, accomplishment through their fantasy sports participation. They also take a more transactional approach, prioritizing rationality and knowledge over team and individual loyalty and other nonperformance factors. It is not, however, just that men's and women's individual experiences and perspectives differ. It is also that a masculine model, where knowledge, rationality, and competition are advantaged over affect and personal growth, define fantasy sports fandom just as they do traditional fandom. In the end, fantasy sports fandom may be more personalized than traditional sports fandom, but it is no less gendered.

Accomplishment and Control in Fantasy Sports

While previous research has noted a shift in loyalty with fantasy sports from teams to individual players, it has often neglected a key additional element—fantasy sports participants experience positive real game plays and performances more directly as success for themselves and not just a beloved team. The virtual control fantasy sports participants exercise and the specific benefits they reap from the performance of "their" athletes can then promote feelings of personal pride, validation, and achievement. Certainly, some women allude to gaining satisfaction from their sound decisions and finding those "diamonds in the rough" (Kels). However, it is men who report with much greater frequency that what they gain from fantasy sports and what they play for is a personal "sense of accomplishment," "satisfaction from doing well at something," and "self-gratification." In feeling like an active participant in the game, men, like Mike, reveal that fantasy sports provide participants with a way "to feel good about" themselves. Likewise, another male participant nicely explained this aspect of fantasy sports when he wrote, "When you build a good/successful team, I guess it's like the feeling for an artist when they paint a good picture. A sense of achievement and return on investment of mental energy." For some men, this sense of personal accomplishment goes so far as to create a symbolic oneness between the fantasy sports participant and athlete, as when Ted described the "euphoria" of victory in this way: "Yeah, I won! This is good; my guy got what I needed."

Related to all of this are understandings of control. After all, feelings of accomplishment hinge on having *built* a successful team and making "*smart* pickups," as opposed to getting lucky. And while fantasy sports offer all participants greater control than regular fandom, men, much more than women, see control as central to their success. In fact, women typically say that their successes or failures are to a large extent beyond their control, even if they put the requisite time into the hobby and have the necessary knowledge. For instance, when asked how much control she has over whether she wins or loses, Jennifer, who invests eight hours a week[57] in fantasy sports, said:

> Oh, none. And that's the thing, and in the end, looking back on this, I will be like, "I have spent an extraordinary amount of hours on something that really comes down to chance." . . . So, in the end, I have no control. I can read as much as I want, I can make those final decisions, but in the end, it's just all gonna be how that player plays today and I have no control over that.

Likewise, Michelle, who spends significantly less time than Jennifer on fantasy sports (about forty-five minutes per week), claimed, "Oh, God. I think it's practically almost all luck [*laughs*]. That's why I think the guys that did all the crazy trading of different players all the time, every week were totally overanalyzing things." And Nicole, who similarly noted she has little control, claimed, "My husband would disagree with me, but I think a lot of it is luck. He *likes to think* that he's in control."

Nicole whose "husband would disagree" and Michelle who discusses those "guys" who overanalyze everything are onto something here. When men reflect on their influence generally, the majority, like Cole who opened the chapter, assert that outcomes are mostly in their control. As Anthony, who spends three to four hours a week on fantasy sports, put it:

> I think I have a pretty good amount of control. Certainly, there is always some measure of luck with injuries or whatnot, but [you have] a pretty good amount [of control]. On a scale of one to ten, I would say it is a seven or an eight; it is mostly what you do and what you decide and who you pick and that kind of stuff.

As Anthony begins to suggest, men are also more likely to think that success—and thus their control over it—hinges on sports knowledge. By knowing more about sports, men feel in control of how well they do. Zone, who invests about three hours per week, was unequivocal in this, saying, "I believe it comes down to knowledge of the sport and knowledge of the league. Period." Frank elaborated:

> The more you understand football, the more you understand schemes, the more you understand positions and how positions are different in different schemes, and who's coming up in the pipeline and who's maybe moving on, you can kind of look and predict, "OK, this is someone who's probably poised to have a pretty good year." And I think at the end of the day, really, it's those people you find that win the leagues for you.

Even those men who note after some reflection that they may not be in charge of their fantasy destinies indicate that they *want* or *need to think*, based on their knowledge and skills, that they have complete control. Zone told us, "I would like to think that I have complete control over the destiny and successes of my fantasy teams, but that is simply just not the complete reality." Or as Jerome, a hard-core player who invests more than ten hours a week in fantasy sports, acknowledged after much reflection, "I think that I think I have more control over it than I actually do. . . . Hopefully, my guesses are better than other people, and hopefully they're slightly more educated guesses; that is the only thing I can hang my hat on. And I don't even know if that's true."

Interestingly, even when men acknowledge that they may not be fully in charge of their fantasy sports performance, they tend to talk about not being in charge only when things go awry, rarely attributing their *wins* to factors outside their control. In fact, men are about half as likely as women to admit that their fantasy sports failures are due to their own inattentiveness, poor decisions, lack of knowledge or experience, or being outmatched by the competition—in other words, largely things within their control. As an illustration, consider how two players—Jane, who spends about seven hours a week on fantasy sports, and Ray, who spends about eight hours a week on fantasy sports—interpret their losses. Jane acknowledged, "A lot of my losses this year are totally attributed to me not starting the right player. And that's on me." Ray, however, offered a view that mirrors many men's: "If I lose to anyone, so be it. It's luck; a lot of it's luck."

Notably, many of the same men who claim their defeats are out of their control often feel directly responsible for their successes and, as research would suggest, revel in the personalized achievement of their victories. Archie, who invests more than fifteen hours a week in the hobby, nicely summarized how many men seem to think about the degree of skill versus luck involved in fantasy sports:

> Just kind of [a] general feeling people have is that when you win, it's because of your skill and smart moves and things like that, and when you lose, it's because of dumb, uncontrollable luck, right? [*laughing*] You claim your victories are the result of skill and wisdom and intelligence and all this, and your losses are the result of "Oh, I can't believe I had such terrible luck." And, of course, it's actually both are equally caused by a mix of skill and luck.

Attributing failure to luck and claiming to have done everything in their control to be successful allows men to CORF of their defeats. Yet if achievement is personalized in fantasy sports, it follows that failure is as well. Thus, by failing to acknowledge that maybe sometimes they are just not good enough or do not work hard enough to win, men preserve their own sense of themselves as knowledgeable, skilled, and successful players. And while Archie characterizes the viewpoint that success is attributable to skill as a "general feeling people have," our data point to this as a feeling *men* have.

Yet this is beyond individual-level sex or gender differences. Hegemonic masculinity dictates that performances of manhood require being skilled, dominant, and in control—hence men's greater proclivity in this space to announce they are in charge and that they desire to be so. Men also are doing manhood as they interpret their success as a result of their skills and efforts and, accordingly, bask in the glow of *their* personal accomplishment. This is why participants like Steve, a dedicated player, describe wins not just as satisfying but also as "validating"—wins validate not just men's choices but also their manhood. But when disruptions to these projections occur (e.g., a loss), ideological repair work[58] must follow ("I was unlucky") to perform institutionalized notions of hegemonic masculinity. Thus, we see men, more so than women, pushing narratives of being in control of their fantasy destinies and gaining a sense of personal validation and accomplishment from fantasy sports—but also failing not because they are lesser but because forces out of their control impacted their ability to win. Men preserve both their individual sense of themselves and their adherence to hegemonic ideals in the process.

Attachments, Loyalty, and Roster Decisions in Fantasy Sports

Although men and women understand their influence over outcomes in fantasy sports differently, fantasy sports as active, engaged fandom provide all participants the opportunity to personalize their fan experiences, particularly as their focus and allegiances shift from real teams to individual athletes. Rostering decisions present a key opportunity for co-creation in fantasy sports; yet this co-creation is gendered. Here, too, men's and women's behaviors reflect and reinscribe gendered assumptions and dynamics.

Fantasy sports heighten interest in and attachments to individual athletes, but they do so in gendered ways. For men, attachments and roster decisions are largely transactional. Real-life individual athletes are involved but as a means to an end—the athlete as a person is of interest only insofar as he serves fantasy sports purposes. Athletes are to be bought, traded, exchanged, and deployed in fantasy lineups, albeit virtually, as commodities without much attention or thought to whom they are as people. As a result, men rarely report having any prolonged, affective attachment to any particular real-life athlete. To the extent that men hold on to players for multiple seasons, it is, as Cole revealed in the chapter opening, because they have a "propriety interest" in those athletes. Similarly, Roland, a hard-core player who told us multiple times that he is "completely dispassionate" in his fantasy decisions, argued:

> If this guy can help me, then that's the most attachment I feel towards him. If he can't, then I have no problem moving him along. Or I feel like I like him and he's doing well, but he can help me get somebody better in return if there's some sort of trade, then I have no problem hitting the eject button on him.

Given this transactional approach, it is perhaps unsurprising that men are clear, often forcefully so, that real-life team affiliations should not be taken into account when making fantasy sports decisions. They largely couch this position in the language of success, as successful players are purportedly those who are statistically savvy and strategic. Importantly, for these men, there is no place for emotions in these decisions. Ray, a Miami Dolphins fan, articulated:

> I think to be a good manager, to win a league, you need experience, you need to take emotion out of the game, don't play favorites. I see it way too often where people are like, "I'm a Niner fan, I'm going to pick all Niners," and they . . . sign up for a league year one, and they'll never play again because they picked based off of who they liked and they didn't do well and to them it's no fun.

Roland, an Eagles fan, was equally concerned with the flip side of this coin—not playing real-life rival team members. He claimed:

> One of my friends, [I] had a long argument with him about it, because he will frequently not play players that are going against the Eagles because he doesn't want to root for them and against his team, where I could care less. If that's the best matchup, I'm starting him. . . . You have to be able to compartmentalize.

Moreover, men who may start fantasy sports as "homers" (predominately rostering players from their favorite real-life teams) come to prioritize competitive fandom over traditional loyalties in their fantasy sports involvement, as Cole indicated doing in the chapter opening. Mike, who plays in two leagues—one with friends and one with strangers—reoriented his allegiances after being the "joke" in his friend league. He recalled:

> It used to be [the] joke in my league that I had all Eagles, like my whole team was all Eagles players. . . . I actually just won my championship for the first time last year and that was after I dropped a bunch of Eagles players. I was doing well in the playoffs [before], but I didn't win—I think it was hurting my team maybe 'cause I had . . . guys that weren't so great, just because I just liked them.

It is not just that being calculating and emotionally detached are approaches men generally take. This dispassionate, transactional approach becomes the narrative of appropriate—and successful—fantasy sports fandom. As Anthony, a Rams fan, notes, fantasy sports are not about making "roster moves with my heart." Rather, playing is about seeing "if you can be smarter than any of the other guys in the league" and pulling for and deploying athletes based on what you "think they are going to do." When an athlete can no longer do what you need him to do, fantasy managers should, in Roland's words, "hit the eject button" on him in terms of their team, loyalties, and affections. In privileging these ways of knowing and being, gender is institutionalized in fantasy sports fandom such that masculine terms define legitimate participation.

It is against this backdrop that women's fan experiences must be understood. To be sure, women also buy, trade, and exchange athletes as part of their fantasy sports involvement, and they do so in ways that they calculate will maximize the potential for their victories. This is expected if they are to compete and thrive in an environment where this is required. For women, however, the individualization of the hobby also involves feeling as though they know *their* athletes personally (that they may even be akin to family) and taking a greater interest in them as people. They are more likely than men to pull for real-life athletes long after they serve no fantasy sports purpose for them, to recognize athletes' off-the-field faults and do-gooding, and to use these factors in making roster decisions.

As an illustration, Kate, a casual player who is "loosely" a New York Jets fan, indicated having "some sort of loyalty" to her fantasy players:

> It's a different kind of attachment [than one to a real team]. But I don't know if I can properly articulate that, like it's *more* individualized and personal. You feel like you know them on a personal level, I guess. . . . It's more that you have researched them individually and know their individual stories as opposed to like a team's history.

This more "individualistic" and "personal" attachment can result for some in feeling a connection well past "their" athletes' fantasy sports usefulness. Jane, a dedicated player, noted:

> There are guys that I see, if he's not on my team this year and he does something great in a game, I'll be like, "Yeah, he's an alumni of my team, that's right." . . . I root for them. I'm like, "That's *my guy*" in a sense—even though he's not my guy, he's not anybody's guy.

Or then there's Lynn, a fantasy sports participant for eleven years, who alluded to forming a connection with players she saw, in essence, grow up. She claimed, "There is some [players], yeah [I'm attached to], especially if it's someone that I drafted their rookie year. . . . They're like my babies." Lynn's affinity for her "babies" reflects an affective approach to fandom that stands in stark contrast to the ways in which men "compartmentalize" rationality and emotional attachments.

A key place women's affective approach to personalized fantasy sports fandom manifests is in their strategies for drafting or picking up players during the season—those athletes for whom they will subsequently spend their time rooting. Again, here, it's worth noting that both men and women predominately practice what Yuksel and colleagues term *impartial selection*. They do what fantasy sports as an institution gendered masculine dictates—focus on performance-related measures so they can compete and win. Despite this, many fantasy sports participants—especially women—take the co-creation and personalization that fantasy sports afford further by considering the off-the-field behavior and character of athletes in making their rosters. In essence, these participants still want to win and compete, but they also want to craft their fan experience such that they can root for and affiliate with people they respect, like, and do not find morally reprehensible.

Notably, women do more to reconcile their desire to win with their desire to avoid players they find problematic—they integrate competitive fandom with affective fandom. Some, like Anne, a dedicated player, "think twice" about those athletes who are a "douche" or "constantly in trouble" and bypass them when other equally viable options are available. Others, though, are unequivocal that they reject some athletes because of certain off-field behavior *no matter what* the consequences are for their fantasy team's bottom line. A host of issues—having extramarital affairs, making racist or anti-Semitic comments, dogfighting, being involved in the sexual or physical assault or murder of another person—move an athlete beyond the pale of rostering for some, but do so more typically for our women who play.[59] Jennifer, who just started playing fantasy sports this year, is one woman who revealed taking into account the kind of person an athlete is in real life when making roster decisions. She also articulated how she saw her stance on this as quite different than that of men she knows. As she explained:

> Brady I hate because he left Bridget Moynahan when she was pregnant with their child for Gisele. Oh, and when I talk about this with the guys, they're like, "Are you serious?" And I'm like, "Listen, I've hated Tom Brady for a long time." And that literally is my 100 percent reason [why I won't ever draft him], he left [Bridget] for Gisele while she was pregnant. . . . Yeah, I understand he's a great quarterback. I could've picked up Tom Brady, but I didn't. Oh, I hate him.

While some, like Jennifer, sidestep athletes with questionable moral character, it is overwhelmingly athletes accused or convicted of sexually or physically assaulting a woman that participants, especially women, avoid. Topping this list is Pittsburgh Steelers quarterback Ben Roethlisberger. Michelle, a limited player, is one woman who rejected Roethlisberger as her quarterback because, as she explained, he is an "awful human being." She continued that she knows that he is a "good" football player who would "score plenty of fantasy points," but "I just didn't care. I don't like [him]." Likewise, Claire, a casual player, expressed avoiding Roethlisberger no matter where she could get him in a draft. In creating her fantasy football team, she said, "I was not picky, except Ben Roethlisberger. . . . The rape allegations—that would be my one [no]."

The personalized fandom fantasy sports afford also means that liking someone personally or thinking him a "good guy" can elevate an athlete in some managers' estimations—and, again, this is more likely to occur among women than men. Jennifer, who refuses to draft Tom Brady, also prioritizes players like Torrey Smith, whom she sees as a civic-minded, stand-up man. She told us:

> He's doing pit bull rescue, and he constantly puts pictures of his pit bull [on social media], and he does all this work with charity, and I have come to be, I have become obsessed with Torrey Smith to the point where three weeks ago, I word for word said to my boyfriend, "I should sit Torrey Smith this week, but I just like him so much." Word for word. And he was like, "You really can't. He's not gonna score a point in this [game]," and I ended up sitting him . . . [but] I still haven't dropped him, even though he has not been doing well, because I just think he seems like such a great guy.

Similarly, Lynn, a hard-core player, claimed that she ranks Larry Fitzgerald highly because "he's a good receiver, but he's also, he's always known as the class act. He's always giving away tickets to every home game and even away games to fans."

On the one hand, these rostering decisions are another way that fantasy sports provide a more personalized, agentic version of competitive fandom. Fantasy sports participants can prioritize rational calculations of players' likely success, regardless of other factors. Or, if they choose, they can take character issues into account. Yet it is women much more so than men who give thought and priority to the real-life athlete as a person and whether they want to root for and be associated with him (even only virtually).[60] Why that is the case likely revolves around two factors: (1) men, more so than women, adhere to, prioritize, and gain respect for following a masculine "winning is everything" transactional approach to fandom that deemphasizes emotions, and (2) women are more connected to and empathetic regarding some of the off-field issues being considered. Both further illustrate the gendered dynamics of fantasy sports fandom.

Central to men's fandom is a focus on winning and a definition of success that requires being rational and calculating rather than emotional. This is not surprising, given that traditional conceptions of hegemonic masculinity are specifically constructed around dominance and stoicism.[61] Thus, to prioritize one athlete over another for nonperformance, nonplay factors is irrational, at odds with larger notions of masculinity, and harmful to one's chances of accomplishing what really matters—winning. For instance, Cole, who opened the chapter, argued:

> I don't really pay too much attention whether there is someone that I would have over for dinner or convict if I was on a jury or something like that [*laughs*]. That doesn't seem to be the point of fantasy sports. . . . I don't think the point of fantasy sports is to make social or personal judgments on the players.

Reflective of the independence and authority embedded in masculinity generally and because of the dominance of men and masculinity in sports specifically, men are confident in asserting this viewpoint. Their perspective on appropriate behaviors and attitudes sets the norm for legitimate fandom in this space. When women argue that considering off-field behavior of athletes is inappropriate, they often allude to some official entity as justifying and thus legitimating their stance. Men do not generally do this, likely because they do not need to. For example, Annick, a hard-core player who has participated for about twelve years, relied on the league's determination of eligibility, not her own, in deciding whether an athlete's behavior made him out of bounds. When asked if she took off-field factors into account, she replied:

> No, and I'll tell you why. . . . It's like [a] Michael Vick question, right? Michael Vick killed dogs, I love dogs, but I have had Michael Vick on my fantasy team because if the league has decided that he is reinstated and they have decided that he can play again, then he is eligible to be on my team. I don't turn a blind eye—I am aware of it—but for purposes of fantasy, you can't afford to be [taking off-field behavior into account].

Notably, some women make an additional nuanced observation—that traditional fandom also requires individuals to turn a blind eye to the real lives of athletes since the leagues do not significantly penalize athletes for their assault of women or other alleged crimes. These managers reveal that even traditional fans need to be unemotional and detached to remain fans of their teams and sports more generally. Such a comparison is not one we heard men make, thus indicating either a general lack of concern for athletes' off-field behavior or a lack of necessity to account for their decision to ignore it. Annick, quoted above, was one woman to make this connection:

> If I ever thought, stopped to think about the real realities of the guys that are our athlete heroes, I would not be a sports fan. I would just be done with being a sports fan because they all—they drink

and drive, they beat their girlfriends, they take drugs, they do illegal things, they get involved in shady situations, they exhibit bad judgment all the time.

Jane, who only takes off-field issues into account if a suspension is possible, also makes this point. She asserted, "Unfortunately, I try to separate the football players from the real-life guy, because otherwise I'd have problems with the football."

In each of these cases, women put forward an account to justify why they do not take off-field actions into consideration, suggesting that they, more so than men, need to explain their unemotional, success-focused decisions—and that they have grappled with this. By being advantaged in a space built on the dominance of maleness and masculinity, the White, middle- and upper-class men who play fantasy sports simply have a greater ability to disregard factors they deem immaterial. In fact, insofar as the ranks of those who created and continue to control the entire fantasy and real sports industry are themselves men,[62] it is not a stretch to say that men are largely in control of determining what counts as relevant and irrelevant. Legitimate fantasy sports participation, as with sports fandom more generally, is defined on masculine terms.[63] Co-creation, then, is deeply gendered. Individually, women and men make different decisions in crafting their fantasy sports rosters, and these decisions reflect expectations associated with the gender frame—that men are to be rational and calculating while women are to consider emotions and the concerns of others.

Co-creation, however, also operates at the institutional level and, again, in gendered ways. Fantasy sports participants fashion their fan experiences collectively through fantasy sports league rules and settings. For instance, nothing stops them from mandating that certain athletes are nonrosterable in their league because of their history of violence against women. Yet fantasy sports participants reveal no cases of their league members collectively saying that they, unlike the professional leagues, will not root for and roster such players as a group. Here, as in the real game, both collectively and individually, violence against women is rendered insignificant and masculine approaches to fandom dominate.[64]

But there is another reason why men may be more likely to ignore and less likely to grapple with the off-field behavior of athletes, particularly in regard to the treatment of women: the privilege of the powerful is not to see or consider the position of the oppressed. In fact, numerous studies demonstrate that men are more likely to accept rape myths than are women; men are less likely to understand the definition of, reasons behind, implications of, and consequences of sexual assault and harassment.[65] Indicative of this is that some men joke about rostering and rooting for athletes accused of rape or intimate partner violence, and some also have team names that make light of sexual assault—something even those women who have such athletes on their teams do not express doing. For instance, Tony, a dedicated player, claimed, "I will crack jokes on the guy if I have like some wife beater on my fantasy team. If I'm at a bar watching a game, I'll just joke like I'm rooting for a wife beater." When asked if that bothered him at all, he replied after a long pause, "I guess to some degree, yes. . . . But it's kind of just the nature of sports. He's good at what he does. . . . It's not really my issue."

Other men, unlike women, comment that they do not know the "real," full story of what happens between the parties involved in sexual assault or intimate partner violence situations, that everyone deserves a "second chance," and/or that athletes have cleaned up their lives. These rationales reflect classic rape myths and frequent justifications for excusing or pardoning perpetrators, particularly those who are otherwise advantaged by their race and/or class.[66] Thus, the accusations become minimized or discounted and the need to consider them reduced. Exemplifying this, Bill, a married father and hard-core player, related:

> I look at Roethlisberger, yeah, he's done some pretty [bad things], especially that whole incident in Georgia, but from what I can tell, he has kind of cleaned his life up. I don't know. I have no idea what he was like before, I really have no idea what he's like now. I don't know the guy, so I would think that "Hey, everybody deserves a second chance." If he did it again, I think he'd be in trouble, but right now I'd say, yeah, I would have no problem picking Roethlisberger. He's married. He just had a baby. You'd like to think that he's doing the right thing there. Let's hope for his sake that he is.

To a large degree, this way of thinking about and discussing purported rape and assault against women, particularly by athletes, mirrors larger discourses on this topic and how traditional fans react to allegations against athletes on their favorite teams. Jessica Luther writes about how, for instance, the media typically "write the violence out" of their accounts of allegations against athletes (e.g., rape is discussed as a "mishap" or "mistake"—or, as Bill said, an "incident").[67] In privileging men and masculinity, the focus is also on the athlete and the team (particularly in reference to how it will affect their on-field performance, ability to play, or chances of winning) and not on the survivors and the impact this violence has on them. Finally, Luther finds that once the authorities or courts decide on the legal issues, accounts turn to a discussion of "redemption" for the athlete accused of sexual violence. Just as the media, institutional entities (e.g., colleges, the National College Athletic Association), and communities of fans reframe and minimize athletes' assault of women, so, it seems, do many fantasy sports players, particularly men. And in doing so, men's dominance is reinscribed in this domain, just as it is in traditional fandom.

Importantly, while the women with whom we spoke sometimes acknowledge how their views and experiences differ from men's, the men with whom we spoke rarely, if ever, acknowledge the gender dynamics we highlight in this chapter. Similarly, not a single participant in our study—man or woman—ever said a word about the racial dynamics at play in this space. Fantasy sports participation involves the virtual manipulation of athletes whom participants use for their own success. The majority of fantasy sports players are White, while the majority of athletes in the most popular fantasy sports are racial-ethnic minorities. That these White participants, regardless of gender, talk about drafting and trading—that is, virtually buying and exchanging—Black and Latino bodies without any mention of race underscores the racialized power dynamics of this space. Our participants' racial privilege allows them not to see or concern themselves with these dynamics at all. That it is White men in particular who frame these largely minority athletes as commodities highlights that these racialized power dynamics are also gendered—even as our participants remain silent on these issues.

From Better Fans to Disgruntled Purists: Gendered Perceptions of Fantasy Sports' Impacts

To this point, we have argued that fantasy sports participation alters traditional fandom by shifting fan allegiances and influencing how participants consume, appreciate, and know real sports—and that it does so in gendered (and racialized) ways. Participants' assessments of the impacts of fantasy sports on real fandom, however, are gendered as well. Women are much more likely than men to argue that fantasy sports participation *enhances* traditional fandom for them and others, arguing in particular that the hobby produces better, more informed fans. In fact, about twice as many women than men discuss improved real sports knowledge and understanding resulting from fantasy sports participation, and they often focus a great deal on this in their narratives.[68] For example, Jane, a dedicated player who has been "passionate about the NFL for a while," told us that with fantasy sports, "there's a lot more interest in the numbers and the stats and the finer details of football, and I think that increases knowledge of the game. And the more that fans know about the game, I think it makes for a more intelligent fan base." Likewise, Lynn, a current Arizona Cardinals fan, claimed:

> It has made me a better fan. I always liked watching football. That was kind of ingrained in me from both my mom and my dad. But other than my team, growing up I was always a Cowboys fan. Other

than Cowboys' players, I didn't know a lot of other players in the NFL. . . . Now I can watch any game and know the players, know what's going on.

Importantly, women, like Jane and Lynn, generally enter fantasy sports with the love and knowledge of real sports characteristic of traditional fans. Yet many, even those who claim to have much sports knowledge—including several with careers in the athletic realm—still report gaining additional understanding and confidence through fantasy sports participation. Men, as detailed in the following chapters, enter not only assuming they and other men are fans and have sports knowledge but also with an orientation toward demonstrating and being recognized as *already having* said knowledge. But, again, the gendered dynamics in fantasy sports are not just about individual difference. Instead, social constructions of masculinity and fandom overlap such that sports knowledge and experience are assumed for men and boys *and* central to the very definition of fandom. This institutional backdrop frames gendered interpretations of knowledge accumulation and personal growth through fantasy sports. For men, fantasy sports provide a way to show off their sports knowledge and fandom, not to attempt to augment it. Because they are marginalized in the very definition of fandom, women are more likely to position fantasy sports participation as enlarging the knowledge they are assumed to lack and that they, themselves, likely underestimate.[69] Furthermore, women's admitting to an *increase* in knowledge may provide them legitimacy as a "real" sports fan in a man's world (detailed in Chapters 1 and 5), whereas for men, an increase in knowledge suggests a lack of previous knowledge, which threatens both their fandom and their masculinity.

Men, conversely, often reveal that they see their and others' sports consumption, knowledge, and accordingly, fandom—traditionally defined—changing in *undesirable* ways with fantasy sports involvement and their dominant presence in U.S. society more generally. They note, for instance, *downsides* of playing are that they "tend to lose track of the real standings and focus mainly" on their fantasy teams, select games to watch based on how many of their fantasy players are in them, and no longer watch games in their entirety or do so less. They also complain that fantasy sports make them "less of a fan of teams and more individually oriented" and makes them "root for players instead of enjoying the game." As one player explained, "My focus is on fantasy touch, and the pleasure of the game is lost." Women often note these changes as well, but they do not generally interpret them as problematic.[70]

For some men, this is directly tied to fantasy sports' impacts on real team allegiances. Because many men prioritize their competitive fantasy fandom over their traditional fandom, men feel and complain about conflicts of interest in fantasy sports—both in regard to their own reactions to these and others'—more often than women who are more likely to let other factors, including attachments to individuals or real teams, into account when deciding their rosters. One man complained that because of such conflicts, "fantasy sports can take the fun out of the competition at times." Tony, a Philadelphia Eagles and Pittsburgh Steelers fan, harshly condemned others for putting fantasy sports above traditional sports fandom:

> To me, that's the most annoying thing. If you are watching like an Eagles-Giants game with your buddy that you grew up with and you're both big Eagles fans, but the guy on the other team, let's say a guy on the Giants is on your fantasy team—just to watch the person be like, "OK, OK, Victor Cruz scored. I'll get some points for Cruz." I'm like, "Dude, your priorities are not straight here!" . . . I can't stand for the people that do that. I think that's the most annoying thing about fantasy sports.

A subset of men goes further, indicating that fantasy sports are "ruining" how the general public watches, understands, and follows real sports. They argue that fantasy sports cause those involved to *lose* an understanding of and interest in the real game as a team sport, the unfolding of games over the entire matchup, and the outcomes of games and their implications. These players complain that fans today increasingly watch only the RedZone channel and that they have "ADD [attention deficit disorder]" when it comes to sports. To them, fantasy sports have fundamentally changed how we understand and interact with real sports in ways that hinder and supplant true (traditional) fandom, which focuses on teams rather than individuals and games rather than plays. Tony complained at length about this issue and the rise in popularity of fantasy sports more generally:

> Nobody wants to watch the whole game; they just want to see the highlights. It's just kind of annoying to watch people's attention span collapse. And you can't really just talk about the actual real game anymore with a lot of these fantasy people. . . . [Fantasy sports] just kind of make a lot of people annoying football fans because they are more interested in more of the fantasy thing and only want to talk about touchdowns and not like any big hits or blocking or how plays develop. . . . What I enjoy about the sport is just not what these other people are looking at.

Another male player summarized the position of these sports purists when he complained that the downside of fantasy sports is the loss of the true nature of the sport. You're not watching the competition of Team A versus Team B; you're watching a bastardization of true competition. In addition, [you] become unaware of why a player or team is successful, and unable to understand the core concepts of sport.

Some men also criticize the casualness and accessibility of fantasy sports and, thus, the extension of legitimate fandom they provide (see also Chapter 3). These players argue that the omnipresence of fantasy sports experts on television, radio, print, and online media and the computerized projections made available on fantasy sports platforms create the sense that *anyone* can participate—even those who are not traditional die-hard fans. As Bob, a hard-core player, claimed, people can now play fantasy sports "with a lot less preparation than you had to do back in the day. You had to sort of know a lot more going into the draft than you do now. So a lot more people, there's a lot more casual players now than there were before."

Relatedly, some men argue that fantasy sports have become "too big" and represent too much of a focus of the sports media. In fact, even admitted fantasy sports fans complain that the media's focus on them has gone too far and an appropriate balance is not being struck between sports coverage for traditional fans and that for fantasy sports fans. As a result, these men worry that traditional fandom is being supplanted by fantasy sports. One male player complained, "I despise the ubiquity of fantasy sports talk during broadcasts and in pre-/postgame shows. . . . The broadcasts are WAY too full of fantasy talk. It's not the reason the games are being played; in fact, it's the opposite, right?" Ted, a dedicated player who also thought that broadcasters focused too much on fantasy sports, griped:

> Broadcasts focus too much on it, I think. They have to; sometimes they have to realize that before the fantasy exists, before the stats exist, the [real] game is the reason, not the stats, not the stats accumulating, [for the] competition. . . . They [the media] lose the context of the game in the league for potential playoff spots in the actual NFL. Instead, it becomes how did this affect your fantasy team? That's how the broadcasts seem to go more and more. And I do not like that one bit, that's bad.

Such fantasy sports purists and staunch traditional fans are not wrong about the commodification of fandom in fantasy sports. Our fieldwork at a Fantasy Sports Trade Association (FSTA) summer conference makes clear that the sports industry is heavily invested in integrating fantasy sports content into their broadcasts and sports-related programming—thus trying to capture both the traditional and fantasy fan. Speakers at the conference discussed at length how television networks have numerous sponsored fantasy segments in their sports broadcasts and programming, which bring in substantial amounts of revenue.[71] Others noted how sports announcers pepper references to athletes' fantasy sports performances into their coverage of live games (e.g., "So-and-so is having a great fantasy day"). Sports broadcasters are also now thinking more about how to "monetize" fantasy sports sponsorships (e.g., by getting paid when Draft Kings are mentioned in a Cubs broadcast). Another FSTA presenter noted that new mobile technologies will further integrate fantasy sports with in-venue sporting events, allowing venues and arenas to "engage" in "real-time mobile fantasy" with their traditional fans as they attend the event—something that he called a great opportunity for "proximity-based marketing."

Importantly, though, FSTA panelists asserted that "alienation of regular fans is not an issue" because the media have been "successful" at striking a "balance" between fantasy and real sports in their programming and commentary. In fact, conference presenters mentioned that if anything, sports broadcasts will come to incorporate even *more* fantasy-related content in the future. In their estimation, they have barely "cracked" the surface of what they can do in terms of real and fantasy sports integration and their capitalization on fantasy sports. For instance, a sports network representative claimed that Matthew Berry, a fantasy sports guru, will play a "bigger part" in what they do on the network in response to audience demand. Some also expressed interest in professional athletes discussing their own fantasy sports participation on air, making them more "relatable" and "likable" to regular fans while further integrating fantasy sports into sports media. Yet these industry professionals may ultimately be missing the mark as they see traditional and fantasy sports fandom as mutually reinforcing in ways that some fans, particularly men who are purists and devoted traditional fans, do not. Rather, even though they love fantasy sports, these men feel keenly how fantasy sports conflict with traditional fandom and worry about their impact on how we interact with and appreciate real sports.

It is not surprising that men are so much more bothered by the intrusion of fantasy sports into real sports broadcasts and fan experiences. The real, true fandom of which they speak so nostalgically—and which, in their eyes, fantasy sports disrupts—is, of course, a masculine domain. It is integral to the social construction of masculinity at an institutional level, men's performances of manhood, and as result, their identities as men. Moreover, as fandom becomes broader and potentially more accessible, some men may feel their once-exclusive domain being encroached upon. Women fantasy sports enthusiasts do not have the same stake in how fandom is defined and generally fail to offer the complaints we heard from men. Women also are the ones now being included, and therefore, it makes sense that they are rather nonplussed about any changing dimensions of fandom resulting from fantasy sports. Men more forcefully resist and feel more keenly than women a threat to fandom's purity.

Conclusion: Gendered Co-Creation, Power, and Personalized, Competitive Fantasy Sports Fandom

Fantasy sports offer a personalized, competitive fandom that gives participants some measure of control and a direct connection between their successes and that of real-life athletes. Within the rules of their leagues (which participants set and modify), participants craft their teams as they see fit—prioritizing rational calculations of athletes' likely performances, real-team loyalties, athletes' character and alleged crimes, or a mixture of some or all of these considerations. Pittsburgh Steelers fans cannot release Ben Roethlisberger, stop the team from signing someone from a rival team, or get them to trade for a stand-up guy like Larry Fitzgerald. In the world of fantasy sports, the fan can conceivably do all of these. Thus, while fantasy sports as a competitive and masculine fandom prioritizes knowledge, skill, and rationality in roster decisions, co-creation opportunities abound in ways unavailable in traditional fandom.

It is also an arena replete with power dynamics—overt and subtle but almost exclusively unacknowledged. The result is that race and gender privilege are reproduced and reinscribed in fantasy sports. Although not explicitly sex segregated like "real" sports and not relying on presumed physical differences that justify men's dominance in athletic pursuits, the majority of fantasy sports participants are men. But the space is gendered in a myriad of ways that extend far beyond numeric representation. The sole accepted definition of success in fantasy sports is winning—a type of dominance fitting with traditional notions of hegemonic masculinity. And while fantasy sports require attention to individual players and sometimes attachments develop to them, letting one's heart govern fantasy sports decisions and rooting loyalties is inappropriate. Some do take into account allegations of criminal and/or immoral behavior (especially sexual assault) in devising their teams. Yet such considerations *are less common than refusing to roster a player from a rival real team.* This bears repeating—fantasy sports participants are more willing to draft someone with a criminal and/or reprehensible background than they are to breach real-team loyalties. And women more commonly take into account team loyalties, athletes' off-field behavior, and athletes' character than do men. This makes sense, as such tactics violate the general (and masculine) expectation of rationality and winning at all costs. Moreover, with men's privilege comes the option to ignore behavior that seemingly does not affect or concern them, such as violence against women. Thus, while fantasy sports, unlike traditional fandom, offer opportunities for participants to customize and control their experiences, our work indicates how the very process of co-creation is gendered in ways not acknowledged in previous research.

Indeed, the very sense of being in control of one's success as a result of one's efforts, abilities, and choices is steeped in notions of White, class-privileged men as dominant, rational, and in charge of themselves and others. Men, more so than women, feel and like to think they are in control. Also fundamental to this is participants' using their knowledge and skills to roster athletes who then contribute directly to the participants' own success. Athletes, in effect, become the property of these managers—*their* guy—if only temporarily and virtually. It is the fantasy managers who choose to draft, play, or sit them and, ultimately, trade or keep them. The outcomes of the athletes' labor belong to the manager insofar as he or she accrues points on the basis of the athletes' performance. As further evidence of this, one need only look to social media, wherein fantasy sports participants attack real-life athletes for failing to perform *for them*. This has led some athletes to respond in turn, as when Martellus Bennett tweeted at the start of the 2017 NFL season, "I don't care about your fantasy football team. Thanks! Sincerely real life football guy."[72]

This, in and of itself, is indicative of power, and these power dynamics are racialized as well as gendered. The vast majority of fantasy sports participants are White—and most are White, middle- to upper-class men—while the majority of athletes manipulated in fantasy sports, particularly in football (the most popular fantasy sport), are men of color. The allusion to slavery, as evident in the much-criticized 2017 ESPN sketch—is thus quite evident. Although research on why Black men and women do not play fantasy sports is scant, this suggests a possible reason—they do not want to participate in an arena that makes them complicit in their own subjugation.

Furthermore, given the prioritization of men and masculinity in this space, it is perhaps not surprising that the group of purists and die-hard traditional fans who resent the intrusion of fantasy sports on real sports and fandom are overwhelmingly men. These players, who "enjoyed it more when not a lot of people were playing it" and when it was comprised solely of "people who really loved football," are nostalgic for the loss of an exclusive preserve, one that "these other people" have now infiltrated. Whether they are conscious of these implications, these sentiments reflect exactly the types of subtle processes that perpetuate institutionalized inequalities across many contexts, including sports.

This all points to one last important detail—that participants leave essentially unacknowledged the power dynamics of fantasy sports fandom. Accordingly, much of what we discuss in this chapter represents what schol-

ars would call subtle sexism and racism—invisible but consequential interactions, dynamics, and structures that perpetuate the dominance of certain
groups and identities and the marginalization of others. In this case, they
reflect and perpetuate the privileges of men, Whites, and those socioeconomically advantaged and particularly those for whom those dimensions
intersect—White, middle- to upper-class men. It is to their experiences that
we now turn.

3

Letting Men Be Men

Jock Statsculinity and Fantasy Sports

rank is an immediately likable, articulate, White, twenty-seven-year-old living in Indiana, who "always" followed sports and was "an athlete"—more specifically, a competitive runner—in high school and college. He recalls how he began playing fantasy sports in his senior year of college, first joining a few public, anonymous leagues to "figure out drafting and make those mistakes" that any new player would make. Frank soon started playing with friends, hoping his experience would help him beat them handily. In reflecting on his entry into the hobby, he is mindful of how fantasy sports filled multiple needs for him as a young man trying to find his place in society. He explains in a matter-of-fact, relaxed manner:

> Coming out of college, wrestling with those identity questions that every college student wrestles with—not sure what I was, where I was going, didn't have a career—I had an English degree; what do you do with that? I had no real sense of direction. . . . [Fantasy football] was a place where I had control. It was a place where I was good. It was a place where I was recognized by my peers as like, "Man, you're really good at this." . . . There was something there that got me very interested in the first place because it was meeting some psychological needs, it was meeting relational needs, it was meeting some different needs in that direction.

Now, Frank has a master's degree, a career in higher education, and is married and expecting his first child. Thoughtfully, he explains that with these benchmarks hit, he is "much more comfortable with who" he is and "probably in a healthier place overall" than he was just a few years ago. No longer is he chasing his self-worth through fantasy sports. Even so, he is still drawn to them and currently plays in eight fantasy football leagues (three of which are with friends, coworkers, and/or family and the rest of which are with strangers). Part of the draw, he tells us, is about escaping the real-life stresses of adulthood and reimagining himself as having the dream job of many boys—that of general manager (GM). He notes, "I do need rest. I work hard during the week and I need a break, and so this is that for me. And it's a false reality, it's a silly construct where we can be a general manager and have that dream job, and it's not real, no, but it does feel real."

Certainly, it is not that Frank lacks other ways to fill his leisure time and to unwind after a hard day's work. He still follows sports, he reads and writes, he is active in his church, and he picks up running from time to time, cycles, and plays Frisbee. But many of these activities cannot fulfill Frank's other needs, in particular, a need to be competitive. As he puts it:

> I enjoy watching football, but it's nice to have something of myself invested in it. It's nice to have some sort of objective. I do enjoy running, and I like being in shape, but it's hard for me to run after twelve years of competitive running—it's hard for me to run without some sort of competitive goal. . . . The drive isn't there, and so that's part of why I do fantasy football. . . . There's a [competitive] goal.

Frank is clear that being competitive is something that is important for him and for men in general, noting it is a "cultural construct" for "men to be competitive longer in life," whereas for "women to be very competitive, it's kind of like, 'Oh, you know, she's kind of a bitch.'" Importantly, though, fantasy sports provide safe, "temperate" competition that, for Frank, does not go "too far" like physical athletic activities have in the past. It is hard to imagine this rather even-keeled professional once got into a fight during a dodge ball game, but Frank sheepishly admits this was the case, calling it "embarrassing." Fantasy sports, unlike the competitive athletic pursuits of his younger days, allow him to "compete without a 100-percent selling out and saying [to himself], 'Oh, this determines my mood and the rest of my day.'" They also allow Frank to maintain competitive pursuits as his physical athleticism and priorities shift.

It is not just the competition fantasy football provides that has kept Frank investing several hours a week in the hobby over the last seven years. He is also clear that he enjoys the cerebral aspects of fantasy football—that he relishes digging into data and "pushing my brain to think in new ways." In fantasy sports, there is always "something new to learn, there's always some new development, some new player coming up, there's always some new nugget." Not only that, but this process also gives him the feeling of control. As he describes, "*I'm* creating a strategy, *I'm* putting together a philosophy of fantasy football and trying to use it to drive success and drive the big picture of how *I'm* competing in the league. . . . *I* can control. . . . *I* can amass the knowledge that's better than other people." And through these efforts, Frank is able to demonstrate visibly that he not only enjoys "the athletic world and competing" but that he is "really knowledgeable about football, about fantasy, about sports in general."

Below the surface of these explanations for why Frank and droves of other men like him dedicate such time and energy to fantasy sports are important glimpses into how involvement is about engaging in and performing masculinity. Gender scholars, such as Candace West and Don Zimmerman, push us to think about gender as something we "do" rather than what we "are." Drawing our attention to men in particular, Douglas Schrock and Michael Schwalbe refer to men's enacting dominance through interaction as a series of "manhood acts."[1] It is through the performance of these manhood acts that men establish masculine identities and reinforce the dominance of men and masculinity as categories of being. Although "all manhood acts imply a claim to membership in the privileged gender group," work on them and multiple masculinities reminds us that gender is contextually dependent.[2] We perform and are held accountable to diverse variants of masculinity (and femininity) in different social settings and situations. A variant of masculinity we call "jock statsculinity" dominates fantasy sports. Across numerous sports and thousands of leagues, participants recognize, value, admire, and are held accountable to this unique model of masculinity.

Jock statsculinity combines elements of the masculinity that emerged alongside organized sports in the late nineteenth and early twentieth centuries in the United States—a masculinity akin to the hegemonic ideal type that centers on one-upmanship, competition, athleticism, control, and aggression—with a more cerebral masculinity—one that reflects being strategic, tech savvy, rational, and adept with statistics and that is associated with socioeconomic power, intellectual prowess, and even nerdiness. Jock statsculinity also harkens back to boyhood for men—reflecting a juvenileness of play, banter, and escape that adult responsibilities and interactions often fail to allow. The masculinity project that fantasy sports entails, then, is a hybrid, existing at the intersections of middle-class masculinity, laddish and sports-based masculinity, digital gaming and nerd masculinity, and boyish masculinity.

Accordingly, jock statsculinity differs from the masculinity available through traditional sports fandom. Traditional fandom masculinity is largely consumptive yet still very much steeped in many of the elements of traditional (sports) masculinity (e.g., competition, aggression, and dominance).[3] Jock statsculinity is qualitatively different in that it combines these elements of traditional masculinity with elements of nerd masculinity and, to some extent, the enactment of boyhood fantasies—and it does so in an *active* way. The active element of jock statsculinity is particularly important, as control is a key aspect of traditional masculinity that traditional sports fandom masculinity does not include to the same degree as jock statsculinity, a point we discuss at length in Chapter 2. Moreover, while traditional sports fandom masculinity certainly includes an emphasis on knowledge, it is not a nerd masculinity. Additionally, the way men employ their knowledge (and thus stake a claim to jock statsculinity) is competitive and results in measurable personal outcomes that further reinforce claims to masculine status. These factors, along with the fact that jock statsculinity involves more than mere consumption, makes it particularly potent.

At the same time, this masculinity project, like that made available through traditional sports fandom, is largely accessible—albeit mainly to White, class-privileged men. Because of the nature of the hobby, aging men, self-described nerds, and nonathletes are able to practice the manhood acts that fantasy sports afford, thus giving them a foothold on legitimate masculinity unavailable through actual athletic participation. Some men are even able to resist elements of jock statsculinity without delegitimizing their presence in this space. Jock statsculinity is thus more compelling than traditional fandom masculinity and more accessible than the masculinity available through physical athletic participation. Notably, however, we demonstrate that fantasy sports' accessibility makes the manhood project less attractive to some men—those hard-core, longtime players who had previously cornered the market on fantasy sports. Jock statsculinity thus presents opportunities for both the expansion and contestation of manhood in contemporary U.S. society.

Masculinity in the United States: Sports, Workplace Rationality, and Digital Gaming

Sports as a defining aspect of and means of demonstrating manhood is a rather modern phenomenon in the United States. In fact, a "crisis in masculinity" in the late nineteenth and early twentieth centuries contributed to the rise of organized sports and physical activity as core leisure pursuits for men in the United States.[4] With the modernization of workplaces, urbanization, and closing of the frontier in the 1800s and into the 1900s, traditional male-controlled forms of masculinity weakened. White middle- and upper-class men's work was especially rationalized; in the new industrial capitalist order, privileged men used their brains, not their brawn, to succeed. Simultaneously, women were asserting their agency in new ways in the economy, in the home as the moral and logistical center of the family, and in the political sphere as they demanded their rights—all of which (coupled with the above workplace changes) fostered fears about the feminizing of U.S. society.

In this context, men, particularly White middle- and upper-class men, required additional ways to assert their manhood, bodily empowerment, and difference from and superiority over women. They needed to prove they remained the ones in charge, the physically powerful, the providers, the tough fighters—and organized sports and physical leisure pursuits provided a solution. In short, as work became separated from men's bodies (again, especially for privileged men), leisure pursuits contingent on the body filled this void. Men could demonstrate and cultivate their physical superiority and gain self-confidence and feelings of power and control in an arena where girls and women were by and large excluded. In their workplaces, these men could be rational and in control, while in their leisure activities, they could demonstrate a masculinity that hinged on bodily agility and strength as well as aggression and violence.

This masculinity cultivated through organized sports and athleticism re-inforced power not only based on gender but also on class, race, and ethnici-ty. Certainly, the working poor at the turn of the twentieth century turned to sports to bolster their claims to masculinity (and still do so today), but since many remained very much engaged in physical labor, working-class men did not need sports and physical leisure pursuits to prove their manhood or their physical strength in the same way as well-to-do professionals or white-collar workers did. Rather, sports and athletics served as an escape from the dif-ficulties of working-class life and as a validation of manhood when economic power was beyond reach.[5] Moreover, the affluent viewed organized sports as offering a civilizing influence over immigrant and working-class boys and men—teaching them discipline and American values. As Jennifer Ring puts it, "middle- and working-class men cultivated competitive athletic cultures to define and assert the changing mores of masculinity in an era of rapid so-cial change. The middle classes sought a masculinity defined by rationality, discipline, and Christian morality, whereas the lower classes asserted their independence from that enforced order and asserted their masculinity by roughness and passionate physical toughness."[6]

In the postwar period, science, math, and technological competence became core foci in schools for boys. In subsequent decades, these develop-ments, alongside the growing technological needs of the military, the com-puterization of work more generally, and the further emergence of the ser-vice economy, necessitated changes in masculine ideals—changes, again, that reflected not only gender but also class and race.[7] More specifically, White middle-class masculinity, which already was associated with ratio-nality, became even more coupled with intellectual acumen and "skill" and progressed to include technological fluency and achievement. Within lei-sure, sports still represented a core arena for boys and men of all classes and races to prove and test their manhood; however, new leisure spaces for boys and men to demonstrate their worth emerged during this time frame. Chief among them was digital gaming, which exploded during the 1970s and 1980s. Despite women's involvement in digital gaming from its onset, industry advocates, and the media more generally, constructed video gaming as a male domain by marketing it as akin to sports, focusing on young men in portrayals of gamers (the "athletes" in this space) and highlighting the masculine skills that digital gaming supposedly hinged upon and developed (e.g., technological fluency, mental agility, competitiveness, aggression, etc.).[8] As just one of many examples, the January 1983 issue of *Life* magazine featured a photo of sixteen of the country's top "vidiots," all of whom were young White men, standing in front of video game arcade machines with five young White women dressed as cheerleaders in the foreground. Such images promoted not only the idea that gamers are men but that they are also like athletes.[9] Hollywood depictions of the boy gamer who uses his smarts to save the day (e.g., as Matthew Broderick's character David Lightman does in the 1983 film *WarGames*) further served to link gender, age, and Whiteness to technological savvy.[10] As Carly Kocurek argues, "an emergent ideal of masculinity—one associated with youthfulness, technological competency, intellectual abilities, creativity, boyishness, and a particular type of militarism" arose during this period—one that was unquestionably tied to digital gaming.[11]

Digital gaming, however, both in its infancy and currently (though to a lesser extent today[12]), is also associated with a maligned social categorization—the "nerd"—and insofar as this is the case, the meaning of masculinity in this space is ambiguous. On the one hand, "nerd masculinity" aligns well with some elements of more mainstream masculinity, particularly rationality and technological competency; moreover, the nerd appears to lack core traditionally feminine characteristics, such as "emotional expressivity and aesthetic consciousness."[13] On the other hand, the prototypical nerd is not athletic, does not engage in physical activities, is not physically fit (but, rather, is slight and weak), and in his social awkwardness struggles in his interactions with women (thus rendering him sexually inept and powerless)—all of which put him beyond the confines of ideal Western masculinity.[14] Accordingly, Ran Almog and Danny Kaplan conclude that "nerd masculinity reflects an ambivalent social location: it is privileged on the one hand" in that it is associated with some ideals of manhood (especially as conceived as a White, well-educated, middle-class professional) "but greeted with derision on the other," as it falls short of achieving other conventional markers of what it means to be a real man.[15]

Just as athletic leisure pursuits developed as historic sources of masculine power were in flux, so too must the emergence of fantasy sports, nerd masculinity, and jock statsculinity be situated in context. The rise of Silicon

Valley and the information economy lends itself to the flourishing of a masculinity centered on rationality, tech savviness, economic power, and Whiteness. One need only look to media narratives of "nerdy" tech entrepreneurs such as Mark Zuckerberg or Bill Gates for evidence of this shift in what powerful men might look and act like. Achieving economic success through the use of one's mind and technological skills means one need not physically dominate others to establish a firm grounding in masculinity.

At the same time, recent changes in men's economic position—a decline in real wages, underrepresentation among educational degree recipients, the "mancession" of the first decade of the twenty-first century—heightened the economic anxiety and difficulties of many men and their families. This, combined with women's inroads in educational, occupational, and political arenas—and continued movement on the part of women and other marginalized groups to de- and reconstruct understandings of gender and tackle sex and gender inequality across various spheres—has produced the (real or imagined) sense that masculinity is in crisis. Of course, it is a particular masculinity that is in crisis—White, middle- and upper-class, heterosexual, patriarchal, hegemonic masculinity. In their analysis of 2010 Super Bowl commercials, Kyle Green and Madison Van Oort argue there are "a number of central themes involved in this crisis, including discontent over the loss of traditional patriarchal status and heteronormative family values, diminishing confidence in failing bodies, and uncertainty over the economy."[16]

Just as the rise of athletic leisure pursuits responded to the crisis in White, middle- and upper-class masculinity in the late nineteenth and early twentieth centuries, so too might fantasy sports address the contexts in which men in the twenty-first century must assert, defend, and redefine legitimate masculinity. What we heard and learned from fantasy sports players through our survey, interviews, fieldwork, and analyses of message boards is that fantasy sports promote the performance of a hybrid masculinity—one that progresses from masculinities of the modern era but that is new in the intersections it entails. Fantasy sports offer a version of the vicarious masculinity Sara Crawley, Lara Foley, and Constance Shehan identified, insofar as men gain status and power through the athletic successes of other men, possessing knowledge of sports, and simply having a male body.[17] In this way, it is similar to traditional sports fandom. Yet, vicarious masculinity here includes, as discussed in Chapter 2, the added element of *direct* involvement in the achievement. Moreover, the competitive fandom characteristic of fantasy sports fandom—in which knowledge, skill, and investment are deployed in a competitive environment with quantifiable outcomes, which are, to some degree, within the participants' control[18]—provides a more productive, potent means of performing masculinity than available in traditional, consumptive fandom. This is something that might be particularly needed as women gain power and "invade" traditional fandom.

To be sure, while fantasy sports allow their participants to be active and competitive in their fandom, they are still disembodied—the competition occurs digitally—and rather passive relative to physical participation in real sports. Thus, unlike athletic participation in which men embody power and thereby accomplish and learn masculinity, in fantasy sports, participants attempt to best one another by outsmarting them. This cerebral quality likens the hobby to some digital gaming (and White middle-class workplace masculinity) in which rationality and analytic skills are viewed as the core of success and where the stereotype of the nerdy and inactive "couch potato" gamer still dominate popular conceptions.[19] Fantasy sports, however, downplay the negative associations with feminized passivity and the nerdy gamer through their connection with core traits of the jock—identification with sports, aggression, one-upmanship, and dominance—and they do so in a way that allows White, class-privileged men in particular to play make-believe like they did as boys.

All in all, fantasy sports offer the potential for a particularly powerful manifestation of masculinity—a performance that mixes and reflects elements of laddish, traditional sporting masculinities and nerdish, gaming masculinities but that also offers a more direct and impactful version of vicarious masculinity than traditional fandom. Jock statsculinity includes the cerebral and geeky part of nerd masculinity, the athletic and competitive part of hegemonic masculinity, the play and escape part of a boyish masculinity, and the reflected part of vicarious, traditional sports fandom masculinity—all in a context that reifies the status and privileges of White, middle- and upper-class men. It is not a static performance of any one of these masculinities but an intersection of them all, and as such, it differs from each. Jock statsculinity moves beyond the common delineations of each of its elements, and for this reason, the masculinity project becomes potentially more, not less, powerful while still remaining relatively accessible.

Jock Statsculinity in Fantasy Sports: The Macho, Sporting Dimension

In the chapter opening, we met Frank, whose narrative is ripe with discussion of how fantasy sports offer him and men like him a means to compete, one-up others, be in control, and demonstrate their worth by succeeding in the appropriately masculine domain of sports. In this way, doing gender in fantasy sports involves the performance of a rather macho, sporting masculinity characterized by control, competition, and dominance, one that we often associate with aggressive, athletic, popular, heterosexual men, exemplified by the prototype of "the jock."[20]

Whether in the workplace, sports, or digital gaming, gender scholars have long noted that competition, particularly head-to-head competition with a focus on winning (often at all costs), is characteristically framed as masculine.[21] Hegemonic masculinity is fundamentally based on dominance and superiority, and although contextually dependent variations on masculinity exist, all manhood acts are focused on claiming membership in the dominant gender group. At the core of men's participation in fantasy sports is just that: competition, one-upmanship, and winning. Men discuss with much pleasure how they play fantasy sports "for the competition" and how a main benefit of participating is having an "outlet" for their "competitive spirit." One male survey respondent, when asked to elaborate on what he gained from playing fantasy sports, summed this up well when he wrote, "What do you gain bowling or playing any sport? Competitive challenges. Using instincts, strategy to play, to beat everyone and do well."

The value of this for many men, as the above player alludes to, hinges on the result of the competition. The goal is to "beat everyone and do well" and, as others noted, to experience the feeling of "victory over those" one has "embarrassed in the league." In particular, beating others is integral to how men think about fantasy sports, largely because victory is integral to how they gain respect and "prove" themselves among other men. CB, a hard-core player who's played fantasy sports for more than a decade, indicates as much when he argued that in "extremely competitive leagues [with] a bunch of guys that take it really seriously, if you do well in those leagues, it's a respect thing. You have got to know what you are doing to even be competitive with those guys." Likewise, others claim that what they gain from playing fantasy sports is to "be able to brag when you beat your friends" or, as Bob, another hard-core player, simply replied when asked how important winning was to him, "Oh, it's what we play for—to prove that you can beat everyone."[22]

Having that win on the scoreboard and, consequently, being able to brag to others about it makes the men we talked to, as Archie put it, walk a "little taller" without ever having to lace up a pair of cleats and get on a playing field. Moreover, men reveal that an additional benefit of winning and having bragging rights is getting to control the nature of the interactions that follow. Brendan explained this idea at some length:

> I might be a little bit happier if I'm gonna get to send off a message to the person who was my college roommate, that as predicted, I defeated him this week. But what's more, I think in all honesty, I don't think that that's a matter of having the victory. It's having the knowledge that we're going to communicate over this and *I'm the one* who gets to initiate and set the tone for the conversation, because he is expecting me to send something to him. Whereas if I lose, I'm

sitting, saying, "Oh gosh, what's this next message from him gonna look like?"

As this suggests (and as introduced in Chapter 2) feeling as though you control the outcome of the competition (and the interactions that follow)—that *your* abilities determine if you win or lose, if you gain those bragging rights—is a large part of the attraction of fantasy sports for men. Even though participants clearly do not actually control those athletes who comprise their teams and who are disproportionately men of color, fantasy sports offer them symbolic control as they shift their lineups, draft and claim players off waivers, and drop them when they underperform. They thus provide participants with gendered and racialized command and dominance, a way "to experience the social power that predominantly White, male owners of professional sports teams possess on a daily basis."[23] Moreover, and unlike regular fandom, fantasy managers—not the real-life teams for which they root—are the ones in direct competition with one another, albeit here on a virtual field. This all targets core aspects of traditional understandings of masculinity—to be an alpha man is to be in charge, compete and win, and always be in control. Recall Frank's statement from the beginning of the chapter about why he first started playing fantasy sports; he claimed, "[it] was a place where I had control. . . . There was something there that got me very interested in the first place because it was meeting some psychological needs. . . . [Fantasy sport] allows people to be involved with a hobby that's wildly popular and football in general but feel *more* control over that." Other men repeatedly echo this same desire and that fantasy sports give them control more so than traditional fandom. Fantasy sports enable them to achieve the "satisfaction of having control over the success of a project" and "the ability to feel like" they "can 'control'" their own teams. This feeling of control augments not only the enjoyment of fantasy sports and traditional sports fandom but also the competition and importance of winning—and the masculinity project as a whole.

Playing with known competitors and the ability to do so without physical proximity or capability, which is less possible in real sports, amplifies the competition and desire to crush one's opponents—and the masculinity that is thereby demonstrated. The majority of our fantasy sports players have at least some knowledge of the identity of their competitors and many are actually friends, coworkers, or loved ones.[24] This dynamic heightens the importance of winning and gaining bragging rights, especially when the competitors are closely connected to one another. This contrasts with some digital gamers (particularly those for whom role-playing games are their favorite genre) who express uneasiness with competing against their friends and prefer competition online among strangers.[25] Men delight in one-upmanship regardless of with whom they play, but they are clear that competing and winning against *men* who are their friends or family members is what really matters. Ted, a dedicated fantasy sports player, for example, notes in reference to his friend league in which all the players are men:

> Winning the whole thing would actually be very important, just because I would look at that as a good achievement, as far as sports fan interest is concerned—picking good players and stuff like that and having them be better than the guys my friends pick. . . . [But] I just keep coming back to the whole friend thing. I've been in other leagues where there's just random people and I never care [about winning]. . . . [The] importance is more about winning when it's just my friends, I guess; it's a little more competitive.

Sentiments like Ted's, which highlight the appeal of competitive fandom in the context of men's close social ties, are common among men. As another put it simply, a main benefit fantasy sports give players is "the satisfaction that can only be gained by trouncing close friends in a totally meaningless endeavor." Thus, unlike environments in which the combatants are relatively or completely unknown personally to one another and are more wholly disembodied, here the existing and future close connections raise the competitive stakes, making this space particularly compelling for the accomplishment of gender.

It is thus not surprising that a common and critical manhood act that occurs within fantasy sports is trash talking, or competitive banter and verbal taunting that occurs before, during, and after a matchup among league managers. Trash talking—something also associated with jock cultures (particularly among male athletes and fans in contact and collision sports[26]) and online competitive digital gaming[27]—is both a welcomed and integral part of men's social interactions in fantasy sports[28] (see also Chapter 5) and a key way they perform a sporting, macho masculinity. The men in our study repeatedly discuss loving to talk trash, with some even expressing that they play explicitly *for* the trash talking. In response to an inquiry about whether smack talking exists in his fantasy sports leagues, Bill, a hard-core player with extensive real sports experience as a youth, is typical of many men when he answered emphatically, "Oh sure!" Alluding to how the length of time he has been playing with his group of friends enables trash talking, he continued, "Mainly because of the twenty-five years [of playing fantasy football together], there's a lot of what I call stupid traditions. . . . And there's a lot of smack talking . . . and things that have happened are definitely brought up again and again and again." Similarly, Otto's voice rose in excitement when he discussed the smack talk that occurs in one of his leagues in which people from his neighborhood participate. He proudly explained, "Every time you see one of those guys, it's everybody's talking crap. . . . You make fun of each other's teams, the other people themselves, their mothers, you name it. It doesn't end!"

Men overwhelmingly characterize the smack talking they encounter as "good natured," and many try to make clear that it is neither overly aggressive nor intentionally offensive.[29] For example, Sam, a hard-core player, relayed that trash talking in his leagues is "mostly . . . good-natured ribbing. You ask them what they were thinking, you tell them [they] have a lousy team, that they drafted a loser, that you're going to crush them."

Moreover, just as with winning, trash talking is something men value (and do) with people they know and particularly with men they know well—"taunting each other" (as Anthony calls it) just does not hold the same appeal if it is done with strangers or acquaintances (or women). An interesting dilemma arises here, however. Men reveal they are most likely to be "more insulting" with the men in their fantasy leagues who are their close friends and family members. Yet this same closeness and familiarity creates the potential for disaster if the smack talk goes too far and thus jeopardizes important real-life relationships (see also Chapter 6). Accordingly, while the closeness of ties fosters smack talk, it also requires men to exercise some restraint to avoid interpersonal problems. This makes the trash talking in the typical traditional fantasy sports league less hyperaggressive, misogynistic, racist, homophobic, and offensive than what researchers have reported in strictly anonymous settings—for example, in some online digital gaming contexts.[30] Brendan, a dedicated fantasy sports player who has played with the same men for twenty years, supports this argument:

> It's never, it's not vulgar trash talking. It's because I guess we know each other well and we're all kind of older, it's mellow commentary, but it is poking fun at somebody for losing or for starting a particular player who we think is going to do poorly or who's been in the news for something here lately. . . . You definitely jump on someone when they're down but not in a manner that they are going to remember it next year or carry a grudge about it or leave the league over it.

Thraka, a dedicated player currently in three leagues, also alluded throughout the interview to how he engages in smack talking mainly with those who are his closer friends. Notably, he clarified that this trash talk, while common, is not aggressive, largely because he would not want to say anything that "would threaten a friendship. . . . It's just [saying to a competitor,] this week you are on the bottom and I want you to know I noticed that."

This balance of trash talking with one's closest of friends without harming relationships is a delicate one. The balancing act is made easier, perhaps, by the common assessment among men that, as Bill told us, "guys" like them have "pretty thick skins" and that with a friend, they know where the boundaries of acceptable insult talk are. Even so, some men clearly fail to achieve this balance, and many respondents, both men and women, report instances where the smack talk among men goes "too far" or gets "too personal" (see Chapter 6). As just one example here, Marie, a dedicated fantasy sports player, claimed that "sometimes" the smack talk crosses a line. She recalled a recent occurrence, highlighting the masculine nature of the exchange and her inability to relate as a woman:

> Somebody was trolling another guy for not playing the Seahawks and then he came back with, "Well, you shouldn't have lost your job." It got ugly. . . . Sometimes I find the things they say to each other rather shocking, but I'm like, "Girls don't talk like that to each other." . . . The things that they write seem out of bounds to me. But it doesn't seem to affect their friendships.

To be clear, all of this reportedly "good-natured" and "mellow" trash talk that "doesn't seem to affect their friendships" is embedded in the institutional context of sports. This context is deeply gendered and historically linked to a particular manifestation of masculinity—hegemonic masculinity—that emphasizes heterosexuality and the denigration of femininity. Although men repeatedly deny that their banter is misogynistic or homophobic, they nonetheless recount exchanges that are specifically couched in gendered and heterosexist terms. In some cases, this evinces in somewhat subtle ways, such as passing reference to exchanges as "ball busting." At other times, players provide explicit examples of the sexist and homophobic language they and others use, even as they deny that such exchanges are problematic. Zone, a dedicated player who participates only in free leagues, for instance, disclosed:

> I enjoy giving and receiving [trash talk]. . . . My favorite line is telling the other team to take off their skirt if they are going to compete with me and that I have a dress waiting for them after the game. Of course, this only works out well if the other player is of the male gender and presumably straight. Otherwise, well, it just doesn't read the same. While I realize this may sound male chauvinistic or gay biased, there is absolutely no bias intended, and I wouldn't make the same post if the other team was played by the female gender. . . . I might make a "pants" comment, though.

That Zone tries to make clear that the trash talking he so enjoys is all in good fun and not sexist or homophobic while simultaneously using sexist and homophobic language underscores how these particular elements of the masculinity project are so deeply embedded in this context as to become effectively invisible.

Moreover, trash talking, as a manhood act, is fundamentally about one-upmanship and exhibiting dominance—here, by making sure your competition knows you noticed that he is "at the bottom" and through "poking fun" at other men. Trash talk is about constant posturing, about actively asserting one's superiority over others and signaling others' inferiority by mocking their choices, their position in the standings, their personality, their mothers, whatever. And this is a uniquely *masculine* project. Ted sums this up best, perhaps, when he characterizes smack talking as the "typical macho" kind of banter that occurs among close friends. He explains, "The interactions are the better the friend is, [the] more [the] trash talk, the more insulting you can be. . . . Definitely trash talking [happens]—typical macho kind of 'your team sucks and my team's great, and I'm smart and you are dumb,' that kind of typical, stereotypical stuff."

Equally noteworthy is that in the disembodied world of fantasy sports, men are asserting themselves nonphysically—and may not be doing so even in person. In fact, while some trash talk is done face-to-face or over the phone, much of it, even in nonstranger leagues, is accomplished via email, chat rooms, "The Smack Board" on fantasy sports platforms (e.g., ESPN's), instant messaging, or social media (e.g., Facebook or Twitter). Ray, a dedicated player who generally plays in leagues with "mostly friends," explained how this reliance on new media heightens the potential for hurt feelings or angry reactions:

> When you don't have the face-to-face communication, body language, tone of voice, that stuff [trash talk] doesn't get communicated well via instant messenger or a forum post, a tweet, whatever. It's really hard to know if somebody's just kind of jabbing you and giving you a little joke your way, and it's real easy to be on the other end, to be offended.

Furthermore, some of what we observed on fantasy sports message boards and chat forums and occasionally heard from our respondents about banter occurring in stranger leagues can only be characterized as hypermasculine and toxic; and it is likely that the anonymity of those involved and the use of new media to communicate in these spaces are partially to blame. As others, particularly Kishonna Gray, have written regarding Gamergate and insult talk in online multiplayer digital gaming, anonymity disinhibits people, pushing them to write and say things that they never would offline.[31] Beyond the anonymity that some online spaces afford, they also give the illusion that as "make-believe" worlds, real-life norms do not apply—so one can say whatever one wants. In addition, some online spaces fail to have anyone policing civility norms; therefore, no official repercussions follow when crossing moral boundaries. Moreover, communication via new media often does not take place in real time nor is it direct. One can send off a text message, email, or tweet or post a comment in a forum and not have to contend with an instantaneous response and reaction (or one at all)—all of which reduces any potential cost of being offensive. And, indeed, the most toxic discourse we saw or heard about in fantasy sports occurred in online, anonymous leagues and settings. Ted is one respondent who recognized that anonymity may give rise to offensive banter among fantasy league members. He explained how after "fooling around" with the settings as a commissioner in a stranger league (which resulted in people's points being changed), he was met with "very, very abusive language, like really bad stuff—really, really bad, grotesque stuff about my sexuality and my proclivity for certain things."

We, too, observed homophobic and misogynistic joking and insult talk on the public online fantasy sports message boards and chat forums we studied, settings in which posters identify themselves via only self-selected usernames. For example, on one advice forum, posters in the midst of exchanges regarding lineup advice casually discussed how certain athletes or other posters are "pussies," "faggots," or "bitches." Other references to athletes (e.g., Alex Rodriguez as "gayRod") or things being "gay" pop up on various sites as well—such as one person who commented on a popular message forum, "This one time, like eight months ago, I saw two guys kissing in a park. And that was the gayest thing I'd ever seen, until I saw this thread."

In line with what Luke Howie and Perri Campbell find in the context of fantasy basketball in Australia, we also found numerous images and memes among user posts and avatars that demean women, as well as language and discussions that focus on women as sexual objects.[32] For example, one day when Kissane went to a forum for lineup advice, she found she had to sift through comments about how Tim Lincecum (former pitcher for the San Francisco Giants) was on his game in the past because some "badass bitch" was "piping" him, but "when she started piping someone else . . . well, he wasn't the same." Posters also discussed how other athletes, such as Tiger Woods, had "too much puss" and that was his downfall. In discussing whether to start Justin Verlander, a Major League Baseball (MLB) pitcher, one poster noted his then-girlfriend "[Kate] Upton looks like a freak, humongous tits and legs like a chicken . . . looks so freaky," to which other posters replied things like, "LOL," "I would eat her ass! Lol," and "And chew the corn." On another day, a poster asked the others on the forum, "You see Gisele [model and Tom Brady's wife] is releasing a coffee table book of her topless shots . . . for 700 bucks," to which other posters replied, "I wouldn't buy it," "double cream Giselle [sic] please," "man I'm hungry," "Yeah, I'm starving," "Too bad the vagina around here has all been eaten," and "lmfao." On a different site geared toward those playing fantasy football, as posters peppered a forum with questions about which of two or three players to start, individuals started to interject names of women such as "Penelope

Cruz or Salma Hayek?" to which a woman on the site replied after some banter on this point, "This is when being the girl on the blog sucks."

All this is not to suggest that the majority of men engage in this caliber of hypermasculine, homophobic, and misogynistic exchange. In fact, our respondents indicate this is not the case, although many engage in subtler forms of such banter. Those that do, though, are quite visible on the various message boards we explored and new media likely heighten such talk. Furthermore, these exchanges reveal that men presume the audience of fellow fantasy sports players consists wholly or largely of other men, further contributing to the continued perception that men dominate this realm. Finally, the misogynistic and homophobic discourse we read and occasionally heard about from our respondents demonstrate that in line with hegemonic masculinity, performing manhood in these online spaces is about being decidedly heterosexual and antifeminine.

Manhood in fantasy sports thus involves focusing on competition, winning, and beating others; feeling in control; and engaging in interactions focused on belittling and, at times, aggressively putting down others. For some, typically in online and anonymized spaces and also occasionally and more subtly in nonstranger leagues, it also means asserting heterosexuality and superiority over women through homophobic and misogynistic discourse. Certainly, aspects of this performance are different than that of the prototypical jock—most notably, the mechanism by which men participating in fantasy sports are competing, one-upping one another, being in control, and establishing their dominance over one another is not a physical sport. Participants also need not even be physically present to engage with one another in these ways or to gain the validation that arises with each manhood act. One, then, may be apt to say it aligns more fully with masculine display in online multiplayer digital gaming. But unlike some in this realm, here the men typically know one another's real identities, often interact in person, and have close connections that need to be maintained off the virtual playing field. All of this renders the competition, the outcomes, and the corresponding trash talk alternately more and less consequential and potentially damaging.

Jock Statsculinity in Fantasy Sports: The Cerebral and Playful Dimensions

Much of the allure of fantasy sports for men revolves around their association with a macho, sporting masculinity that is closely aligned with traditional conceptions of hegemonic masculinity. Fantasy sports, though, also build on other masculine ideals—those of a cerebral, even nerdy quality—

and provide access to a boyhood masculinity that allows play and escape from the real world.

To start, men in our study, much more so than women, discuss playing fantasy sports because they "love" the cerebral aspects of the game. They also more often assert that success in this space hinges on their intellect and ability to understand and analyze statistics. Otto, a hard-core player who works in an engineering lab at a university, is representative in this regard, as he told us, "I enjoy being successful at analyzing statistics, I guess. That's the part [of fantasy sports] that I really like to do. . . . I take other people's ratings and manipulate the data before the season to help me figure out my draft strategy. Once the season does play, I digest actual NFL [National Football League] statistics."

Men are not only more likely than women to see themselves and their mental skill sets as deciding fantasy sports outcomes but also, as discussed in Chapter 2, are adamant that they make their fantasy sports decisions "rationally" by focusing solely "on the numbers," something we heard much less frequently from women. Fantasy sports is not a realm where one should consider, for instance, the off-field behavior of athletes, largely because doing so might jeopardize the chances of success—something that many men prioritize and presume to be within their control. And unlike real sports participation, there is no need for physical dexterity here—just mental acuity and nonemotional focus. The resultant sense of power and gratification men gain through being successful in this way, therefore, is both new and old—new in the sense that it combines the cerebral with the athletic in a nonphysical playing field; old in that it reflects long-held understandings of men as rational, nonemotional, and good at math.

To be clear, although men are using and valuing their brains rather than their brawn, the everyday interactional processes in this space still denote a macho, sporting manhood. These men, while "brainy," practice dominance as they point out to one another, often through the aforementioned trash talking and bragging, that they are superior. Men promote this narrative of themselves—that they are smarter and more knowledgeable than others—expressing, like Dino, that their sports knowledge is "usually at the top" in their fantasy sports leagues and that even those who professionally advise readers and viewers on fantasy sports matters do not, in his words, "know much more than I do." Just as the digital gaming nerd revels in his "specialized and encyclopedic talk about game titles, game genres, and the histories of game series,"[33] men who play fantasy sports clearly relish showing off to us and to their fellow players their knowledge of sports, their ability to strategize, and their statistical chops. In essence, it is not enough to have sports-related and strategic knowledge and merely enjoy sharing it—what scholars call mavenism. Demonstrating one's manhood involves "schwabism," or having this knowledge and enjoying having others know that one has it.[34] Men repeatedly reveal themselves to be schwabists, focusing on the pleasure they receive from being able to *show off* the superiority of their "intellect and guy instincts" to the others in the league. Sam, a novelist and hard-core fantasy player, explained what he likes about fantasy sports:

> Putting my intellect and guy instincts up against others. . . . A guy will say, "That was a stupid move" or "What a bad trade," and when I can later *show him that I was right*, that I picked a "stud," when I win the league or do well, I have bragging rights. It's a lot of fun . . . [to] *show the rest of the league that I'm smart* and can play the game.

Our statistical analysis of the survey data further supports the link between sex and schwabism, as our male players score significantly higher than our female players on our schwabism scale. That is, male players are significantly more likely to report having knowledge for the purpose of showing it off. Notably, believing that men are better at fantasy sports than women is also positively associated with schwabism in our survey data, suggesting that those who hold more traditional views of sports as a masculine domain are particularly invested in showing off their knowledge to others.

Clearly, men highlight and celebrate fantasy sports' cerebral qualities. Some, however, go further and directly connect the hobby to nerdom, a masculinity that is maligned in some respects but that aligns well with dominant constructions of masculinity in the modern era—Whiteness, workplace power and professionalism, nonemotionality, technological competence, and high intellect. Some, like Roland, a sports writer and hard-core fantasy player, unabashedly self-identify as a "total fantasy nerd," and others, sometimes without directly identifying themselves as "nerds," are quick to note how fantasy sports are akin to other "geeky" pursuits, in particular Dungeons and Dragons or tabletop miniatures games. Archie, a new player who invests a great deal of time in the hobby, explained that fantasy sports are "Dungeons and Dragons for jocks" because each has "the stat aspect of it, like the obsession with statistics, and people can play it entirely that way, but it also has the role-play aspect, and I kind of imagine my team." Also recognizing this connection was another male player who recalled a tweet from Chris Kluwe (former NFL punter) that said, "Fantasy sports are Dungeons and Dragons for guys that find third baseman statistics more interesting than slaying an Umber Hulk with a +5 Holy Avenger." This respondent continued that he found this tweet "completely true, as a person that has a foot in both arenas."

What distances fantasy sports players from stereotypical nerds, however, is the hobby's explicit connection to real sports.[35] As the participant above notes, what the fantasy sports player is excited about is "third baseman statistics"—something decidedly masculine—and that might give men who play a sort of "jock insurance" as C. J. Pascoe terms it.[36] In essence, by having one foot in jock culture, fantasy sports players have more leeway to admit to and practice less hegemonically masculine behavior and traits. Moreover, the role-play aspect to which Archie refers is also housed within sports and associated with racialized and gendered power. Fantasy sports players are reimagining themselves as professional sports owners, GMs, or coaches—*White men*[37] who have immense power over athletes who are disproportionately men of color in football, basketball, and baseball. Accordingly, men, but not women, frequently express that this role-playing attracted them to fantasy sports in the first place and continues to do so now. As one male player put it, fantasy sports participants value the "chance to pretend to be a real GM," or as another claimed, fantasy sports "fulfills my desire I had growing up to be a part of professional sports."

Given the dearth of women working at the upper echelons of men's elite sports and the scarcity and smaller scale of professional women's sports, that White men but not women express a desire to role-play GM through fantasy sports makes sense. Girls and women have had little reason to aspire to professional sports careers and, therefore, do not focus on this role-realizing element of fantasy sports. Furthermore, Black boys, who may hold dreams and expectations of playing professional sports,[38] may not imagine themselves as the GM, given their relative absence in power positions in sports. This offers a potential explanation for their lesser participation in fantasy sports relative to White men, who speak at length in their interviews about this draw of fantasy sports. An example is Jerome, a thirty-four-year old who works in the film industry. He explained:

> I love watching baseball, but I actually love following baseball more, like the behind the scenes and reading what the GMs are doing and all of that stuff. . . . Why I love it [a fantasy baseball league] so much was because for me it now, it fulfills that [desire to be GM]—like I am part of a league, I make decisions.

After some reflection (and even though he does not think of it this way daily), Jerome acknowledged that it's all make-believe: "Deep down, I realize what I'm doing is pretending like I'm part of something that I would love to have been part of, which is real baseball. . . . I think it's ridiculous that I somewhere in my head equate that what I do is equal to a guy who works in baseball."

As is the case with schwabism, this make-believe world involves displaying dominance, boasting, and bragging. In Anthony's words, men, as "sports wannabes" who "never got anywhere close to being able to really do anything like that [manage a pro team] in real life," can garner in fantasy sports tangible proof that they would have been successful GMs, if only they had realized their boyhood dreams. Men often told us how their managerial skills are on par with (or better than) those professionals they emulate—that their records are "better than NFL teams that are really good" (Otto) or that winning in fantasy sports helps prove you can do "a better job of building a team than the real guys did" (Bob). These references to being comparable or superior to what amounts to mere dozens of sports professionals in the whole world (there are thirty-two NFL and thirty MLB GMs, all of whom are men and the majority of whom are White) are striking and represent a clear performance of hegemonic masculinity. As White, middle- or upper-class men, they are already at the pinnacle of the status hierarchy in the United States and yet their bravado about their abilities imagines them even higher—on a level that only a select few ever occupy (and often for only a few years at a time) and that is decidedly masculine, male dominated, and White.

Notably, this level of self-assuredness is characteristic of men more generally and something that develops in boyhood as they come to understand and internalize the *boy code*. When this "kicks in, boys seem to become *more* confident, even beyond their abilities. . . . Boys *find* their voices, but it is the inauthentic voice of bravado, of constant posturing."[39] Accordingly, boys learn through the boy code that "they are supposed to be in power, and thus they begin to act like it."[40] Their (over)confidence carries over into multiple realms, from overestimating their intelligence[41]—even in the face of contradictory evidence—across various contexts (e.g., in education, workplaces, and everyday life) to overestimating their leadership skills in the workplace or sports.

The posturing in which men engage is also tied to dynamics within the larger (real) sports world in which, as Michael Messner argues, public display and recognition of athletic prowess is intricately tied to self-worth and masculine identity.[42] This is made all the more challenging insofar as masculinity is a performance and not a static identity; it must thus be constantly demonstrated, as one's claim to it is always tenuous.[43] In real sports, cultural understandings of men (and boys) as inherently more athletic and physically imposing than women work in all men's favor, but even still, male athletes must constantly prove themselves or suffer the hits to their self-esteem, self-concept, and manhood. In fantasy sports, where cultural beliefs about the inherent intellectualism and rationality of men work in all men's favor, but particularly White men's, men must still repeatedly prove and brag about their superiority—here by asserting their *mental* superiority in understanding and analyzing statistical data and sports information. Thus, in this space, sports affinity (and masculinity) ties not to physical prowess and dominance but intellectual acumen and knowledge—and, as we've previously discussed, in more impactful ways than traditional, solely consumptive fandom.

Imagining themselves as GM also gives men a way to be playful during a time in life, adulthood, when opportunities for play are limited. Highlighting the gendered and childlike nature of this, one male player wrote that men play fantasy sports "to vicariously live the life of a sports General Manager that we won't get to live out in reality. Same reason little girls dress up as princesses." Notably, such role-playing, whether among children or adults playing Dagorhir,[44] is often a shared project. Archie makes this clear when he offers several examples of how league members "banter back and forth" about their teams to reinforce that they are real managers running teams. He explains:

> I was joking [to another league member] about "Well, I hope you gave them [fantasy sports team] a good pep talk before the game" and things like that, and then all his players played really well that week except for Tom Brady, his quarterback. And he was like, "Yeah, I gave a great pregame pep talk, but Tom Brady was too busy preening in front of the mirror.". . . And I'd talk about how I was firing fantasy trainers like Spinal Tap drummers because every week, every week it'd seem like I'd lose two wide receivers to injuries in the first quarter. And I'd be like, "I gotta get a new trainer."

Understanding themselves as GMs, who not only strategize but also give pep talks and hire trainers, becomes possible because men, typically White, class-privileged ones, engage in this play together. They thus mutually construct and continually reinforce a narrative that they all are real coaches, managers, and owners.

Moreover, much of the trash talk and other banter in fantasy sports looks and sounds like juvenile chatter that one might expect among boys. Kissane was struck by this as she recently read an exchange between some fantasy sports players online. After one user wrote, "Early slate pitching is awful," another immediately responded, "Your face is awful," to which others chimed in with "lols" and other equally juvenile comebacks such as "Your mom is awful." Instead of envisioning two White middle-aged, professional, middle-class men (who, given the demographics of fantasy participants, are likely those engaging in the exchange), she pictured a handful of boys teasing and poking one another as they walk home from school. And it's clear that these sorts of give-and-take exchanges are common in our respondents' interactions with other league members, offering them an additional way to harken back to a time before adult responsibilities set in, to take part in juvenile play in an easy and inconsequential way and to consequently perform boyish masculinity. According to Erik Barmack and Max Handelman in their book *Why Fantasy Football Matters (and Our Lives Do Not)*, "the whole trash-talking and chest pounding and borderline immaturity that guys revel" in in fantasy sports is something "they can't otherwise do in adult society."[45] Such talk allows men to be childish and so do fantasy sports.

This harkening back to boyhood, when one could play, engage in juvenile chatter, and pretend to be whomever one wanted, serves a further purpose. It allows men to escape from or unwind after the day's adult activities into a space that is both relaxing and masculinized. Men, and not women, focus on using fantasy sports as an escape. Notably, they largely emphasize needing a respite from two particular parts of their lives: work and fatherhood—the combination of which is a key marker of modern manhood. Nicholas Townsend argues that to achieve full manhood, men today must accomplish the "package deal"—they must be gainfully employed, have children, own a home, and be married.[46] The fatherhood pillar of manhood, however, is more than it was a couple of generations ago. In addition to being a good provider, today's fathers must also attempt to spend time with and be emotionally close to their children.

Men and women also now expect egalitarian marriages in which they will share in the household labor.[47] Thus, as Kathleen Gerson argues, current expectations "press men to give more time and energy to both work and family."[48] And there's evidence that men today as a group are doing more housework and childcare than previous cohorts, although they still lag behind women.[49] Therefore, men who express using fantasy sports for escape are, somewhat ironically, using one form of gender display—one that perhaps relies on nostalgia for a more traditional masculinity—to escape the dictates of another, more modern and seemingly onerous, one.

Men seeking escape through fantasy sports are also operating within the aforementioned broader context—that which contributes to notions of a crisis in masculinity—in which men are seemingly losing out to women in the home, workplace, and education. In her book *The Stronger Women Get, the More Men Love Football*, Mariah Burton Nelson argues that in such a context, sports, especially those that seem exclusively male, become more central to men's building and practicing of masculinity and their claims to (natural) dominance over women. Real sports provide men a means of escape from increasingly "feminized" spaces and women's demands for equality, attention, and power. As Nelson puts it, "sports offer a pre–civil rights world where white men, as owners, coaches, and umpires, still rule"—and wherein women may be strong, "but they are still weak*er*" than men.[50]

Similarly, fantasy sports offer their men—largely White, married, middle- and upper-class professionals with children—a way to "blow off some steam," to get "away from the reality of life," and to "escape from normal day-to-day dull drudgery and/or stress"—and, potentially, a respite from women and increasingly feminized spaces (see also Chapter 6). Anthony, a fifty-two-year-old casual player who is a partner in a law firm and married with three children, is one respondent who uses fantasy sports as escape. At the end of his interview, he told us he wanted to add the following comments:

> What can I say? It is a good release. It is something that I do either early in the morning or late at night as a relaxation thing. It's a hobby when you are done with the crap from the day, and the kids and the bills and the work and the bosses and all that—it's like escapism. I do that for the last half hour of the night, and it is almost like a make-believe world—you go to your league and you look at the standings and you're, whatever, in fourth place or whatever and you look at the schedule and say, "Wow, if I could win this game this week, I can get ahead of this guy." It's like an escape, you know? [It's] harmless, doesn't cost any money; you don't have to leave the house, it's not like gambling, booze, drugs, or whatever. You're not going to the casinos, it's pretty healthy, and just something to focus on and forget all the other crap for an hour.

Notably, all of the "make-believe," escapism, and playfulness of fantasy sports aligns it well with digital gaming and, to some extent, nerd masculinity. Many digital games also allow their participants to perform and play around with alternative identities and to live out fantastic situations. Indeed, one of the marginalizing aspects of the stereotypical nerdy gamer is that he is too preoccupied with fantasy worlds (a criticism we also heard about fantasy sports players). Additionally, Derek Burrill argues that digital gaming, like Burton contends about football, represents a means by which adult men can be boys and escape the real world of adult responsibilities, feminism, and class.[51] Fantasy sports likewise allow for this sort of "digital boyhood" and escape, through which adult men can enjoy engaging in expressive forms of play but, importantly, do so while remaining firmly grounded in the appropriately masculine domain of sports and emphasizing the masculine, instrumental aspects of play (playing to win).[52] And here, unlike the play of their youth when they likely were participating in sports, digital gaming, and role-playing masculine statuses (e.g., pretending to be cops and robbers), no physicality is involved. Last, the quantifiable results of this role-playing and its connection to real sports and athletes provide participants with both a feeling of control and a sense of realism that is often absent in other fantasy worlds and situations.

All in all, men reveal that fantasy sports provide a powerful means by which they can assert and reimagine themselves and one another as being in control, as having superior intellects and sports acumen, and as competent authorities in professional sports. As such, fantasy sports provide a means by which men are not mere spectators of the accomplishments of other men but rather producers themselves who perform a cerebral, yet still macho, masculinity that is rooted in fantastical escape. In fantasy sports, men, regardless of physical ability or age, can play like boys, banter like teenagers, and assert and show off their cerebral prowess as rational, adult men who are self-proclaimed experts in statistics, strategy, and sports information. In this way, the masculinity is both potent and largely accessible—something to which we now turn.

Fantasy Sports Accessibility: Opening Up Masculinity

As a hybrid masculinity, jock statsculinity offers opportunities for inclusion, variation, and contestation. Some men, more typically those who are highly committed to the hobby (i.e., dedicated and hard-core players), seem to fully encompass and promote jock statsculinity. Others, typically casual and limited players, more minimally embrace jock statsculinity. Yet none of the men with whom we spoke reject all elements of jock statsculinity. Indeed, the majority adhere, display, and continually construct the greater part of jock statsculinity but not all its components completely. Thus, just as legitimate fandom is defined on masculine terms, those with the most power and the greatest stake in its accomplishment—men who are hard-core and dedicated players—define legitimate masculinity in this context. All players, regardless of their commitment level, are accountable to the dictates of jock statsculinity.

To be sure and in no small part due to the disembodied nature of the hobby, self-described nerds and aging, busy, injured, and/or physically non-athletic men are able to perform the manhood acts that fantasy sports afford and gain respect for them in ways not available in real athletic pursuits. In particular, for many self-described athletic men, fantasy sports fill "a void" that is left after they can no longer physically compete anymore due to age, time, and/or physical capability. Fantasy sports allow them *to continue to* have access to the macho, sporting elements of jock statsculinity—namely, sports participation, competition, and dominance. For example, Anthony, who "back in the day" "played all the major sports," disclosed:

> I am over fifty years old now, so I can't actually go out there and play with the younger people anymore [in real sports], [so] this is as close as it gets to competition. . . . At my age with work and kids and all that, I don't really have hobbies, and I don't have time to be a golfer and stuff like that. . . . [Fantasy sports players are] a bunch of people like myself who used to play sports and now they have grown up to be doctors, lawyers, stock brokers, whatever, but they still need their competitive fix.

Another male player who, like Anthony, no longer plays real sports due to age and other responsibilities, emphasized the importance of the interactional practices that constitute these manhood acts:

Fantasy sports allows people to come together and bond over a similar interest; it allows owners to trash talk, boast, belittle, trade, and let men be men. It fills a void, that we all had when we were younger and allows us to do something for ourselves, and it all centers around sports. It beats a book club!

Importantly, these men—typically White, professional middle- and upper-class—have claims to masculine status through other legitimate sources. The player quoted above even identifies himself as "the only breadwinner in the family," and Anthony notes it is those doctors, lawyers, and stock brokers who are playing. But for these participants, as with many men, fantasy sports provide access to a particularly salient masculine space and identity—sports and athleticism—when physical participation is no longer possible. And just as hegemonic masculinity explicitly includes a rejection of femininity, jock statsculinity is accessible yet still expressly for and about men—"it beats a [presumably women's] book club!"

Jock statsculinity's inclusion of strategy, knowledge, and statistical expertise necessarily makes it also accessible to the unathletic "stats geek" who is interested in the more cerebral aspects of the hobby. For these self-professed "nerds," fantasy sports might be a way to gain legitimacy in a masculine, competitive environment in which full inclusion had previously eluded them or was limited to consumptive fandom—a much less potent version of status in athletics. These men who, as Archie noted, have grown up in a "jockocracy" and thus have been taught to appreciate and value sports, are able to make legitimate claims to masculinity in the fantasy sports context because they do not need "athletic ability to succeed." As one male player summarized, "As someone who was never good at playing sports, at least I can show I would have made a good GM!"

In these ways, the performance of jock statsculinity is more accessible than that of real athletic participation because the manhood acts involved are open to a greater variety of men. This is in keeping with the notion of multiple masculinities, which allows men to variously emphasize different elements of the ideal type. Men also can and do make legitimate claims to jock statsculinity while refusing to perform or even by explicitly condemning some of its characteristic elements. In his analysis of men's elite ultimate Frisbee, Hamish Crocket found that some men enacted what he termed moderated masculinities, emphasizing support, cooperation, and collaboration; minimizing sexist and homophobic banter; and not shying away from intimate physical contact with men.[53] Likewise, in some men's narratives we see their resisting the full extent of jock statsculinity in this contested terrain or, at the very least, that their thoughts and behaviors are, at times or in some respects, at odds with some of the expectations of manhood explored in this chapter.

For example, although winning, competition, and dominance are embedded in the performance of jock statsculinity, some men reject or distance themselves from these elements while still remaining legitimate participants. By virtue of being men in a masculine arena, they benefit from a gender structure that privileges men's experience—this (and their advantaged status in terms of their race and class) may paradoxically be exactly the reason why they can reject some aspects of the hegemonic ideal as their overall dominance in this realm (and in larger society) remains unquestioned. For example, Bedric, a miniature role-playing game enthusiast who admitted members of his fantasy league "aren't the coolest people, but we're also not isolated geeks," downplayed the importance of winning. He asserted, "I wouldn't say [winning is] important at all at this point. . . . Since we are all learning and all [are] basically just trying to have fun, just being part of the experience is enough for me."

Other men express that they do not feel the need to one-up or damage others to elevate themselves. Bill, a hard-core player who kickboxes to "stay somewhat in shape," claimed, "[Aggressive smack talking] is not my personality anyway, like I'll definitely join in the banter, but I'm not looking for ways to trash somebody else to make myself look better." Thraka, a miniatures gaming devotee and dedicated fantasy sports player who told Kissane that he would be "happy to be your nerd world tour guide anytime," alluded to not feeling the need to take advantage of women to prove something to the rest of the league. After contrasting himself with another man in his league who is "a huge trash talker and kind of a jerk," he noted, "I don't feel when I trade with her [a woman in the league] that I need to go ridiculous with my trade proposals. I don't have to actively try to make her swallow something awful because I have to prove to the rest of the league that I'm tough or something."

Some men extend their rejection of such acts of dominance to policing the behavior of other men and keeping those in their leagues "in check" by making sure the tone of the trash talking is acceptable and that it is not misinterpreted. Ray, an information technology consultant, claimed, "[As commissioner of a fantasy football league,] I have to monitor it as well, make sure that the trash talking doesn't get out of place." Jerome, who also told us that fantasy sports allow him to develop and enact aggressive traits that run counter to his normal personality, recounted how he had to step in when members of his league attacked someone who had just joined after he made what was considered a bad trade. He explained:

> The new guy, who's a friend of mine, who I got to join the league, emailed me and was like, "Jeez, this is a lot of stuff directed right at me." And I had to send an email to the group being like, "Hey, guys, hey, we're all just doing this for fun, and if you don't like the trade,

that's one thing." So every now and then, I would say like once a year, something goes over the line.

In still other cases, we see the development of what might be considered localized norms for enacting jock statsculinity. For example, several men assert that the smack talking in their leagues, while still prevalent, is often about self-deprecation rather than demeaning others. Drew, a casual player who works in information technology and also does a "fair amount of online gaming," mentioned that the participants in his league will "talk a little bit of lighthearted grief to one another" but that "it's usually us talking grief about ourselves more than actually talking smack to any of the competitors." Steve, a dedicated player who works for a *Fortune* 500 company, also characterized "a lot" of the smack talking in his leagues as "self-deprecating." He said, "Just talking about how awful my team is or will someone please take this guy off my hands? There's not a lot, none of the leagues I'm in are people particularly mean." Paul similarly claimed:

> Being in North Dakota we don't do a whole lot of trash talking—it's just not our culture, I guess, so like in the friends and family league, the winner almost always sends a "Well, it was a good game; it was sort of close" or whatever text to the other person, and then you kind of both self-deprecate a little bit.

This is not to say that the variability of practice tied to jock statsculinity is not contested or problematized, even among those men engaging in alternative performances. In fact, men who express notions at odds with the dominance embedded in jock statsculinity understand, and often highlight, that they are different from other men and, at times, lament this. For example, Dino, who "played almost everything" sports-wise growing up, told us:

> I'm not like one of those people who always wants to beat this [or that]. . . . [I] wouldn't say I have that gene that I always want to beat someone; I'm always more in it for a good game than beating people. And I don't really like that about myself sometimes, because I'm not realizing full potential of things sometimes because I'm not going for first place.

Tony, who seemed to both embrace and reject other players' seriousness around fantasy sports and their aggressive smack talk, later in his interview acknowledged, "I do feel like a nerd when I do play fantasy; when I'm not playing fantasy, I make fun of fantasy nerds all the time." Tony's ambivalence and Dino's seeming disappointment in himself highlight the power of hegemonic ideals even as expanded notions of legitimate masculinities take hold. Even in supposedly rejecting elements of a macho, sporting masculine performance, some are in fact affirming it or, at the very least, feel the weight of being accountable to it.

Fantasy sports are a contested space for enacting masculinity in other ways. Specifically, the relative perceived accessibility of jock statsculinity in fantasy sports makes the manhood project less compelling for some men—those hard-core, longtime fantasy sports players who had previously cornered the market on the hobby. This is perhaps unsurprising, as a sizable body of research, including classic work on women's entry into previously male-dominated workplaces,[54] demonstrates that whenever possibilities arise for new people to gain entrée into formerly exclusive spaces, dominant groups engage in a series of interactional and symbolic practices to contest their entry and protect the space and, by extension, their place in it. Scholars have noted such dynamics in both sports and digital gaming. Deirdre Hynes and Ann-Marie Cook, for instance, argue that as soccer's governing bodies seek to engage casual fans, hard-core male fans lament the sanitization of the sport and what they see as a loss of the authentic match-day experience.[55] Similarly, Betsy DiSalvo finds that digital gamers distinguish between authentic and inauthentic gaming by denigrating casual and social games and those who play them.[56] And much has been written on how sports fans, both men and women, identify legitimate and illegitimate participants—often disparaging those seen as new to sports fandom, in particular women.[57]

As we introduced in Chapter 2, a sizable minority of players—almost all of whom are men—push back against fantasy sports' popularity and seeming accessibility. Despite being avid fantasy sports fans themselves, such men complain about its present-day prominence and indicate, sometimes directly, sometimes indirectly, that the exclusivity of the hobby has been lost. Men who have been playing the longest and have some of the greatest levels of current investment most commonly express such sentiments. These players feel a certain level of ownership over this space, and the entrance of newcomers—many of whom are women—threaten this. Thus, even though a larger audience and therefore greater recognition for one's fantasy sports' achievements might accompany greater accessibility, this subset of players view this differently. Instead, the hobby is less special and potentially less competitive and, as a result, less powerful as a masculinity project. The potency of jock statsculinity, particularly in comparison to claims to masculinity available in traditional fandom, partially hinges on the exclusiveness of the space. Charlie, a longtime, dedicated player, for example, complained that fantasy sports are no longer reserved for "hard-core" sports fans. He explained about the rising popularity:

I don't know that I love it. I probably enjoyed it more—and again this is part of my personality—I enjoyed it more when not a lot of people were playing it. You kinda have this thing that you do and that people aren't as into, and now it's everywhere and everybody's playing. I thought of myself as a pretty hard-core fan that was into this. . . . Now, it's just kind of a part of sports. . . . Everybody thinks they're an expert now.

Otto, a longtime, hard-core player, was a bit stronger in his opinion regarding the hobby's popularity and also referenced how fantasy sports have lost their specialness. He argued:

I'm actually getting to the point where I'm a little disgusted with fantasy football and the popularity of it, how many people are involved. . . . I don't like the rising popularity. The thing about fantasy, when I first started to play, I liked it because it was so unique and a really abstract way to look at the game. . . . It was an obscure little side thing that people who really loved football did just to be able to get a little more out of the game than what you'd get from just watching it.

In lamenting the loss of a seemingly more authentic version of fandom, men rely on the masculinized definitions of fandom that privilege knowledge over affect discussed in Chapter 2. They bemoan the degraded knowledge of the fan base that accessibility has supposedly brought, arguing that "fantasy sports are not good for breeding better sports fans." This provides a symbolic way to ward off the encroachment of newcomers—both those perceived as, and who may even self-identify as, "unathletic White men" and, as we will discuss in Chapter 4, women. Although these men present their concerns as being about the integration and dilution of fantasy sports (and sports fandom more generally), these discursive and symbolic practices unveil something larger. In bemoaning the inclusivity of modern-day fantasy sports, these men are also revealing and reflecting on threats to the masculinity project and their place within it. In essence, with the opening up of jock statsculinity to the men (and women) casually participating in fantasy sports, some men push back and argue fantasy sports no longer hold the same appeal as they once did when only certain men—themselves included—had exclusive access to them and the resultant masculinity and power they provided.

Conclusion

In this chapter, we have explored how fantasy sports provide men with a means by which they can achieve and perform a variant of masculinity we call jock statsculinity. Jock statsculinity contains elements of traditional, hegemonic, and sports-based masculinities in that men utilize the hobby to exert control, compete, and exercise dominance. Elements of nerd masculinity combine with this, as the competition and dominance center on testing and demonstrating intellectual acumen and knowledge of statistics and sports, rather than physical strength or abilities. Jock statsculinity is boyish as well. Through their participation, men play, act juvenilely, and relive their childhood dreams of being involved in professional sports. One of our players, Frank, with whom we opened the chapter, nicely summarizes much of this when he claimed:

> I think there's a lot of levels that fantasy sports are very attractive on. It's control, it's augmenting an activity you are already interested in, it's competition, and it's relational, it's social, and I think it just makes a lot of sense why it's so popular when you look at how many may be needs that you are meeting.

These "needs" that Frank suggests fantasy sports meet are to a large degree about masculinity and manhood. While certainly our respondents do not typically specifically equate their play with achieving and policing masculinity (although some do), the frequency with which men slip into gendered and sexed language in discussing their fantasy sports involvement (e.g., their common use of "guys" or "ball busting") is striking. Moreover, men focus a great deal on how fantasy sports provide a mechanism by which they can be powerful and in control while directly highlighting their superiority to others, often through trash talk and posturing—essential components of masculinity. Additionally, and as research on vicarious masculinity suggests, these players make explicit their ties to real sports—that they are akin to real-life managers, sports experts, and/or former athletes. In doing so, they bolster their claims to masculinity even though they do not (or cannot) actively assert themselves through physical play. Although emphasizing these connections to real sports make them similar to men who are everyday sports fans, men fantasy sports players, as competitive fans, can also use and continually point to tangible successes in the hobby (e.g., their win-loss records) as direct proof of their (superior) masculinity in ways unavailable to the average fan. Thus, fantasy sport serves as a particularly salient site for masculine performances.

Fantasy sports, moreover, provide a foothold in sports (and the related possible accomplishment of masculinity) for men who might otherwise be outside the confines of some aspects of the prototypical masculine ideal—those self-professed "stat geeks" or "unathletic White guys" who through an active relationship to sports can prove themselves in ways that go beyond just being a sports fan or spectator. To use Andrei Markovits and Emily

Albertson's language, fantasy sports blur the line between "doing" and "following" sports;[58] and thus, we argue, they present a particularly potent site for the accomplishment of masculinity. This accessibility, though, is not welcomed by all players, and some, particularly men who have been playing a long time, are quite displeased that their exclusive hobby, which set them apart in their sports expertise from the masses, is now seemingly open to all.

Finally, that many men express using fantasy sports as a way to escape or get relief from what one might argue are the demanding aspects of modern masculinity—namely, being a good provider *and* involved in family life—is fascinating and telling. Not only does the hobby provide a respite from work and family as a leisure activity that is decidedly masculine for a group of already very privileged men, but playing GM and engaging in juvenile smack talk provide them with a way to return symbolically to their boyhoods when they daydreamed of being sports professionals and played ball on sandlots, driveways, and neighborhood fields and courts. Sports in general "are about a return to boyhood" and "recall the bucolic American past, unhurried by the drive of the corporate clock. They remind us of the purity and innocence of play."[59] Fantasy sports allow men simultaneously to escape and embrace important components of the masculinity project. They provide them with a respite from the demands of paid labor and family life that twenty-first-century men must concurrently manage. They do so, though, through embracing other hypermasculine pursuits and behaviors—sports, one-upmanship, and trash talking—that perhaps remind them of their youth and allow them to feel in control. Thus, the attraction of fantasy sports for many men seems to be a response, in part, to changing notions of masculinity and the demands on men in contemporary U.S. society.

Men's turning to fantasy sports as a masculinity project may also represent a reaction to the broader social context in which men and masculinity are presumably in crisis and in which they are increasingly subject to women's power and demands for attention and equality. A resultant focus on fantasy sports makes sense for several reasons. First, fantasy sports represent a preserve centered on those men's sports from which women are excluded and deemed naturally ill-equipped to play. Second, participation involves adopting jock statsculinity and, thus, traits culturally associated (often essentially so) with men and maleness, affording a level of control and command beyond that available in traditional fandom. Finally, men still overwhelmingly dominate fantasy sports. This is unlike fandom in those professional sports to which men had turned as women got "stronger" to escape and distinguish themselves as superior. Yes, as traditional fans, men are still able to gain vicarious masculinity by rooting for and associating with male athletes; however, women have infiltrated the ranks of the traditional fan—particularly men's beloved football. Men need a new, impactful outlet to perform and construct masculinity, and fantasy sports seems to fit the bill.

Jock statsculinity provides men with a rather accessible but, by virtue of being active and having measurable outcomes, potent form of masculinity. It is more fully inclusive of the core elements of traditional masculinity than traditional sports fandom masculinity while also involving the additional elements of nerd masculinity and boyhood masculinity. What happens, though, when women engage in fantasy sports, an arena fundamental to the construction and performance of jock statsculinity and that, as we already know, involves some men who are less than enthused about its growing popularity? In the next chapter, we consider how gender stereotypes frame women's participation in fantasy sports, how they are understood and treated, and how they respond.

4

Playing in a Man's World

Perceptions and Experiences of Women in Fantasy Sports

Jane, a thirty-year-old White divorcée living in Chicago, recollects that growing up, she "never really played sports. I tried, but it's not my thing." Rather, she spent her "teen years kind of like a punk rock feminist contrarian," which involved, in part, her being "thoroughly against" anything related to the Pittsburgh Steelers in an effort to counter "everyone" in her Pennsylvania hometown. By her late teens, however, Jane had left this contrarian phase behind, got "back into football," and developed into a self-described "passionate" National Football League (NFL) fan. She agreed to join a fantasy football league at the request of a work colleague some years later, despite some reservations that participating would "detract" from her passion for football. As this current online sports columnist tells it, "I figured I had a lot of knowledge about football, so what the heck, [I] might as well do it."

By the time we talked to her, Jane had been playing fantasy sports for three years, but she was no longer in the league that drew her into the hobby. Instead, she now participates in two fantasy football leagues composed of "heavy-duty fantasy football people" who live "all over the country." Jane takes her participation in these leagues seriously, devoting "probably too much" time (upward of an hour a day in season) to them, and getting frustrated when she makes "a bad decision."

Moreover, as someone who feels "fairly in control" of her fantasy football destiny, Jane takes a strategic and detail-oriented approach to the game.

She methodically investigates athletes' last few years of play, any "coaching changes that might change the philosophy of how they [the NFL teams] use their offense," and players' history of consistency in performance and playing time across games. As Jane spews out particulars about any number of players or details her fantasy sports strategy with ease, her knowledge of sports and particularly football is evident—and she knows this, telling us confidently, "I know this stuff." Although she reveals that not making the playoffs this year makes her feel like "maybe I'm kind of an idiot," she also indicates that one of the things she enjoys about fantasy football is that it provides "a good way" for her "to demonstrate my knowledge of the league."

Undeniably, Jane is a fierce competitor who gains much satisfaction from doing well in the hobby. She wants to beat the best—those whom she calls the "New England Patriots" of her fantasy football leagues—explaining that "if I can beat somebody like that, sure that's a nice ego boost." Moreover, winning is "pretty important" to her because "if anybody is gonna take part in competition where there are winners and you're doing it, you wanna win. . . . It's just [about gaining] bragging rights, to be the woman in the league full of dudes who beats them all."

In many ways, Jane sounds a lot like the men we have already discussed in this book: she has a lot of sports passion and knowledge and wants to display this, she dedicates much time and energy to her fantasy sports teams and approaches the game rationally and seriously, and she wants to win and gain bragging rights by outstrategizing her opponents, particularly those who are the most skilled and successful. In these ways, she adheres to the (masculinized) dictates of legitimate fantasy sports fandom. Jane's last comment, though, highlights an important facet of her fantasy sports involvement that sets her and her experiences apart from that of many of her peers—in both of the leagues in which she plays, she is the *only* woman. While many of the women with whom we spoke play in slightly more mixed-gender leagues, all women—those who play *and* those who do not play—confront in fantasy sports a context that is highly masculinized and in which they are almost exclusively painted as outsiders. Moreover, despite the variability of women's behaviors and attitudes, sweeping generalizations about women abound and a lens of gender polarization, in which the differences between men and women are highlighted and exaggerated,[1] frames those women who play.

Indeed, throughout the interview, Jane articulates that her being a woman means that she is perceived and, sometimes, treated differently as a fantasy sports player and football expert more generally. She starts our conversation about this by noting that her gender is actually "advantageous" because, in her words, the men in the league do not

> really expect a lot out of that one woman who is in the league, and
> [so] it's a good opportunity to kind of show off a little bit and be like,

"Hey, you're underestimating me and you shouldn't. I know exactly what I'm doing here and probably more than some of you." But, obviously, it's a whole man's thing. . . . I'm not going to be entirely taken seriously by everybody in a fantasy league, at least at first.

She also notes, however, that this feeling of being underestimated is not one she has gained directly: "For the most part, it's not like anybody's been like, 'Oh, you're not gonna be able to win this league 'cause you're a woman.'" Even so, Jane feels keenly that other league members view her as "kind of [the] other" and that "it's a man's world of sports and fantasy sports in particular." She claims that because fantasy sport is a man's world,

> there's not a lot of expectation that a woman would even want to do it or be interested, let alone be good at it. It's just there's an inherent advantage to being a man involved in a sports-related pursuit, 'cause he's a *man*. I think it's more of like an internalized kind of expectation.

Jane recounts several experiences that suggest she is judged by a different set of standards than men. For instance, despite the care she takes in developing a draft strategy, she still gets "some trash talk like on draft day, like, 'Oh, I see you drafted Tom Brady; he's so dreamy,'" to which she feels the need to reply, "He's a reliable quarterback who knows what he's doing." Additionally, despite her formidable sports knowledge, Jane reports, "every trade [request] I've gotten has been like ridiculous—just like they think that I'm dumb . . . like they're trying to get the best of me because I'm a girl." She also notes that some men assume when a woman joins a league that her husband or boyfriend is "gonna run her team" or that she would help him, and thus forsake her own ability to win, by trading with him in ways that are "not gonna be fair."

These occurrences are not the only ways that Jane feels the salience of her gender in this space. She also reveals that while she does engage in some trash talking, typically, "it's the guys amongst the guys" doing it. Moreover, she explains that this banter is what one expects from "dudes" in sports, including the "homophobic jokes." The latter, Jane argues, "[is] just something I'm not going to engage in. . . . I know it's all like good natured and stuff, but I don't need to validate some of those comments." Furthermore, as a sports writer, Jane has been the target of direct verbal attacks herself, much like other women have experienced in this profession. Jane writes on the Internet where "people are a lot more brazen in their anonymous or potentially anonymous comments," and as a result, she has received comments such as "Go back in the kitchen" or "This is why women shouldn't write about sports." Feeling that "nobody wants to hear" fantasy advice "from a woman," she rarely confronts her critics; she says, "You kind of want to engage that person, and you're just like, 'Forget it.'"

These incidents and her general understanding of the gendered expectations in sports leave her unsurprised that many women do not engage in the hobby. It is, after all, as she explains it, "a man thing" to participate, a hobby "geared towards men." Yes, she knows there are "lots of female [sports] fans out there," but in her estimation, fantasy sports' focus on "men's sports," those in which men are "hitting each other," helps solidify them as a man's hobby. Additionally, Jane sees the "geeky and nerdy" aspects of fantasy sports as not "really appealing to a lot of women." For these reasons, she asserts that the "boys' club nature" of real sports is "distilled even further when it comes to fantasy sports."

While Jane often does not directly confront many of the things that bother her in fantasy sports, such as the homophobic jokes made among men or her and other women's being underestimated, she is not a shrinking violet. Rather, the gendered expectations regarding fantasy sports and their boys' club atmosphere "motivate" Jane to do better and to challenge prevailing understandings of women through her success. She is all about "proving that 'Hey, I'm a woman and [one] who cares [about sports]; I can still hold my own"; this, she says, is "very important" to her. She wants others to see "that I am all in on this football stuff. And I'm not just here talking about it and just saying like, 'Oh well, this player's good and this team is good and this is a good matchup.' I'm. . . also walking the talk." In essence, Jane wants to be visible as a woman *and* a legitimate and able competitor, and this serves, at least in part, as a motivation for her to put the time and effort into fantasy sports.

Jane's account reveals many of the opportunities and obstacles that exist for women in fantasy sports. Just a decade ago, women were few and far between in this space, but they now participate to a greater extent, although in varying contexts and to varying degrees. Most in our study, like Jane, play in leagues in which they are the sole or one of only a handful of women, but others play in leagues with more even gender composition or in leagues with only women.[2] Women also report myriad reasons for participating and a range of commitments to fantasy sports, from hard-core players involved in multiple leagues for a decade or more to novice players with little previous athletic experience. Among those women who win or place highly in their leagues, we find both self-described "girly girls" and those who position themselves as "one of the guys." Yet, regardless of their backgrounds, attitudes, behaviors, or skill, women confront a space in which they are cast with a broad brush of largely stereotypical similarity, framed as outsiders, and seen as lesser. In short, women in fantasy sports enact a reality that suggests femininity is dynamic and variable, but they do so in an environment that is still decidedly masculine, even as that masculinity becomes open to more men in this space.

More concretely, what we argue in this chapter is threefold.[3] First, like other male/masculine-dominated spaces (e.g., digital gaming, real sports, and workplaces), prevailing gender beliefs that favor men and disadvantage women dominate. In essence, expectations about femininity and women in the abstract run counter to both notions of the typical fantasy sports player and performances of jock statsculinity. Thus, while fantasy sports are theoretically accessible to women, the larger gender frame of the domain as masculine is quite strong. Moreover, structural barriers, some of which are directly tied to these gender beliefs, impede women's full participation.

Second, given the power of the traditional gender frame in fantasy sports, those women who play often feel the salience of their gender acutely and, at times, confront men who seem to push against women's intrusion into a sphere that was until recently largely their own. They question women's competency and motives, discount their successes, and at times, create hostile and intimidating environments. Whether women enact behaviors or self-identify according to a dichotomous traditional gender frame, they are nonetheless held accountable to these expectations. Furthermore, men set the interactional rules, variously accommodating, isolating, ridiculing, and/or ostracizing women.

Third, women react to all this in ways that both reproduce and resist traditional conceptualizations of masculinity and femininity,[4] often simultaneously. Frequently, their agency reinforces notions of women as less knowledgeable and less interested in sports, fragile and in need of assistance, or ill-suited to fully participate in the hobby and the interactions that surround it. Some retreat from male- and masculine-dominated leagues or interactions or ignore misogynistic assumptions and comments. Women also engage in "conflicted agency," as they position themselves as "nonregular girls" or use damaging stereotypes about women to their advantage (as Jane suggests she does). And some participate in "mediated agency" in which they enlist the help of men (or allow men to assist them) to improve their fantasy sports experience. While ultimately all of these responses may result in a better environment for these women, they leave fundamental power dynamics in place by reaffirming that men set the interactional rules and are in charge. Moreover, these responses fail to challenge notions of what it means to be a woman/feminine or a man/masculine in fantasy sports or more generally, nor do they resist constructions of gender as binary.

Women, though, often by their very presence, also push against notions that women do not belong here. Some women (though not many) at least occasionally directly challenge what they see as sexist behaviors in fantasy sports. Some, like Jane, immediately and forcefully resist accusations that they pick up players because they are "dreamy," while others play up their femininity while also highlighting their power (e.g., through their choice of team names). Many women, like Jane, also visibly embrace aspects of jock statsculinity. They focus on winning, are competitive, identify as sports fans, and aim to show off their sports-related knowledge and skills—and strive to prove their worth within the confines of the model of success jock statsculinity dictates.

The gender dynamics here interweave with race, class, and sexuality. The women who play are overwhelmingly White, highly educated, and class privileged. Among those with whom we talked, they are also typically heterosexual and cisgender (i.e., their gender identity as women matches their sex categorization at birth).[5] They may be outsiders in terms of their gender, but they are insiders in terms of their race, class, sexuality, and cisgender identity. They are, thus, better positioned to assert their agency, to choose how they do so, and to stake a claim to belonging in the dominant group than those not so privileged. Notably, while heteronormativity in fantasy sports (and U.S. society more generally) opens up opportunities for acceptance for heterosexual women, it also contributes to women's illegitimacy. Gender and sexuality intersect to marginalize women, as men assume romantic desires and aims drive their participation.

All in all, what this chapter puts forward is a portrait of fantasy sports as a contested terrain[6] in which women push back, sometimes forcefully, against larger understandings of gender but ultimately still fail to fully disrupt them. Increased women's participation does not automatically result in increased legitimacy. What is more, gaining legitimacy takes work, work that most men, like those we profiled in the previous chapters, do not have to engage in to the same degree or at all. In fact, given that jock statsculinity is broader and more open to the masses of elite men than masculinity that hinges on active participation in real sports, men might have to work even less hard in this space than in real sports to gain legitimacy. And although jock statsculinity is perhaps more accessible than traditional hegemonic masculinity, as a cultural type, it is still superior over all expressions of femininity. As such, women, despite their varied backgrounds and experiences, feel like outsiders who must repeatedly prove themselves.

Male-Dominated Spaces, Marginalization, and Agency

By and large, women fantasy sports players, particularly those featured here, are tokens, making up a relatively small percentage of those participating in their leagues. As such, Rosabeth Moss Kanter's classic study of tokenism, in which she explored a sales division of a *Fortune* 500 company that was overwhelming male (more than 85 percent), provides an important backdrop for our work on fantasy sports.[7] In this and any such skewed environment, Kanter argues that three tendencies—visibility, polarization, and assimilation—influence social dynamics and, in turn, how tokens respond.

According to Kanter, the limited number of tokens makes them highly visible (and thus, overscrutinized). This places enormous pressures on them to perform well, and they often respond by working doubly hard and over-achieving or, conversely, by trying to shirk the limelight. Furthermore, to-kenism fosters "group boundary heightening" and social isolation as domi-nants play up the supposed differences between themselves and the tokens and/or may quarantine the tokens by limiting their interactions with them. Some tokens simply accept such polarizing dynamics, while others try to become "in" with the dominant group. Last, Kanter argues that dominants view tokens in line with stereotypes associated with their social category, which produces "role entrapment." Dominants may misunderstand tokens as fulfilling roles that align with stereotyped expectations, or they may treat tokens consistent with the roles and statuses they expect for members of that social category. Tokens themselves may find it easier to act in accordance with these expectations than to resist them.

While Kanter established the dynamics of tokenism, others extended her work, arguing that the content of the token status matters a great deal, such that tokenism is gendered and racialized. More specifically, Christine Williams's research demonstrates that tokenism in settings in which men are the tokens do not generate the same (deleterious) dynamics as those in which women are numerical minorities.[8] Moreover, Adia Wingfield's research on Black men nurses reveals how tokenism operates differently (and in disad-vantageous ways) for them than for their White counterparts.[9]

Sociologist Cecilia Ridgeway's assertion that gender frames our inter-actions further helps us understand the gendered processes that underlie the experiences of women as tokens. Gender, Ridgeway argues, is always an important (and instantaneous) way in which we perceive and classify people and, accordingly, is one of the primary means by which we organize the social world.[10] In the absence of information to override them, gender beliefs—or larger cultural assumptions about how men and women are and what men and women should do—shape our behaviors, expectations, and sense of the rewards that we and others deserve. The effects of gender beliefs on assessments of others and individual actors' behaviors, though, will be *greater* in realms in which gender is presumed to be relevant to the task at hand. Therefore, in settings that are culturally typed masculine, "gender beliefs will bias judgments and behaviors more strongly in favor of men."[11]

Empirical studies on women's treatment in male-dominated fields, in which women are often numerically or symbolically tokens, provides sup-port for Kanter and Ridgeway. For instance, in line with gender beliefs about women, researchers found that individuals assume that even those women who are involved in real sports as participants, coaches, or fans are inferior in their sports-related skills, knowledge, interest, and experience.[12]

For example, Michael Messner demonstrates how women coaches, like Kanter's tokens, are forced to demonstrate their competence repeatedly, are mistaken for team moms, are offered unsolicited advice on how to perform their role as coach, and are scrutinized more heavily than men coaches who are generally assumed competent by default.[13] Researchers have observed similar dynamics in digital gaming and live-action role-playing games. For example, James Martin and colleagues demonstrate how women participating in Dagorhir (a live-action game) are typically limited to subservient positions within the group, have few character options, have their skills and motives for participating questioned, and are supposed to give way to men on the "battlefield."[14]

But women, even when tokens in masculine fields, have agency. Given the power of the gender frame, however, the extent to which their actions alter the overall gender structure varies and is overall fairly limited. Sharon Hays distinguishes between two types of agency—that which is structurally reproductive and that which is structurally transformative.[15] Reproductive agency involves actions that range from being unremarkable to having trivial consequences but leaves underlying structures unchanged. Conversely, structurally transformative agency affects "the pattern of social structures in some empirically observable way."[16] Although reproductive and transformative agency are presented as two distinct categories, Hays emphasizes that agency "occurs on a *continuum* [emphasis original]" and may not even be conscious.[17]

The literature on digital gaming demonstrates the reproductive nature of much of women's agency in masculine-dominated fields. For instance, Catherine Beavis and Claire Charles note that women often liken themselves to men (e.g., by asserting they are "like a boy" or "not the girlie type") and express feeling satisfied when told they play well "for a girl."[18] Some also express liking the visibility their token status affords them and that being a "girl" in this space makes it "easier" for them.[19] Furthermore, Kishonna Gray finds that some women of color respond to the intersecting oppressions they experience in online gaming spaces with self-segregation.[20] Likewise, Amanda Cote reports that some self-identified female gamers leave online gaming entirely, avoid playing with people they do not know, or camouflage their gender while playing in response to the harassment they face.[21] Each of these documented responses fails to counter gaming as a male and masculine domain and leaves larger gendered understandings of women as ill-equipped to compete against men unchanged. Accordingly, Cote surmises that a key limitation of the coping strategies of female gamers is that they help to "construct online spaces as 'for men.'"[22]

Women involved in real sports also engage in what might be construed as reproductive agency. Some women verbally assert that they are more akin to men than women, as women gamers do, or position themselves as outliers by criticizing other women and vocally devaluing femininity.[23] Moreover, some women normalize or ignore the homophobia and sexism they see and experience.[24] Other women in sports use stereotyped expectations about women to their advantage by, for instance, using their sexuality to gain free coaching in skydiving[25] or by launching softballs over the heads of men who play too shallow whenever a woman bats.[26] And women engage in what might be considered "apologetic" behaviors in response to the contradictory mandates of being an athlete (e.g., being aggressive and developing a muscular performance body) and a woman (e.g., being passive and accommodating toward others and focusing on appearance).[27] Again, in all these cases, women largely fail to disrupt gender beliefs about women in sports or femininity more generally.

However, some women in sports and digital gaming assert themselves in potentially transformative ways. They challenge gender beliefs of women's lesser skill by making it obvious they are women while simultaneously demonstrating their expertise in sports or gaming or by directly pointing out that their skill is superior to those men who question or harass them.[28] They challenge gendered understandings of women and earn the respect of men by showing that they can "both take insults and dish them out" in gaming arenas.[29] And they attack the misogynistic and homophobic environment of masculine settings by directly confronting and correcting those engaged in offensive discourse and behavior and redefining proper participation as not including hypermasculine displays.[30] While often quite taxing, all of these efforts hold promise for transforming larger understandings of gender and power dynamics in these fields.

The transformative power of such agency and whether individuals in these contexts read it positively or negatively hinges, at least partly, on class, racial, and heterosexual privilege. As just one example, White, heterosexual, class-privileged women can at least embody some of the assumed qualities or look of a "regular sports fan" and employ the "social, cultural and economic capital to partake in the kind of serious leisure expected" of an authentic fan.[31] Accordingly, such women have the "power to assert their rightful place as supporters" of sports and gain legitimacy in ways those who are Black, lesbian, and/or poor may not be able.[32]

With this as backdrop, this chapter details what "playing in a man's world" is like for women. Insofar as fantasy sports reflect a version of competitive fandom, women must contend with not just gender beliefs that position them as illegitimate sports fans but also the gender belief that they lack the competitive chops necessary to be successful. Moreover, the very structure of fantasy sports makes it hard for women to transform inequities and the gender beliefs that underlie them. When women are successful in their fantasy sports leagues, their accomplishments are not physical (like those of women athletes) and are therefore less visible. Men may, therefore, dismiss or explain away women's successes, including by assuming that as heterosexual women, their male partners must be making decisions for them.

Yet women exercise agency in this space, and here the structure of fantasy sports is as enabling as it is constraining. In fantasy sports, women play side-by-side in the same leagues operating by the same rules as men and are able, virtually at least, to play the role of manager of a professional men's sports team—all of which are extremely rare in real sports.[33] Moreover, when women and men do play side-by-side in fantasy sports, they are often doing so with known others, not anonymized strangers who might be more apt to see them and react to them only in stereotypical terms. The women involved also generally fit the larger raced and classed profile of the legitimate sports fan, affording them opportunities to assert their legitimacy.

The structure of fantasy sports and the resources at women's disposal thus offer an arena to take seriously Hays's contention that agency exists on a continuum. Indeed, larger gender beliefs about women loom large in fantasy sports, and accordingly, women as symbolic and numeric tokens are marginalized and react in ways that are largely (but not always) reproductive. Yet we see evidence of transformative agency as well, with women simultaneously asserting their legitimacy and femininity, albeit a conventional, White, class-privileged femininity. Although previous work has largely focused on agency as either reproductive or transformative, women in fantasy sports both resist and reinforce gendered arrangements, often simultaneously.

Abstract Views of Women's Place in Fantasy Sports

Just as in other male- and masculine-dominated spaces (e.g., digital gaming and real sports), prevailing gender beliefs that favor men and disadvantage women dominate in fantasy sports. When asked to reflect on why most fantasy sports players are men, a majority of our respondents, both women and men, turn to well-worn binary expectations about femininity (and masculinity) and women (and men) in the abstract. Collectively, they articulate that women do not participate in fantasy sports because women find real sports unimportant and uninteresting, have other more feminine interests and obligations that occupy their time, and are less competitive and statistically oriented than men.[34] Whether these stereotypical and dichotomous understandings of gender are accurate (though much research suggests they are not), they ultimately serve to reinforce the space as male/masculine and provide an overall frame by which men judge and evaluate particular women.

To start, both men and women assert women in general are less interested in, knowledgeable of, devoted to, and experienced in real sports (particularly sports in the institutional center) than men. These represent important criteria for performing jock statsculinity; and in invoking such beliefs, our respondents are essentially arguing that fantasy sports are not any different than their real counterparts in terms of their gender dynamics. They also are relying on a definition of sports fandom that is itself gendered—that it is about sports knowledge and experience, both attributes associated with men. Charlie, a college-educated White man, for instance, in reply to questions about women's underrepresentation in fantasy sports, wondered aloud, "What percentage of serious sports fans are women? It just, it's a direct correlation. . . . I don't think that it's fantasy that they're not into; I think it's just [women are not] heavy sports fans." Mike, a self-described "real athletic" kid, essentialized women's underrepresentation when he argued, "In general, I think women don't really know football that well, so I don't expect them to be interested in it, so I think that's sort of natural. . . . I figure a lot of girls don't really know how it's played or the rules or some are just not into it." Jennifer, a single White woman who was heavily involved in sports growing up, pointed to larger structural forces contributing to gendered interest and experience in sports:

> Why are women underrepresented in sports? Why is there absolutely no female sport that will ever be like football? I just think it's because of society. I think it's just, there aren't as many girls into sports and there aren't as many girls in football; it's just something that's been perpetuated over the years. . . . I would say it's [the gendered composition of fantasy sports is] like a magnified reflection [of how sports in general are gendered]. Girls aren't automatically like, "Yup, I want to devote all this time to a fantasy football league."

Some, almost exclusively women, suspect that a lack of sports knowledge leads to women's being too "intimidated" to play fantasy sports. More than half of the women used this specific phrasing when describing women's reluctance—including, in some cases, their own initial hesitation—to participate. What's perhaps most interesting is just how powerfully the gender frame shapes perceptions of women's "fit" in this space. Abstract notions of women's lack of sports knowledge are so strong that they influence views even in the face of actual evidence to the contrary. Lindsey, who played tennis, golf, basketball, and softball as a youth, for example, alluded to women's thinking they might need more knowledge than they actually do to play fantasy sports. She argued, "I think it may be a misconception [among women] that you do need to know more about the sport, the rules and follow the players off the field and on the field on your own before you can play fantasy. I don't think they [women] realize that once you have a fantasy team, those things just happen naturally." Marie, a fantasy sports participant for more than eight years, concurred, indicating that even sports-knowledgeable women like herself might feel intimated about joining:

> I think it's intimidating [for women]. . . . Like before you ever play, you're like, "I don't know the rules. I don't know how it works. I don't want to make a fool out of myself." At least that was my thoughts before I started. [Kissane: "And so even you? You admit that you knew sports."] Right, but I didn't have the fantasy [knowledge]. . . . I think women get more intimidated [than men do].

As these and other women recognize, a real lack of knowledge may contribute to women's reluctance to join fantasy sports. However, a lack of confidence in their knowledge alongside fears that in entering a space dominated by men they will, as Marie states, "make a fool out of" themselves also play a role. This reflects the more general confidence gap between men and women, which is especially pronounced in male-dominated areas. Girls and women underestimate their abilities, and as a result, only a select group, typically those high in confidence and/or ability, enter and persist in male-dominated arenas.[35] Given that players repeatedly characterize fantasy sports as a male and manly domain, many women are, thus, reticent to join the ranks of participants. Only those who most closely adhere to the dictates of jock statsculinity and legitimate fandom, like the sportswriter Jane featured in the chapter opening, likely do so. Yet, even these women risk feeling intimidated and, as we shall shortly demonstrate, find men question their knowledge and abilities at every turn.

Women's presumed inferior knowledge, experience, and interest in sports are not the only issues. We also heard, almost exclusively from men, that women in the abstract just are not statistically oriented, and this results in their presumed lower interest in playing fantasy sports. As just one example, Brendan, a fantasy sports participant for twenty years, thought that women "do not pay much attention to statistics . . . and the fantasy sports are very numbers driven which might not fit in with what they [women] really want to do." As a key component of jock statsculinity is interest and competence in statistics, Brendan, and others who spoke similarly, are positing an incompatibility between femininity and statistical acumen/interest as well as between womanhood and fantasy sports.

Others, again typically men, point to what they see as another categorical difference between men and women—that women, often biologically, lack a "competitive nature." Ray, a player for more than seventeen years, typifies this belief, explaining:

> I think a lot of it [why women don't play fantasy sports] is the fact that guys are more competitive hands down. I mean, how many times have

you seen two little boys walking home and one of them goes, "Hey, I'll race you!"? You don't see girls doing that. It's just genetically what boys do.

Ted, a more recent convert to the hobby having played for about five years, reinforced this idea of a competitive difference between men and women, again seeing this as reflective of a clear gender binary but allowing for potentially more social causes. He offered, "There's a competition [in fantasy sports]. Like I was saying, there's a *manly* one-upmanship, teasing and taunting thing that I think societally women just don't; it doesn't appeal to women exactly in that manner."

While not asked this directly, our interview respondents often without prompting suggested a number of "girly" pursuits that they think occupy women's interest and time instead of fantasy sports. These activities—noncompetitive, nonsporting interests that frequently revolve around aesthetics and supportive domestic functions—are at odds with fantasy sports and jock statsculinity and again reflect the kind of binary, dichotomous approach that dominates the gender frame. Some, like Drew, a casual fantasy sports player, suggest that women are into crafts and decorating in lieu of fantasy sports. He explained:

> Women are involved in Pinterest over fantasy sports. Whether it's nature, nurture, or whatever, at least in our current culture for whatever reason some niches are—fantasy sports branches are predominately male, while Thanksgiving decoration and doilies or whatever's on Pinterest, that's just, it's just a niche that's predominately female. . . . Men and women are different—there you go.

Others, most notably men who are also parents, argue that women have responsibilities and interests in the home that preclude their playing fantasy sports. Their discussions of these issues center on two themes that further illuminate and reinforce the ways in which gender operates in this space. First, many make dichotomous distinctions—obligations associated with home and family are demands that women, but not men, face or perhaps more accurately, that men can more easily avoid. Bob, a married father of two children, for example, told us:

> I think guys are more hobbyists than women are, and it doesn't matter what you look at. Guys tend to have hobbies and women don't. I think that women, and it's not to be sexist, I think they're more interested in their homes and raising the kids and then they put everything else aside to do that.

Anthony, a married father of three, recognized that women who have children face demands that he does not (though, like Bob above, he fails to problematize this):

> Not to be chauvinist, with women, especially if they are in their thirties let's say, they are probably mothers, they have children. They are making lunches, getting kids off to school, dealing with that kind of stuff, and don't have the luxury of sitting in front of the computer for an hour or two at seven or eight o'clock at night [to play fantasy sports], while I might be. Because at that point in your life, if you have little kids, you [women] have to give them baths and get them ready for school or do their homework.

Claire, a forty-three-year-old married mother of two and one of few women to discuss this barrier to women's play, recounted how she quit playing fantasy sports for several years because of the kids: "Yeah, I wasn't really able to sit and watch the games and just too busy." She continued:

> My husband has hobbies. He likes his hobbies; men don't give them up as easily as women [when they have kids]. . . . I think just in general women get caught up in their kids; they get caught in the day to day and forget [anything else]. It is nice that they are getting older; I feel like I can do fantasy and do more things for myself now than I ever did, go out with my friends, hang out, socialize that type of stuff because they are more independent, but when they are little, you're just exhausted. . . . I think women don't have as much time [as men to play], I really do. I think women are just more caught up in the day-to-day activities.

Second, most frame women's supposed prioritizing of family-related commitments over leisure pursuits such as fantasy sports as a choice they make freely rather than a structural obligation. The presumption, grounded in biological essentialism, is that women are *interested* in tending to their families over having hobbies. Clearly, though, women do not give up their leisure time to perform household duties in a vacuum, nor are their "decisions" to perform carework merely a reflection of feminine interests. Larger gender beliefs regarding men's and women's expected roles in the family, while changing, still push women to have less leisure time in general and to take on family-related tasks more so than men. Indeed, although women's lack of participation is frequently framed as being due to a desire or need to care for their families, men's participation is often positioned as a necessary escape from the increasing obligations of contemporary marriage and fatherhood. Rebecca, who is married but does not have any children, alluded to this when she claimed, "I would venture to guess that women have other things that occupy their time or that are *required* to occupy their time" that prevent their playing fantasy sports. Thus, while many frame women's lack of fantasy sports participation as a result of gendered preferences, gender and family scholars encourage the consideration of those larger gender beliefs that propel women into the home and away from hobbies, such as fantasy sports, in which they might otherwise participate.

These assumptions regarding women's lack of interest or compatibility with fantasy sports give rise to another structural barrier—men, who control access to most leagues that are not all-woman, fail to invite women to play or inform them of league openings when they arise. Kate, a single, casual fantasy sports player who tried nearly all sports as a youth, explains:

> Often, it's like they're [men are] the ones that create the league . . . and they ask their friends that they know are interested in sports [to join] who also happen to be men. So I think it's kind of like self-fulfilling. . . . It's largely a network [thing that blocks women].

Some players go further, suggesting that men, regardless of their views of women's interest in the hobby, have a vested interest in preserving the space as male-dominated and masculinized. As discussed previously, men employ fantasy sports to shore up a masculine identity and escape the demands of their work and family lives. Therefore, bringing women into this space threatens these functions and serves as a rejection of the powerful, framing belief that men and women each need their own, separate spheres. Thraka, who currently cohabits with his girlfriend, is one respondent who recognized this. He noted:

> I can kind of see how guys that are maybe married and you have a wife and two or three kids and you need something that is your own identity, so you don't want your wife playing in that league. . . . [Some men] will grunt and scratch twice as often if it will get you out of the room, dear. And I don't agree with that, but I can see how some guys would feel that way.

Likewise, Annick, a single woman who is a hard-core fantasy sports player, elaborated on her observation on how men do not want women to "encroach on their turf":

> If you were a girlfriend and you wanted in [a fantasy sports league], I think the worst thing you could do would be to ask your boyfriend, "I would like to play in your league." If anything, you'd have to find somewhere else [to play]. Because to me, that would be like saying,

"I want to now completely invade your space that you have had as
your own space." And I so think that there is a whole, yeah, there is
a whole male territory versus female territory.

And it is not a stretch to see the connection between fantasy sports as men's
"turf" (e.g., a space numerically dominated by men) and fantasy sports as a
site for performing masculinity. Although jock statsculinity has opened up
routes to legitimacy for an increasing number of men, fantasy sports and,
by extension masculinity, remain the province of men and thus must be de-
fended from the potential invasion of women through masculine performance and exclusionary practices.

Overall, fantasy sports, like real sports or digital gaming, are viewed as
"men's turf" and a space where "obviously" women will be less involved than
men. Thus, rather than being gender neutral, fantasy sports in the abstract
are a preserve for men, just as real sports have been traditionally constructed.[36] Unable to default to physiological differences as the explanation for
differing rates of play in this sporting endeavor, men and women turn to
long-held gender beliefs about social and psychological differences between
men and women. They posit that women are less interested in, experienced
with, and knowledgeable of sports and that they are less likely to have a competitive drive or obsession with statistics that would presumably push them
to play fantasy sports. Rather, women are said to be into shopping, gossiping,
home decorating, scrapbooking, and caring for their families. Although not
physiologically based, these differences are no less dichotomized or essentialized in the minds of our respondents. With these understandings (and
with the view that men need spaces to call their own), not inviting women to
join or refusing their entrée in leagues with men appear justifiable.

Furthermore, in many players' accounts (especially men's), we saw hesitation and discomfort. At times, our players stammer and stumble through
their points, reduce the forcefulness of their claims by asking rhetorical
questions or phrasing their views as speculative, and preface their accounts
with assertions that they are not "chauvinistic" or "sexist." These iterative
strategies likely relate to a woman's interviewing them but also suggest ambivalence surrounding this topic.[37] Some seem to understand that the beliefs they espouse are mere stereotypes that may not hold up to the reality
of women's current involvement in sports or that of specific women they
know (and in some cases love). That these players continue to espouse essentialized and dichotomous views despite these hesitations speaks volumes
about the power of the gender frame in this space. These gendered assumptions and views of constraints on women's participation serve as important
background for understanding the experiences of women who actually play
fantasy sports.

Beyond the Abstract: Understandings and Treatment of Women Who Play Fantasy Sports

Abstract understandings of women's incompatibility with fantasy sports permeate down to the local leagues, influencing how women experience the hobby and their place within it. Although the state of play and experiences these predominately White, class-privileged women encounter and live out appear less toxic than what women face in some online multiplayer digital gaming contexts, they are still marginalized and understood differently than men. Like women athletes and gamers, women fantasy sports participants are highly visible, have their competency and motives questioned and tested repeatedly, have their successes discounted, and face hostile and intimidating environments. But what distinguishes this from real sports participation is the disembodied nature of the criteria by which men scrutinize and exclude them. In theory, the attributes that constitute jock statsculinity are as accessible to and attainable by women as they are by men. Physically, nothing is precluding women from being competitive, interested and knowledgeable of sports, aggressive, strategic, tech savvy, rational, adept with statistics, interested in escaping adult responsibilities, and attracted to experiencing a childlike play. Despite this, women still find that they are not treated and perceived as men are and, instead, suffer much of the same fate as women athletes or sports fans. In short, while women may be able to exhibit the characteristics associated with jock statsculinity, the status accorded to men in this space still eludes them.

Indeed, many of the perceptions regarding and experiences of women in fantasy sports mirror those found in other settings in which women are tokens. More specifically, as women in fantasy sports, a setting in which the default player is a man,[38] women find themselves to be highly visible, with men at times directly remarking on their sex, gender, or minority status. Women, for instance, report hearing things such as, "Oh, you're such a female!" when doing things men also do (such as picking up a coveted player in the draft) or being subject to "lots of jokes" about their being "one of the few 'token' girls in the league." Those women playing in leagues with mostly men, especially those who are true tokens (i.e., they are the only woman in their leagues or one of only two) are most likely to report experiencing sexism and being treated or perceived differently than men.

Women note that because of their visibility, they are subject to intense scrutiny and that men use a different set of standards to judge their behaviors and attitudes than they do players who are men. Marie, who plays in three different fantasy sports leagues, felt this keenly, noting that "every move I made, if I dropped somebody or picked somebody up, people were looking at it different than they would if a guy did. . . . Just maybe evaluating what I did with a different lens than they used for the other guys." Similarly, a female survey respondent complained:

> Men believe that women don't follow the stats as closely as guys. . . . [So] if a woman were to make a slightly random or chancy pick/move, guys are more likely to say, "She doesn't know what she's doing," but if a guy were to make that move, then they would think, "Oh, that's so interesting. I wonder what made him choose that player. Maybe he knows something I don't."

We, too, have felt the visibility and overinspection associated with being women in this space. When we attended a Fantasy Sports Trade Association (FSTA) summer conference, the very first words uttered to us by another attendee was, "Hey, you're women. Why are you here?" Moreover, we noticed that men attendees and security personnel repeatedly examined our credentials whenever we entered the conference area, but we did not see men's badges scrutinized at all or to nearly the same degree. As two of only a handful of women attending,[39] we certainly benefited from having no lines at the women's restroom. Furthermore, networking was made easy as other attendees quickly approached us with introductory lines such as, "I haven't met you yet." But we noted to each other that we felt uneasy and under constant surveillance. Throughout our two days at the conference, we had the sense that we were being watched and sometimes directly caught men staring unabashedly at us. We witnessed other women receiving similar attention, in particular a tall blonde woman who seemed to catch the eye of most attendees whenever she moved through the conference rooms.[40]

While not our experience at the conference, women who play fantasy sports, at times, must also contend with men who, as Annick put it, seem bent on being "real jerks" to them. These occurrences serve as a potent signal to women that they do not belong. As Lynn, a hard-core fantasy sports player, simply articulated, "The guys still see it as their domain." She continued, "[When] I first went online to [fantasy sports] message boards . . . [the] guys were rude and crude and did everything to push the girls away." Recall that the performance of jock statsculinity involves the exaggerated display of machismo, typically through insult talk, obscene language, and verbal swagger. Thus, it is possible those men Lynn encountered were publicly performing jock statsculinity for one another more so than targeting her in particular. Nevertheless, many women cite such hyperaggressive, macho performances, core interactional and institutional dynamics of fantasy sports, as creating an intimidating and unpleasant environment in which to play.

Some men acknowledge that women find the aggressive smack talk and sexist language in fantasy sports unappealing, although they also frequently suggest that the problem lies not with the discourse itself but with women who just "can't take a joke" or are too thin-skinned. CB, a hard-core player, complained about this, while also noting how experiencing women in fantasy sports is a rarity. He told us:

> I was talking smack. There is a girl in one of my leagues and it's not unheard of, but I only have one or two leagues where there is a female playing, and I was talking smack to her and she got offended. And I was like [*said in a dismissive and annoyed tone*], "Oh, OK. So I can't talk smack to her anymore."

Similarly, Thraka recalled that one of the three women in one of his leagues "dropped out because the trash talking was too aggressive." He continued to explain, however, that "none of the guys would have felt that way" about the trash talking, but that "from a different set of sensibilities"—that is, from a womanly sensibility—such talk is not experienced as "good fun" but rather is interpreted as "mean." The nonchalant way in which many men (even those like Thraka who are less invested in a macho-aggressive type of masculine display) discuss instances in which men offend women in their leagues reveals how normalized such macho talk is among men. It also highlights how women, and not the performance of masculinity itself, are positioned as the problem.

To be clear, women experience a range of toxicity in general as well as variation across different settings in fantasy sports. Many face very little or no directly hostile backlash to their presence; although even in these environments, men still frequently view women as inferior and speak to them accordingly. Conversely, some women encounter particularly objectionable language and interactions with men in certain fantasy sports settings. Women experience this latter extreme almost entirely on fantasy sports message boards, both public general use ones and those attached to leagues in which the managers do not know one another personally. Paul, a White, married man who currently plays in five leagues, took note of how toxic some online fantasy environs are, indicating that the "comments that fly around" on the fantasy sports message boards he frequents are "pretty bad sometimes." He went on to explain at some length how anonymous leagues and message forums create a particularly hostile environment for women, like his wife. This he saw as akin to online gaming environments. He argued:

> A lot of the leagues are pretty aggressive, especially the anonymous leagues, just like [in] online gaming. You give major anonymity to people and they just spout all these, there's a lot [of] racism and sexism that comes out. . . . Because of some of the language, and stuff is very sexist, I'd say that's a huge turnoff [for women]. I know that does not appeal to my wife at all. . . . A lot of the women kind of keep

their heads down in the forum, they kind of go to the sites [the public fantasy sports message forums], they go there looking for things, they get their information, and then they keep their head down. They go in and out, so they don't get targeted for some of the semi-creepy things that happen.

Women are well aware that public fantasy sports message boards are often hostile to their presence, and for this reason, it is little surprise that most of the women in our study do not report visiting them for fantasy sports–related information and camaraderie. Lynn, whom we quoted earlier, claimed the "crude" response she got after innocently asking after her draft, "How'd I do?" on a public fantasy sports message forum "turned [her] off" and resulted in her avoiding the site for about "a year or two." Other women, like Jane who opened the chapter and who uses a username that marks her as a woman on a public fantasy sports message forum she frequents, explain that they have just come to "expect" sexist and "excessively nasty" responses when they participate in anonymized online fantasy sports environments. And certainly, our own observations of online and anonymous fantasy sports message and chat sites (described in Chapter 3) reveal that those women who choose to use them will encounter hypermasculine and misogynist banter.

Kissane, who has played fantasy sports for more than ten years, was quickly met with the exclusionary environment of some fantasy sports message boards when she posted a link to this study's survey. Beginning a series of comments positioning her as both threatening and unqualified, one user wrote:

> Rebecca if you'd like to discuss any of your survey questions in open forum this would be an excellent place to do so. You may actually gain more detailed information here than in your survey. I particularly am interested to discuss the questions regarding my views on Men & Women [sic] in the home & at work. I have no problem answering those questions, but fail to see the correlation between those questions and any views relating to fantasy sports.

Then another responded:

> Sure, I filled it [the survey] out. Now, time to take the phone off the hook, slug some whiskey while I rough up my last trailer park friend, tell the wife to screw off, kick the dog, then lay comatose on the couch and watch like 10 whole NFL games back-to-back. . . . Only then will I feel gratified.

A third user then commented, "I think my wife helped with coming up with many of those questions!" after which another contributed to the exchange with, "I said I agree women are better served staying at home and raising their children. This would most definitely solve part of the teachers union's problems." To say the least, Kissane got the message loud and clear—your presence as a woman in this space is noted and your motives and understandings of men and fantasy sports are to be questioned.

The majority of our respondents, however, typically play fantasy sports with friends, family members, coworkers, and acquaintances and are not in anonymized leagues. This likely reduces (but does not eliminate) the potential toxicity of both virtual and in-person interactions in this space. This dynamic also promotes quarantining women from some of the worst smack talking and sexist and obscene discourse. Known others might feel the need to protect women in ways strangers do not. As illustrative of this, Caroline, a married woman who plays in one league, indicated that her husband stepped in (without her prompting) when another manager created an offensive team name he knew would upset her and another woman in the league. She explained:

> We had probably one team name that was vetoed . . . because it made fun of the rape allegations against Big Ben [Roethlisberger], and we have a team member who has been a victim. . . . I don't even think my husband would tell me [the name] because he knew that I would be upset.

Caroline's husband knew that another league manager had been a survivor of rape and this team name would be upsetting to someone he cared about; thus, he sought to protect both women from the offensive team name.

It therefore makes sense that despite repeatedly hearing from men about the frequency and joys of smack talking in fantasy sports (and as a way to display jock statsculinity), women rarely reveal engaging with men in such interactions or even being privy to them. In fact, women discuss how the smack talk "is either nonexistent or really toned down" when they are around or, as in Marie's case, how the men in her leagues "don't do it [trash talk] at me, so I don't do it at them." Even when women engage in trash talk or are unopposed to doing so, men reportedly handle them with kid gloves because they are women. Lindsey, a twenty-seven-year-old magazine editor, for instance, thought she was "treated probably with more courtesy than I would have if I had been a guy." She continued, "There were some things I wrote on the smack board or whatever that I think people kind of just take with a grain of salt because no one's gonna like fire back hard at a girl." Likewise, Lynn, who has played fantasy sports for more than ten years and is currently in "eight or nine" leagues, reflected, "A lot of the guys that are from [one league] that I play with, they can be some good trash talkers, but for some reason they are pretty easygoing on me. I don't know if it's because I'm a girl and they're afraid that I'll get upset or cry or something."

Much of this behavior, which some might deem chivalrous, represents benevolent sexism. Peter Glick and Susan Fiske argue that sexism need not always be overtly hostile. Rather, individuals may hold stereotypical and restricting views of women that are "subjectively positive in feeling tone (for the perceiver)" and that "tend to elicit behaviors typically categorized as prosocial (e.g., helping) or intimacy-seeking."[41] Just as with hostile sexism, however, the foundations of benevolent sexism rest in masculine dominance and stereotypical gender beliefs. Accordingly, benevolent sexism is not benevolent in its consequences but, instead, reaffirms masculine power and understandings of women as inferior. Among fantasy sports participants, such seemingly benevolent behaviors ultimately reinforce the space as one in which men set the terms of interactions. The nature of these interactions remains for the most part unchanged and decidedly macho even as masculinity is broadened in this space. The gender frame remains highly salient. In being shielded from such exchanges (even if done for benevolent reasons), women are positioned clearly as women (and not just players) who are fundamentally different from men. Abstract and stereotypical understandings of them—that they are too emotionally fragile or nurturing to take and engage in smack talk at all or in the same way as men do and thus are in need of protection from such offensive exchanges—define women as unsuited for this space and prevent their full inclusion.

Women take note of how they are visible, scrutinized, and excluded or protected from smack talking to a greater degree than men. By and large, though, these dynamics do not overly trouble them. A more sizable issue is that they feel that they are "looked down upon because you are a woman trying to play a man's game" (as Nicole put it) and, correspondingly, that men view them as "jokes" or "easy wins." Mindy, a married woman who plays in a couple of leagues, one of which is an "all-female" league, reported being mocked by "a few guys" and one in particular who commented on Facebook, "Oh, do you have any openings in your all-female league? I'd love to play; I'd love to win some extra cash.'" A female survey respondent similarly commented, "Sometimes I feel like male managers think female managers are a joke. I know in the past, I have been offered trades that no sane person would offer . . . like the trade was being offered to 'trick' me as the female."

That men do not take them seriously as competent fantasy sports managers is a major downside of playing fantasy sports for women and is something they experience as very frustrating and, at times, infuriating. These views of women players as incompetent mirror abstract beliefs regarding women—that femininity on the whole is incompatible with both fandom and jock statsculinity and therefore women cannot and, perhaps, should not compete with men in this sphere. Men purportedly do not see women as measuring up across all of the core aspects of jock statsculinity. For instance, they judge women players, as they commonly judge all women, as lacking sufficient sports-related knowledge, experience, and interest. One female player made this connection, noting:

> The stereotype is that women aren't as good at sports—or like sports as much as men. And that's simply not true. But it's the prevailing thought in our society. So of course the men in my league don't believe that I'll be as good as them. But I am :)

Other women offered similar assessments, like Jane did in our opening or when another female player claimed, "It has been assumed that I do not know the sport and/or statistics. It has also been assumed I don't know which players to put in because of this." Still another wrote, "I feel that I am often offered unreasonable or dishonest trades because other managers believe I am not knowledgeable enough to know the value of particular players or their current injury status."

Sometimes these perceived differences in assumed knowledge lead to women being subject to condescending comments and uninvited assistance from men, the latter of which represents an additional example of benevolent sexism. Brittany, who invests a good deal of time and money in the five leagues in which she plays, explained, "I was the only girl [in one of my leagues]. . . . They're like, 'Are you sure you understand what we're doing? Are you all right?'" Similarly, another female player wrote, "I also receive unsolicited advice constantly about who to start and how to manage my team." Much like women's protection from aggressive smack talking, it is possible to interpret these interactions positively, as instances in which chivalrous men are trying to assist women. And while that may be true in some individual cases, women generally interpret this sort of behavior as an insulting suggestion that they are inferior and need help to play. More importantly, such exchanges both reflect and perpetuate an environment dominated by men and masculinity in which men question women's skills, competency, and their very legitimacy.

The dictates of jock statsculinity mandate that men are not just sports savvy but that they are also smart, strategic, and rational—traits that women told us their peers assume they do not possess. One female player simply reported, "Men don't think I'm as smart as them, and sometimes . . . they can be extremely condescending towards me." For others, their presumed incompetence is more specifically situated. Reflective of the gendered heterocentrism that dominates the space, some women reported accusations that romantic attraction, not knowledge or strategy, guided their fantasy sports selections.

Jane, with whom we opened, was charged with picking up Tom Brady as a quarterback because he is "dreamy," while another female respondent told us men assume she "will pick teams based on 'cute guys' or 'cute outfits,' not based on player skill." Success does not ward off such criticism, with one female player saying, "I'm told I'm illogical—despite the fact that I've come in first place twice already, second place twice, and am currently in first place at this point in time in the playoffs."

Moreover, jock statsculinity is about being competitive, and here, too, women claimed men think they come up short. This is perhaps not surprising, given that competition itself—and its relationship to interactions with others—is defined in masculine ways. Competition is a cornerstone of men's friendships with other men. Gendered expectations that paint women's relationships with others as nurturing, cooperative, and selfless, on the other hand, frame women. As a result, while competition is positioned as inherent to friendship for men, it is considered antithetical to friendship for women—women must choose between being competitive and friendly while men do not. Reflective of this, some women hear derogatory comments that they put their relationships with others over playing to win, thus suggesting that they are not appropriately competitive. For instance, Caroline, a casual player who has been playing for about three years, claimed, "When the other girl and I play each other . . . she and I have been friends forever . . . they [men in the league] were giving us a hard time that I would tank for her, and I don't think they would have said it to any of the guys."

Other times, women receive comments that suggest they are not playing for competitive reasons but rather for relational reasons—for example, to find a boyfriend or connect with their husband. As a case in point, Lynn, who is cohabitating with her boyfriend, was bothered that she had to prove she wasn't using a message board as a "dating service" before the men "kind of embraced" her. She explained:

> When they [the men] saw that one, I knew my stuff and [two,] I wasn't there [on the message board] to pick up on guys, I guess is what they were afraid of [the message board becoming a] dating service or something, and once they saw that that's not what I was there for and I knew what I was talking about, then they kind of embraced me and came around.

Similarly, when Kissane advertised this study's survey on various fantasy sports message boards, rather than being approached as an expert researching the field, some men bantered about her availability. One user posted, "I took your survey; now if you could complete mine: A/Are you spoken for? B/Are you being courted proper?" Here again, we see a lens that is both gendered and heterosexualized as framing women's experiences. It is not just that women are illogical, but their presumed attraction to men dominates their thoughts and actions.

What's notable here is that these views of being less competitive, rational, and sports savvy are attached to women who *play* fantasy sports, who one could argue have already demonstrated their holding these traits by their decision to participate. Relatedly, and worth repeating, is that men are afforded default competency in fantasy sports. They embody jock statsculinity until they prove otherwise. When asked if it mattered whether he was playing a woman or a man in his league, Dino replied:

> No, not at all . . . 'cause I know the one [woman] who has placed [highly in the league], I know she sort of knows what she's doing, but if a woman has just started playing, yeah, I actually will treat her as a woman beginner, yeah, as opposed to a man beginner. . . . If I'm being honest [about how I treat a woman player], it's gonna depend on the woman, how much I think or I know that she follows sports or not.

To be sure, women are transgressing boundaries when they participate in fantasy sports. But what happens when they transgress those boundaries even further by winning? While some men evaluate the success of women as unproblematic or merely "surprising" or "funny," "losing to a girl" is of grave concern for others. Because hegemonic masculinity involves demonstrating superiority over marginalized masculinities and femininity, the threat of a man losing to a woman looms large. Doing so demonstrates weakness and a failure in the performance of manhood. This dynamic holds even as the contours of legitimate masculinity broaden. Accordingly, we heard how some men hate losing to the "girls" or are incredulous that such a thing could happen to them. CB, who rarely encountered women in his leagues, spoke directly on this, admitting that he is one of those men who does not "like to lose to the girls." Likewise, Anne, a single, thirty-one-year-old paralegal, claimed, "Sexism totally exists. So I think that some of the guys in the league, whoever they lose to, they are pissed about it obviously, but I do think that there are some of them that are extra pissed when it is to me or to this other girl." Others, such as Lynn, hear from the men in their leagues when they win, "I can't believe I lost to *you*" or "I can't believe I lost to *her*." Moreover, women's success becomes another tool and opportunity for certain men to assert their own masculinity by deriding those men whom women defeat. As Claire, a casual player, recounted, "We would hang out with them [men in the league], and they would be like, 'Oh, you lost to *the girl*.' It was pretty bad for them."

Thus, some men's responses to women's success include becoming "pissed" off or expressing astonishment, as well as using such moments to demean other men. In addition, though, men fail to recognize at all or explain away women's efforts and demonstrations of competence—and they do so in ways that they do not for other men. This aligns well with research on women's experiences in the workplace, real sports, and digital gaming. In fact, Joan Williams and Rachel Dempsey argue that success itself is typed masculine—that is, when we think of an effective professional, we envision a man and, accordingly, "most of us unconsciously link men with the idea" of success.[42] And because of how our brains organize and process information, behavior that conforms to expectations—for example, men being successful—tends to be noticed, remembered, and attributed to stable traits reflective of who a person "really" is. Behavior that violates expectations, conversely, is ignored, forgotten, or attributed to external factors. In essence, if we expect men on the whole to be successful in a given setting, we will see, normalize, and remember their successes more than women's, and women will have to prove their competence repeatedly. Sociologist Judith Lorber reminds us that there is nothing natural about this—these gendered divisions arise not from biology or physiology but from "cultural meanings, social relationships, and power politics."[43] Yet the existence of the categories male/man and female/woman allow and encourage us to see the differences we believe are there.

Research on real sports demonstrates this process. In her study of coed softball players, sociologist Faye Linda Wachs found that observers confront superlative play on women's part with ideological repair work—activities designed to right what one sees with one's eyes on the field of play (skilled players who are women) with the gendered expectations one "knows" to be true (women are not athletically skilled).[44] Because success, particularly in domains dominated by men, is masculine, women's success in coed softball must be grappled with and contested in ways very similar to what we find for women in fantasy sports.

Frequently, successful women hear that luck is the reason for their victories—as one female player wrote, "I am in one league with 10 teams and I am the only girl. They seem to think [when I win that] I get lucky instead of being skilled at picking and fielding a team." Other times, women's wins are unexplainable, suggesting that luck is a deciding factor, or that the only plausible explanation must be that women cheat. As illustrative of this, one man posted on a fantasy football message board (in response to Kissane's entry publicizing the study) the following, which suggests that women's successes are joke-worthy and demand explanation:

> I have a weird track record when playing against a female opponent. It seems I lose more often than not. Going back about 5 years I have only won a small percentage of match ups vs female opponents. Let me know what your data has to say about that because I am pretty sure they are all cheating.

Women players also hear that they are not "real" women, are lesbians, or are mere anomalies among women. When such women are successful, the larger frame that women, at least heterosexual women, are uninterested and unskilled in sports remains unchanged. This is something that scholars studying women in other athletic contexts have also discovered—for instance, that "sportistas," when recognized as credible fans, are often defeminized and inducted into the "bro" zone or seen as "exotic,"[45] or that successful women athletes are assumed to be lesbian.[46] Reminiscent of this sort of ideological repair work, Marie indicated that men in her leagues deem her atypical of her gender to manage her seemingly contradictory characteristics (i.e., that she is both a woman and a good fantasy player knowledgeable about sports); she explained, "I don't think they [men in her leagues] see me that way [as a woman] anymore. I'm just kind of the random anomaly of a girl. Like, 'Whatever, she's not really a girl.'" Another female player revealed in the survey that the "first comment [when people know she plays fantasy sports] is 'You must be a lesbian.'" And, relatedly, some women note that they are seen as not just atypical or lesbian but as different from the "standard" woman in problematic ways—that, as in the words of one of female player, they are perceived as "*too* boyish or competitive."

Men also make allusions to women, particularly those who do well, as atypical of their sex and gender. Drew, who plays in one free league, noted one of his friends who plays is a "tomboyish" woman who "usually" engages in "more masculine" pursuits. Likewise, David, a married hard-core player, revealed, though exhibited much discomfort in doing so, that his wife who plays fantasy sports is an atypical woman. He explained:

> I will say that my spouse's disposition toward it [fantasy sports] does not strike me as characteristically female. . . . She has a[n] aggressive tactical disposition, which is—I'm not, I mean, that strikes me as, some might say—a sort of characteristically male as opposed to female disposition and my, obviously, reaction has been that my dear wife has a quite aggressive tactical disposition indeed.

An important difference between fantasy sports and real sports, however, is that because of the virtual and cerebral nature of the hobby, observers do not see participants' abilities directly or physically. Rather, fantasy sports managers demonstrate their skill through their decisions, and their play typically occurs through the use of new media. These facets of the hobby lead to another form of ideological repair work: assertions that successful women are not the ones actually running their teams or dictating the roster decisions—men are. Women gamers confront similar assumptions when highly skilled. As one female fantasy sports player put it, "Some people don't expect you to do well, or assume that if you do, it's because a man is helping you." Another female player complained, "[I] deal with jokes that my husband manages my team for me. My first year playing, I won the championship and people still give my husband the credit." That men are given credit for women's successes (and for controlling their teams more generally, as Jane mentioned in our opening) rectifies the seeming contradiction between women's successes and the assumption they cannot compete with men. It also reaffirms men's dominance, excludes women from full inclusion and legitimacy, and reflects the gendered heteronormativity of the space as women's presumed romantic relationships with men determine their victories.

Thus, while exceptions exist, larger gender beliefs about their inferiority and outsider status mark the narratives of women. While their race, class, and sexuality likely afford many some protection, these intersectionally privileged women, at times, face hostile and misogynistic environments and men who view and treat them as less interested and less knowledgeable of sports, as "easy wins," and as fragile, noncompetitive, and nonrational players. When they do well—and many are indeed exceptional players—men are taken aback and sometimes angered but typically engage in ideological repair work to thereby ignore or explain away these seemingly anomalous wins. Overall, despite a broadening of legitimate masculinity in this space, the larger gender frame that establishes a clear binary and attaches often stereotypical expectations to men's and women's interests, aptitudes, and competency in and for fantasy sports deeply influences men's and women's experiences. It is this environment women must navigate—and in which they, despite their outsider status, can and do respond.

Reproductive and Transformative Agency in Fantasy Sports

Women range in the degree to which and the manner by which they push back against their marginalization in fantasy sports. At times, they engage in agency on the reproductive end of the continuum—that is, their actions largely fail to transform understandings of gender. Other times, however, they engage in more transformative agency—countering gendered assumptions, power, and structures in ways that may ultimately shift perspectives and arrangements. Importantly, their responses are not all or nothing, with some women engaging in both reproductive and transformative agency, even simultaneously at times. Equally important, these women exercise their agency from a privileged position. Largely White and class advantaged, these women have resources and the potential for legitimacy that women of color and/or women of lower socioeconomic status typically do not. Accordingly, their fellow fantasy sports enthusiasts may interpret and receive these women's reproductive but especially their transformative agency more favorably than that of women in less privileged positions.

To start, women commonly engage in reproductive agency via retreat. Instead of actively fighting against sexist assumptions and hostile conditions, some women, at least some of the time, quit male- and masculine-dominated spaces and forms of interaction, leaving men to play unimpeded by women's presence. Sometimes, as we have already documented, retreat means avoiding public fantasy sports–related message forums, avoiding the forums on their own league's pages, or avoiding trash talking with men more generally. Other times, retreat involves dropping out of leagues with mostly men in favor of all-women leagues or quitting fantasy sports entirely, as Claire's mother-in-law did because "the smack talk that goes down in that room [among the men] is just to the point where my mother-in-law was in the league at one point and dropped out. She was so offended."

Other women weather disagreeable environments but do so by excusing sexist and homophobic displays as part and parcel of fantasy sports or men's behavior more generally. Such spectacles, to these women, are not to be taken "personally" or are not "worth" confronting. This resigned acceptance is reproductive in nature as women in these instances fail to challenge the gendered dynamics of fantasy sports, leaving men, again, to proceed and think unchanged. Anne, who plays in one league with mostly men, brushed off offensive comments:

> I have been in the league for so many years. . . . They're not going to say something offensive [to me], [but] they're offensive in general, I mean they're thirty-something guys, so you know what I mean. Some people's team names are horribly offensive. I'm not personally offended because I know them well and that it is all just for the laugh of it.

Marie also takes a position of ignoring things that bother her—here because she worries about escalating the issue. After complaining that men assume she knows little about sports, she explained she rarely tries to actively counter these assumptions: "I think that could make it worse. Then it just eggs it on." While perhaps making their playing experience easier, women who ignore those things that offend them are merely doing what Williams and Dempsey argue women do in workplaces—defusing "any potential threat to masculinity that a female might present, by reassuring men that increasing gender diversity won't require them to change their behavior or rethink their assumptions."[47]

All agency in fantasy sports, however, is not wholly reproductive. Women respond to their outsider status and stereotypes of women in sports in ways that are simultaneously reflective of reproductive and transformative agency. We use the term *mediated agency* for instances in which women use men to better their fantasy sports experience and play. This sort of response accepts men's power and knowledge (a largely reproductive approach) but also positions them as allies who might ultimately help alter the gendered dynamics of the space (a more transformative approach). That women who play fantasy sports are often doing so with men they know well who are similarly socially located makes mediated agency possible. These women, thus, have resources at their disposal that other women in spaces dominated by men and masculinity may not have. As a quintessential example of mediated agency, Jennifer, a casual player, revealed that she asked her boyfriend to step in and address an offensive comment made in her league. She explained:

> [A man] said something so offensive about women. And I went to an all-women's college, I am as feminist as they come, and I said to my boyfriend, I was like, "You need to email him and tell him that crosses the line and that can't happen." And he did, and he also posted something on the message board and said, "Remember, we are respectful men, and there are ladies in this league."

Clearly, Jennifer seeks to transform the climate of this league—but she does so in a way that reproduces power dynamics by assuming men control the interactions in the space and must protect women. As another illustration, a female player noted in the survey that what she gained from playing fantasy sports was "feeling cool when I can brag about my fantasy prowess to male friends or when my husband brags about it for me." Again, take note of the contradictory nature of her statement in receiving pleasure from bragging about her prowess to men (an assertion of power) and from her husband's bragging for her (a mediated assertion of power). Such behaviors are reflective of the somewhat contradictory space fantasy sports occupy. They potentially present opportunities for women's inclusion while simultaneously being environments that remain dominated by men and masculinity. It is thus not surprising that using men as intermediaries is one way women exercise a degree of agency.

Women also frequently engage in what we call conflicted agency. Here, women reinforce or accept gender stereotypes about women but then (1) use those stereotypes to gain an advantage or (2) position themselves as atypical women to whom the stereotypes do not apply. To illustrate the first, some women gleefully claim they do not counter assumptions about women as inferior because this creates a situation in which the men "never see the ass kickin' coming!!!" Similar to Wachs's female softballers who allow men to play shallow so they can then hit the balls more easily over their heads, women, like Jane expressed doing in our opening, strategically allow men to assume they are not in the know when it comes to fantasy sports. As Brittany, a dedicated fantasy sports player, explained, "They don't expect as much from me. . . . I ended up being able to use that to my advantage.

They think that I know less than I do, but it gives me a better playing field." Notably, this response is both reproductive and potentially transformative. It is reproductive because it depends on leaving stereotypes about women's inferiority unchallenged. It is potentially transformative, however, in that each time a woman does "kick ass," the other players may be forced to reckon with women's capabilities in this space and, accordingly, adjust their assumptions.

As illustrative of the second type of conflicted agency, many women position themselves as "atypical" women or "one of the guys." Unlike others who consider sports fanship and competitiveness as part of their identities in rather gender-neutral and transformative ways, women in these instances explicitly assert that they are unlike typical women. Jennifer, quoted above as employing mediated agency, claimed her father "made" her "into a tomboy"; regarding her fantasy sports participation, she said, "I like the fact that I was an exception or I played it up." Annick, who is one of our most hard-core players, also positions herself as breaking down stereotypes and the relevancy of sex and gender in fantasy sports while simultaneously suggesting she is atypical of women. Reflecting this sort of conflicted agency, she noted:

> I love my longtime league. Yes, I'm a woman, and yeah, it's fun that I've won it the last two years being the only woman, like I don't consider myself, I'm not a token by any stretch, I have established my credibility whether I was male or female. It is fun [to] have the big steak dinner [the winner gets with the other managers], but wearing a dress and being a girl, that is fun. But I don't; it [my sex/gender] doesn't play into the day to day at all, I mean at all. It's just, I am just one of the guys.

Thus, these women seek to mark themselves as competent fantasy sports players (and as sports aficionados overall), but in doing so reinforce notions that the average woman is not as knowledgeable or interested in sports and cannot compete like them. Much like Matthew Ezzell's women ruggers, these fantasy sports players identify with men rather than other women and thereby, raise their status in a domain dominated by men and masculinity.[48] Moreover, when White and heterosexual, they can stake claim to being an exception to their gender without risking the same negative assessment and consequences that others, particularly Black or lesbian women who are already stereotyped as too masculine, might face if they employed this strategy.[49] As such, conflicted agency, while potentially transformative in that individual women gain acceptance or demonstrate competence, does little to disrupt what it means to be a woman or the notion that men and masculinity define legitimacy and acceptance in fantasy sports. And insofar as it is

White, heterosexual, class-privileged women who can claim to be "one of the guys" while playing fantasy sports, it does nothing to disrupt the intersections of race, class, sexuality, and gender privilege in this space.

Some women, however, engage in behaviors or express attitudes more reflective of transformative agency. In doing so, they challenge fantasy sports—or sports more generally—as the province of men and, by extension, their exclusion and marginalization. This opens up the possibility for genuine change in the gender dynamics of the space. Given that women to whom we spoke embody some aspects of the authentic sports fan—White, class privileged, and heterosexual,[50] they may not only feel more comfortable in asserting agency in such ways but also in laying claim to legitimacy than others who are outsiders on multiple fronts. Some, like Jane in our opening, often forcefully claim that they are sports fanatics and that sports are central to their identities without also making reference to being "atypical" like those aforementioned women. With such declarations, these women, like Michelle, a newcomer to fantasy sports but a self-described "sports nut" and "football junkie" who is "willing and able to participate in just about any athletic endeavor you might want to throw at" her, counter notions of sports as a province reserved exclusively for men. Others also actively assert other masculine-typed qualities, such as their competitive spirit or their desire to one-up others, again as Jane did, without saying they are anomalous for their gender. Anne, for instance, claimed, "[fantasy sports] get [at] that level of being a competitor even though you're not actually competing. . . . I played basketball, I played soccer, and so I was always competitive my whole life, and then, so that [fantasy football] gives me an outlet for it. . . . It gives me an outlet to beat somebody, I guess."

Other times, women participate in behaviors or express attitudes reflective of jock statsculinity as they simultaneously highlight their gender. By doing so, they suggest more directly than others that women, not just atypical women, can embody these characteristics. These women, for instance, are clear that they engage (or would engage) in what might be described as masculine bravado while also making visible that they are women. Jennifer, who was also someone who engaged in conflicted and mediated agency, claimed:

> Winning is very important, and that's the thing: if I was to win this whole thing, I would get so much satisfaction, and my post on the message board would probably be like, "Suck it. You're all dudes and a girl just won her first year of fantasy football." . . . If I win, I would probably buy something like superfeminine, like I would go buy a hot pink purse just to post on our message board and be like, "Thanks, guys, for buying me this purse."

Relatedly, women also often employ strategically chosen team names that satirize gendered expectations, flip them on their head, or reference girl power, much like roller derby girls do with their personas or female football fan groups do in Europe.[51] For instance, we heard of women naming their teams things like "You're Losing to a Girl," "Queen of the Turf," "Nobody Beats Our Johnson," or "Vaginal Hubris" to both demonstrate their power and gender while also ridiculing misogyny within the space. Notably, such assertions of power and bravado are likely read more positively when highly educated White women express them than if Black women were to do so. Insofar as stereotypes of the angry Black woman pervade historical and contemporary popular thought and cultural imagery,[52] such displays might result in being judged as too angry, aggressive, or outspoken and accordingly dismissed. One need look no further than the treatment of Serena Williams for evidence of the dismissal and demonization of a successful, agentic Black woman in sports.[53]

Moreover, just as in the male-dominated workplaces where women confront challenges to their organizational "fit" and respond by working "twice as hard to get half as far,"[54] women in fantasy sports also voice that they work "doubly hard" to prove that men's assumptions about women are incorrect. Their underestimation gives them, as Annick explained, "a little bit of a chip on your shoulder" which, in turn, pushes them to "do the best you can, and you wanna crush those boys." Or as Lynn explained:

> You have to have a bit of a thicker skin . . . and prove that you're worthy enough to be there before the guys embrace you. . . . [Women] have to prove even harder that they're not picking their players because they look cute in their pants or whatever. . . . You have to work, I think, almost doubly hard than the guys to prove your knowledge. . . . [Being the only woman in the league] makes me want to beat them even more to prove that I'm not the token female, that I can hang with the big boys and I know what I'm talking about. . . . I'm representing all of womanhood here.

Indeed, though not common, some women find that some men recognize or even accept them as legitimate fantasy sports players, thus suggesting the structural impact characteristic of transformative agency. Lynn, quoted above, was one woman who alluded to such a progression. She revealed:

> I've been playing with most of them [the men in the league] for so long; I think they're a little bit better about it [dealing with my success]. . . . Now it's like, even at draft time, they can tell that I guess I've proven myself. Instead of [questioning my skill], it's, "Damn it,

you took that player before me" or whatever. And I kinda always take pride in that.

Annick, also quoted above, expressed a similar idea—that men in a league in which she currently plays recognize her ability. She described part of a dinner conversation she had with members of the league: "Everyone said, 'Look, on paper your team looked great . . . but you knew those were risky picks that could have really done poorly,' and they said, 'Congratulations, you made all the right calls and it all worked out.' So I appreciated that."

Thus, while often women engage in agency that is reproductive or, at best, mediated or conflicted, there are glimpses of their enacting transformative agency. In at least a few of their leagues, some gendered understandings and dynamics shift. The overall narrative here is reminiscent of what other scholars have found in real sports and in digital gaming. Women do, at times, contest how they are being treated and defined, but they often do so in ways that ultimately leave the spaces masculine and dominated by men. Yet, women have some resources at their disposal to counter gendered assumptions and the misogyny in some of their leagues that others in spaces dominated by men and masculinity may not. These are well-educated, middle- and upper-class, White professional women who fit into the space in terms of their race and class and are often playing side-by-side with men who can act as allies. Moreover, the more tangible nature of competitive fandom here may provide them with more power to advance their claims than women sports fans more generally—even if their victories are still subject to ideological repair work. As Sharon Hays postulated but few have demonstrated, women's agency exists on a continuum—reflecting, reinforcing, and countering gender all at once, sometimes simultaneously.

Playing in a Man's World: A Summary

Despite both an expansion of legitimate masculinity and increased participation of women, fantasy sports, like real sports or digital gaming, are still decidedly framed in the abstract and experienced by women as "men's turf." In discussing why women are less likely to play than men, our respondents turn to well-worn stereotypes about women. Women are less interested in, experienced with, and knowledgeable of sports and less likely to have a competitive drive or obsession with statistics than are men. Rather, women do what women are supposed to do—shop, care for their children, and engage in domestic and aesthetically oriented hobbies (such as decorating), all of which takes them away from fantasy sports as a potential leisure activity. Such abstract views reflect a larger gender frame that establishes men and women as distinct and highly differentiated from each other.

Demonstrating the strength of these larger gender beliefs, women, whose participation in fantasy sports would seem to counter the stereotypes, often experience the hobby as exclusionary and find men frame them as outsiders and judge them lesser than men. Women, at times, have to deal with offensive and sexist language and interactions and contend with "real jerks" who are "rude and crude" and do "everything to push the girls away." Even more frequently, they face high levels of scrutiny and questioning of their competence and motives and have their successes discounted or explained away.

Women in fantasy sports, however, do not typically describe encountering situations akin to the hypermisogynistic environs that many women sportswriters and media personalities and online digital gamers face, particularly those who are Black and/or lesbian.[55] With the exceptions of some online public message boards and anonymous fantasy sports leagues, for the most part, more subtle and indirect manifestations of sexism exist in fantasy sports. That women are largely playing with people they know (and often know well) likely both quarantines them from extreme misogyny and reduces its prevalence in their leagues, as men and women interact with those they care about and understand beyond abstract stereotypes. Roland alludes to this sort of dynamic when he explained that his wife, who is "crazy about" fantasy sports, is "very much our equal at every level, especially in fantasy." He continued:

> A large part of that [equal treatment] has to do with our relationships with these people. They know her, how bright she is, so I don't think they would look at her like that [as inferior] anyway. But, or specifically because they know her, but in general, I don't think they have those ideas about—I guess what I'm saying is that I don't think we have a bunch of misogynists in our league.

Women's insider status in terms of their race and class also likely affords them some protection from extreme and direct sexism as well as opportunities for inclusion and legitimacy.

Women respond in varied and often contradictory ways to their status in fantasy sports—and indeed, part of the privilege of this group of women may be that they have the ability to choose how to exercise their agency. They retreat from hostile and masculine environments and exchanges and ignore or brush them off as personally harmless. They try to use the stereotypes regarding women to their advantage, enlist the help of men to better their experience, or position themselves with pride as atypical women who deserve respect. Some push back against stereotypes of women and the masculinized environment of fantasy sports. They do this by stretching gendered understandings of what a successful fantasy sports participant looks and acts like, mocking or repositioning gender assumptions through their strategic choice of team names, and actively and simultaneously flaunting their successes and gender. While not the predominant story, women players do sometimes gain the respect they seek and are seen as equal competitors by *some* men in their lives—even if these men may not grant that women in general are legitimate sports aficionados and competitors. Women express feeling pride, satisfaction, and sometimes, power as a result of gaining such legitimacy. Thus, just as fantasy sports play is empowering for men, it is for many of these White, class-advantaged women as well.

Overall, the account of women and fantasy sports is both old and new. It's old in that masculinity, albeit expanded, still dominates and long-standing abstract beliefs about women hold sway here (e.g., that women do not know sports, that they are emotional and fragile, and that they are not rational) and profoundly affect the experiences of women who do play. But much is new here—the interpersonal dynamics enmeshed in a virtual game create space and the resources for some women to gain legitimacy and to avoid some of the worst forms of sexism witnessed in other male-dominated spaces. And women push back and engage in agency that at times is more reproductive, other times more transformative, and still other times mediated or conflicted. The story, therefore, is a multifaceted one that reflects how the terrain of fantasy sports is contradictory and contested but still one in which women are relative outsiders.

5

The Social Aspects of Fantasy Are Huge

Gendered Social Capital in Fantasy Sports

In many ways, Jerome, a White thirty-four-year-old man, exemplifies the jock statsculinity we outlined in Chapter 3, as he is a competitive sports fanatic who relishes the cerebral aspects of the game and loves playing general manager (GM). He has been involved in the hobby for some time, having participated since the age of nine when he and a group of neighborhood friends held their first draft in someone's barn. In the precomputerized era during which this took place, Jerome served as the league statistician, collecting and recording all the group's data each morning. Even though he recalls this time fondly, he explains that he took a ten-year hiatus from fantasy sports, during which he felt he did not "need" them because, as a die-hard Cubs fan, he was already "so focused on it [sports]." He returned to fantasy sport, however, in his midtwenties partly because, in his words, it "fulfills something in my life I don't have anymore"—namely, the aspects of competitive fandom not available through just watching sports.

But Jerome, who is now married with one young child, also returned to fantasy sports for another reason—they provide a means of connecting with others.[1] Since he has moved cross-country more than once to pursue academic and career opportunities, a level of geographic mobility not uncommon for middle- and upper-class individuals of his generation, fantasy sports may be particularly useful in this regard. Of his motivation to pick up the hobby again, Jerome, who currently plays in five leagues, at least one of which consists solely of high school friends, reveals, "It was initially social, because it was like, 'Oh, I can keep in touch with all of these friends who I

don't normally keep in touch on a weekly basis with,' which is awesome."
And, he acknowledges that in some ways, he has realized his goal of connecting with others through fantasy sports, telling us, "I'm in their life a
little bit and they're in mine." He continues, "Now that more of us have got
married or whatever, now we know [by playing fantasy sports] that every
now and again in an email they'll be like, 'Oh, by the way, how is your wife?'"
Moreover, Jerome has made new or realized nascent connections through
his participation. While he originally only personally knew two other participants in his basketball league, now he has "met two of the other people in
different circles than being in the league." He also feels that if he "saw" these
league members now, he "would have something to talk about" with them,
suggesting that the ties he is making have the potential to move beyond the
confines of the league.

For Jerome, and many men, though, connections through fantasy sports
are paradoxically both limited and deep. On the one hand, he hesitates to
fully acknowledge that he has been able to stay in touch with his friends
through fantasy sports, at one point going so far as to say, "We did it as a
way to keep in touch, and we don't really keep in touch via the league. It's
just every now and then, we check in." As a further case in point, Jerome
reveals that he was unaware that a fellow league member and friend "had
a baby . . . but I knew that he drafted Jackson in the second round." Moreover, Jerome predicts the newer connections he has made through fantasy
sports will remain shallow. Upon finding out that one of his fellow fantasy
basketball league members lived in a nearby town, he recalls, "In my head,
I'm like, 'Oh, that'd be fun to get together,' but in my head I know we're not
going to. But we could."

On the other hand, Jerome repeatedly discusses fantasy sports as a way
to "bond" with others, particularly other men. In fact, he ultimately draws
a distinction between staying in touch and bonding, saying, "This is how we
stay in touch on some level, how we bond more actually than stay in touch.
It's how we bond." As someone who played basketball and soccer in high
school and had a standing Sunday pickup game of football throughout his
youth, Jerome, like many men, acknowledges throughout his interview that
fantasy sports have taken the place of real sports in his life. But the place
they take is not just one of occupying time. For Jerome and other men like
him, sports serve an important function in providing a mechanism through
which they can feel connected with other men without "delving deep." Jerome explains it this way:

> Society has drilled into our [men's] heads we bond by playing sports
> when we're growing up, and then when that's over, we bond by now—
> we have this other thing we can do. . . . So maybe part of it [the at-
> traction of fantasy sports] is just this societal thing of how we, how

does one bond with their peer group and with other members? And you bond in a way you don't have to [delve deep], there's not a lot of delving deep into [each other's lives].

To be sure, Jerome and his friends do not seem to be having the deep personal conversations that would allow them to recognize major milestones in each other's personal lives, such as his friend's having a baby. He and other men freely admit that they spend some amount of time merely discussing the nuances of sports strategy, such as the merits of a particular pitcher, or engaging in sports talk more generally. Furthermore, their interactions are characterized by a high degree of trash talking, which Jerome refers to as "good natured" and "playful joking" that is "pretty constant" in at least one of his leagues. While Chapter 3 established such competitive banter as key to the performance of masculinity, Jerome positions such talk as integral to his forging deeper connections with men in his circle of friends—trash talking, according to him, is both "how we [men] poke fun but also how we show affection to each other." This approach to bonding and connecting to others differs from that of women, and Jerome recognizes this. He notes that his wife "hates, cannot stand any even good-natured trash talk. . . . She just doesn't like that type of interaction." Rather, Jerome thinks she, and other women, "bonds other ways" by, for example, talking "on the phone for an hour and a half every two weeks" with friends and family. Frequently separated by distance and no longer able to play physical sports, yet still embedded in a culture that emphasizes the role of sports in both masculinity and men's connections to other men, Jerome and his friends bond through competitive trash talking.

While some of Jerome's experiences of relationship building through fantasy sports are similar to those of women players, there are some key distinctions. Take, for example, Brittany, a thirty-one-year-old, self-described "numbers kind of person" and avid fantasy sports player who "enjoys watching sports." Brittany is newer to the hobby, "getting involved" about four years ago after having talked about it with "friends at work." Initially, she joined a league she heard about through a blog she reads, but shortly thereafter, she explains, "I ended up joining leagues at work. And now my biggest league is some people that I met through work." Currently, like Jerome, Brittany participates in five leagues in multiple sports (football, ice hockey, baseball, and golf) with managers who are connected to her in various ways and to varying degrees. She plays in two online leagues in which she does not have any previous connection to the other managers, but her other three leagues involve work colleagues and family members.

Brittany's boyfriend participates in three of the leagues in which she also plays, allowing this "highly competitive" couple to share information with each other and spend time together through the hobby. Unequivocally, fantasy sports represent a key shared activity for them, and one that is positive even though they need to set ground rules such as forbidding "smack talking at night" when they compete against each other. In reflecting on the forty-five minutes or so that she spends on fantasy sports daily, Brittany is quick to preface her remarks with "thankfully, my boyfriend and I both are interested in it" and therefore can "watch the fantasy show on NFL network" together. And when asked if she knows what she would do with her time if she did not play fantasy sports, Brittany is puzzled; laughing, she responds, "No. And it's funny that you ask that because my boyfriend and I usually ask like, 'What do our other friends that have significant others that aren't interested in sports talk about? So what do they do?'"

It's not just her boyfriend that Brittany connects with through fantasy sports, however. She claims that, like Jerome, what she also gets out of playing is that she has "made a lot of friends both in person and through blogs and everything like that. I have people that I can speak with and that I have known for years and that we have something in common and it also gives me something to talk to people about." She continues, "I think it's a good way to socially interact; it's a good common ground for people that have a common interest and a way to get groups of people together that wouldn't otherwise."

Despite a negative experience with a fellow manager whose "unnecessary and out-of-line" cursing "turned [her] off to the league," Brittany, like other men and women, is clear that her overall involvement in fantasy sports has opened up new, positive connections with others and fosters bonds with friends she has known for years. Importantly, it also offers a way for her to forge ties with men in the workplace. She explains:

> It's a good starter for conversation. While a lot of people may say that they [fantasy sports] are kind of stupid, it really does help you to get to meet a lot of, as much as I hate the word *networking*, it really is a good networking tool. . . . Professionally, even I have been able to open up my horizons and talk to people that I may not have spoken to before just 'cause of the sports knowledge that I have gained.

In her estimation, fantasy sports act as a sort of cultural currency and way for her to enhance her connections to professional colleagues. Despite having "always" loved to watch sports and "always" having "known about sports," Brittany now has more confidence in her knowledge and feels sure that she is "able to carry thorough conversation." But what's critical is not just that she is surer of her sports knowledge but that she feels "a little more confident" in general. She explains that "even in other situations and not just talking about sports," she believes she sounds "a little bit more intelligent" and more a "part of a group."

Brittany's newfound confidence and ability to discuss sports with men at work is something that helps her gain entrée into spaces dominated by men and masculinity. Importantly, Brittany knows that such inclusion is not automatic. She notes that many women likely do not play fantasy sports because men, who have played in leagues for a longer time, do not invite women to join their leagues when spots arise, nor do they expand their leagues to accommodate interested women. She explains that women who want to play face the problem that "a lot of the leagues, like the leagues that my boyfriend is in, have been going on for a really long time, some of them from like the early '90s." This means that "to find a league that has a spot open is really hard." Brittany is fortunate in being able to join a work league and one composed of her boyfriend's family, each of which contains mostly men. But she still does not play in leagues composed of groups of men who have been friends for a long time, like those in which her boyfriend and men like Jerome have been playing for many years.

All in all, for Brittany, like Jerome, fantasy sports surely offer a way to connect to others—both those with whom she already has a relationship and those she does not. But unlike men like Jerome who emphasize how fantasy sports participation allows them to bond with men in their friendship circles often through highly competitive trash talking, women like Brittany frequently discuss how the hobby connects them to men (e.g., boyfriends and husbands, brothers, and fathers) merely via sharing an activity, having a topic of conversation, and increasing time together. Moreover, White, upper- and middle-class women like Brittany strategically deploy their fantasy sports participation to gain entrée into other circles dominated by men, particularly at their workplaces. Thus, while men and women may differ in their purposes and methods of connecting with others through fantasy sports, they do share one important thing in common—in a space where men and masculinity dominate, the targets of everyone's connections are men, and specifically, White, class-privileged ones.

Implicit and sometimes explicit in Jerome's and Brittany's accounts is that fantasy sports represent a relatively privileged and homogeneous world for interactions and connections. Here, typically, White, middle- and upper-class men and women compete virtually (and sometimes side-by-side) with known and similarly socially located others. Women reap relationship benefits from these interactions, leveraging their participation to develop connections with men and gain entrance and acceptance in male-dominated and masculine realms—albeit, race- and class-privileged ones. That these largely White middle- and upper-class women play alongside men similar to them in many ways may provide greater opportunities for their inclusion than other environments in which they are outsiders on multiple dimensions. Yet, the connective potential of fantasy sports seems particularly tailored and important to White, class-privileged men, whose friendships tend to be more focused on shared leisure activity than their working-class counterparts[2] and for whom work and family dynamics, geographic mobility, and the dictates of hegemonic masculinity complicate social connections.

Social Capital and Fantasy Sports

The emergence of modern fantasy sports—online, accessible, and increasingly popular—fills an important niche in the contemporary social landscape in the United States. In his seminal book, *Bowling Alone*, Robert Putnam argues that individuals have increasingly become disconnected from friends, family, neighbors, and community.[3] This results in steep declines in access to and use of the potential benefits—feelings of value, important resources, emotional support, advice, and a sense of belonging—embedded in social ties, otherwise known as social capital.[4] Many of Putnam's examples of this decline in social capital, such as belonging to civic organizations, meeting with friends, and participating in bowling leagues, require physical presence and proximity. As Putnam himself argued, the loss of these types of connections is tied to demographic and economic changes, and the White, middle- and upper-class men and women who constitute the majority of fantasy sports participants likely experience these changes accutely. White, highly educated, wealthy, married, professional individuals are more likely than those of other demographic groups to experience geographic mobility.[5] In fact, education and income are the largest determining factors in the distance individuals live from their hometowns,[6] which may leave such privileged people physically removed from at least some of their social ties. Moreover, those in professional occupations are more likely than others to put in very long workweeks.[7] Long work hours may preclude participation in civic groups or social activities that have set meeting times and may rule out even something as simple as dinner with friends. Relatedly, Putnam and others, most notably Ray Oldenburg,[8] argue that we have seen a general retreat from brick-and-mortar "third places"—those settings, such as pubs, cafés, and libraries, where people can socialize outside of home ("first places") and work ("second places") and thus build social capital. Scholars detailing this decline often focus on the rise of both traditional and new media, noting how these occupy much of our leisure time and leave less space for socializing in third places.[9]

Fantasy sports seemingly erase many of these barriers to the creation and maintenance of social capital—they can be played virtually and at any time, thus removing limitations of time and distance. Moreover, like some digital games, such as massively multiplayer online games (MMOs),[10] they use new media in ways that may connect people rather than isolate them, perhaps acting as a sort of virtual third place. And they connect individuals both to those they already know (often well) and those they do not.[11] For these reasons, fantasy sports participation may be a particularly crucial mechanism for connecting with others in a world in which face-to-face interaction is increasingly difficult.

The world of fantasy sports, however, is also gendered, and given that a large body of research indicates gender differences in social networks and ties, it may present different interpersonal opportunities for men and women. Men tend to have a greater number of weak ties[12]—those to associates and acquaintances—than women. Thus, on average, men have greater levels of bridging social capital. Bridging social capital links people who are different from one another, thereby promoting the sharing of information and resources across groups and the expansion of opportunities as well as the development of diverse yet inclusive communities.[13] Weak and bridging ties are also typically more instrumental in nature; that is, they are developed or can be employed to gain resources one does not currently possess—to obtain "tangible resources, knowledge, and information for instrumental purposes (e.g., task advice)."[14] For example, instrumental social ties might be deployed to access information about a desired job or to identify a childcare provider.

Women's networks, however, tend to include more strong ties—those with high levels of contact and emotional attachment. Such ties provide greater levels of bonding social capital, connections and resources that flow through relationships in fairly homogeneous networks and that afford belonging and support but not necessarily better opportunities. Strong and bonding ties are more expressive—that is, they are developed or used to consolidate already possessed resources or to defend against resource loss (e.g., in physical or mental health, personal identity, or life satisfaction).[15] Those pursuing expressive objectives through their social ties may be in quest of an interesting and happy life, one in which they feel emotionally supported, befriended, and a sense of belonging and identity validation. The goals here are more affective than task oriented (though, certainly, feeling loved and happy may indirectly help individuals accomplish other goals). Individuals in one's network may serve both instrumental and expressive functions. Moreover, whether pursuing instrumental or expressive aims, individuals "will fare most favorably if they know people with the time, money, energy, or knowledge to help them achieve these ends."[16] Thus, class, race and ethnicity, and gender intersect to influence whom we know and the types of resources we might be able to access from them.

In what follows, we demonstrate that fantasy sports fill an important gap for the White, geographically mobile upper- and middle-class men and (to a lesser extent) women who dominate the ranks of players, as time, distance, and other commitments make face-to-face interactions increasingly challenging. To understand the types of connections men in particular might form through their fantasy sports participation, one must understand that this all unfolds under the backdrop of masculinity that we have previously discussed. Scholars have noted how the rigid demands of hegemonic masculinity, most notably its grounding in unquestionable heterosexuality, make intimate connections between men difficult.[17] Specifically, insofar as building emotional connections with others is considered a feminine trait and doing so with other men puts the presumption of heterosexuality at risk, same-sex friendships potentially threaten men's claim to ideal masculinity. Men thus enter this context at a deficit in terms of their relationships with other men. Sports, however, as a bastion of masculinity, provide a safe space for men to foster close relationships with other men, while simultaneously demonstrating their masculinity.[18]

Jock statsculinity, although broader than a traditional masculinity associated with real sports, emphasizes rationality over emotions and incorporates the (implicit, at least) assumption of heterosexuality. Accordingly, fantasy sports, like real sports, present the opportunity for men—particularly White, class-privileged men—to develop not just casual relationships but expressive, strong ties. In fact, men use the term *bonding* to refer to their fantasy sports–facilitated relationships with other men. Yet fantasy sports do something that active participation in real sports cannot. They provide this opportunity without regard for age, physical capability, or geographic proximity. This is particularly important for men given cultural notions suggesting that their friendships focus on shared activities.[19] With fantasy sports, some of men's relationships with other men have moved from the locker room to online spaces.

Given the general exclusion of women, Blacks, and individuals of lower socioeconomic status, though, the relationships and interactions promoted through fantasy sports participation offer yet another exclusive and elite sphere for social capital–building for White, class-privileged men. Fantasy sports provide opportunities to interact, share information, and feel an affinity with similarly positioned men, just as the round of golf or after-work drink at the downtown club affords.[20] Such relationships and interactions, in turn, reproduce privilege through a phenomenon sociologists call homosocial reproduction. Typically used to describe organizational dynamics, homosocial reproduction refers to the process wherein managers, for instance, select people like them and/or similar to those already inhabiting the setting for open positions.[21] Homogeneous social networks frequently facilitate homosocial reproduction—that is, people hang out with people like them and, subsequently, may think of these people in their networks when openings or promotions arise. The social characteristics of a given organizational setting and the power structures within thus get reproduced over time. Accordingly, inasmuch as fantasy sports facilitate ties and affinities among similarly socially located men, they also help reproduce race, class, and gender relations.

Fantasy sports, though, can also play a role in contesting some of the above dynamics. For those women who do play, there is the potential to develop the types of weak or instrumental ties that typically characterize men's relationships. A large body of research, much of it reviewed in the preceding chapters, documents women's marginalization in male-dominated environments. By removing physical barriers to women's participation, fantasy sports allow some White, middle- and upper-class women the opportunity to diversify their networks and leverage their fantasy sports participation and the knowledge gleaned from it as a sort of cultural currency to further their careers or to gain status more generally *among men*. This strategic use of fantasy sports represents still another way women engage in transformative agency, dismantling to some degree power dynamics in the workplace in particular. Yet, it's also important to highlight that the objects of their connections are almost exclusively White, class-advantaged men. Thus, despite their potential for inclusivity and transformative agency, fantasy sports remain a deeply gendered, classed, and racialized space in which power rests firmly in the hands of intersectionally privileged men.

Augmenting Strong Ties, Fostering Weak Ties for Both Men and Women

Both men and women use their fantasy sports participation to connect with romantic partners, friends, and/or family members and, by doing so, enhance preexisting strong ties. For some, like Brittany in our opening, fantasy sports participation adds a shared hobby to the list of ties and activities connecting heterosexual individuals to their romantic partners—something relatively rare in a world in which workplaces, social networks, household responsibilities, and leisure pursuits remain largely sex and gender segregated. One female player alluded to this draw and benefit when she noted:

> I started [playing fantasy sports] when I moved in with my husband, knowing that he played, and figuring that if I enjoyed it, it would be a fun way to spend more time together. I ended up loving it, and the fact that my husband and I share it as an interest has added to our relationship.

Similarly, David, a hard-core player who has been involved in fantasy sports for more than seven years, revealed how they are enjoyable in large part because he shares them with his wife:

> My wife and I do this together. . . . We have a lot of fun doing it. . . . It's critical that my wife is into it. That makes it so much more en-

joyable 'cause it's a, it's one of *our* activities. . . . Part of the reason I am prepared to spend that amount of time [on it] is because it's something we do together. I wouldn't want to just be like, "All right, honey, why don't you just, you make dinner and I'll go upstairs" and [I] wouldn't be doing that. But the fact that we sit together, and she has the computer and I have the iPad, and we can sit together and do fantasy baseball for two hours, that's cool. . . . This is *our* hobby.

For these couples and others, fantasy sports offer a shared activity that does not require a set time and place to interact, something particularly helpful for professional, middle- and upper-class individuals working long hours and managing other responsibilities. Additionally, because men and masculinity dominate fantasy sports, they present a safe space for men to engage in the more expressive components of strong ties, including those that involve prioritizing time and connection with one's wife. These experiences, though, are not universal; many men experience fantasy sports as something that competes with family time (see Chapter 6), and others use it as a way to escape from family life. But for some, fantasy sports participation represents time with, rather than time away from, their spouses and offers the opportunity for greater connection, increasing their willingness to spend time on the hobby.

Commonly, fantasy sports are about connecting with existing friends and acquaintances. Indeed, interacting with friends is a large part of the fantasy sports experience, as both male and female players in our survey report higher levels of bonding when playing in leagues with friends than in those comprised primarily of acquaintances and strangers. Individuals, like Brittany and Jerome, discuss frequently and at length how fantasy sports forge and solidify friendships by offering players a common interest that provides conversational material and a sense of camaraderie. As with the bonding that occurs between spouses, fantasy sports increase the frequency with which participants interact with their friends—both those with whom they might otherwise touch base (often in person) and those they might not. Cole, a college professor who has played fantasy sports for more than eight years, is exemplary of the former, highlighting how fantasy sports serve an expressive function by creating a "shared project" among friends he regularly sees. He claimed:

It creates stronger social ties. . . . Even for people that you interact with quite regularly on a face-to-face basis, I think it strengthens social ties in a number of ways—there is a shared project; I think it can be a good, something consistent as a topic of conversation. I think any social group has, and all personal relationships have, cer-

tain topics that they keep coming back to, and this [is] a particularly amusing, relatively low-stress one that people can talk about and
bond over that doesn't have the same stakes or other things to do
with work or personal life or other things like that.

Others focus on how fantasy sports support relationships with friends
they see less often or not at all, such as Brendan, who travels a lot for his
pharmaceutical-related job. In regard to his friends who live across the
world, Brendan said, "The folks that I know in the league are people that I
knew from high school or college, and I am much more drastically in touch
with these people because we're playing fantasy sports than I am with anybody else who I went to high school or college with." And it is here that we
can see clearly how fantasy sports may fill an important niche in the twenty-
first-century social landscape. With high levels of geographic mobility and
demanding work lives, particularly among the demographic most likely to
play, fantasy sports help participants maintain strong ties, even in the absence of face-to-face interaction. While certainly friends and family can and
do connect via social media, phone calls, and other communication avenues,
fantasy sports are somewhat unique in providing a substantive means of and
reason for such interaction (i.e., something to "do" together) for both adult
men and women that does not require physical presence (like real sports) or
even simultaneous availability (like many digital games). So while participants often do get together in person with their friends over fantasy sports,
they do not have to in order to reap the expressive social capital benefits of
the hobby.

Additionally, fantasy sports present opportunities to create new social
ties and, sometimes, like we see with Brittany, transform weak ties into
strong ones—turning what were once-tenuous ties with coworkers, acquaintances (e.g., friends of friends), or strangers into full-fledged friendships. Fantasy sports provide fodder for conversation and a reason to interact among
previously known and unknown individuals. As Frank, a dedicated player
whose job in higher education involves travel and sometimes fourteen-hour
workdays, related, they are an "easy topic of conversation" and "can build
relationship, create interactions." As a result, some fantasy sports players
find that they gain access to "a whole pool of people" they "wouldn't have
otherwise met," with whom they become "very good friends" (Bob) and for
whom they develop "strong feelings" (Lynn). This is achieved partly through
being in the same leagues; however, notably, new media platforms (e.g., message boards, Twitter, Facebook) also help promote the development of new
ties through fantasy sports. Fantasy-related platforms may act as virtual
third places, where conversation is the main activity, people can come and
go with few entanglements, participants value wit and playful banter, there

are regulars, and one feels at home.[22] Otto, a married laboratory manager and hard-core player, exemplifies this idea:

> There's a couple hundred people that patronize that [fantasy football] website's message boards pretty much religiously, and I'm one of them. . . . You read that website every day, you read other people's posts, the different threads that go on, you make your comments, and quite frankly over the years, I've pretty much, even if I've never met them, I know them and I know their personality and I know all about their personal life and this and that. And they know a lot about me. . . . I've talked to close to twenty people from that one fantasy website, I never would have met those people or spent time communicating with them [otherwise], and then there's probably another hundred or more that over the years we've gotten to know each other online.

Fantasy sports also provide a point of conversation among those who are—and likely will remain—strangers. It is rather amazing how often fantasy sports players find themselves talking about the hobby and their teams across a variety of settings, from bars to the deli counter at the supermarket. With each of these seemingly insignificant exchanges, they further extend opportunities to engage with others socially, to feel part of a group, and to build social capital. Paul, a self-described "nerd" who works at an Internet service provider, noted this aspect of the hobby:

> It gives you something in common with people that you might not necessarily have that much in common with. . . . My wife, where she was shopping for a coat, and I was tagging along with her the other day and there was a guy standing there checking his phone and he muttered something under his breath about a player, and I was like, "Oh, yeah, I'm sweating him today, too." And then I had this half-hour conversation with this guy that I never saw in my life.

Likewise, Annick, a single, forty-two-year-old hard-core player with a law degree, commented on how fantasy sports connect individuals to others that they do not know at all or know well:

> I feel like the social aspects of fantasy are huge. When you go to watch a game anywhere, when you do venture out on a Sunday to watch a game or you're out at a bar on a Thursday night, people are asking you, "Why are you watching this Bills-Browns game on Thursday night football?" . . . And then it becomes a conversation. . . . It becomes a common bond and a common way to have conversa-

tions and be social and interact with other football fans. . . . There is a communal experience that comes from participating, whether it's with your own league or even perfect strangers. Because you all are kind of sharing this together. . . . I have just met so many great people through it.

In such ways, fantasy sports produce social benefits in rather gender-neutral ways and on multiple fronts for both men and women—among romantic couples, family members, longtime or new friends, coworkers, acquaintances, or even strangers just meeting online, at a store, or in a bar. The social interactions they provide link participants to people with whom they otherwise may not have conversed and give them a sense of belonging to a larger community. What's more, fantasy sports participants become tied to friends of friends or friends of family members through their fantasy sports leagues. Even if they are not actively interacting with these other individuals in person or through message boards, they are now part of the same social network. Thus, fantasy sports, like others have argued in regard to some types of digital gaming such as MMOs or for subgroups of gamers such as teen boys,[23] offer a way for participants to extend their number of weak ties—those ties that are less emotionally and time intensive and involve less mutual confiding but that are critical in opening up opportunities for individuals and expanding the types of ideas and information to which they are exposed.[24] Importantly, however, this extension of weak social ties occurs alongside the reinforcing of preexisting strong ties and the development of new strong ties. Accordingly, fantasy sports players feel a sense of belonging, increased support and intimacy, and improved satisfaction and happiness as a result of the connections their fantasy sports involvement develops and enhances.

Overall, these connections, because of the relatively homogeneous nature of fantasy sports leagues,[25] are largely expressive and reflective of bonding social capital. And while these connections may be to those of the other gender, they are almost exclusively with others of the same race and class background. Fantasy sports may introduce participants to a "whole pool of people," but that pool is not necessarily diverse. This distinguishes it from other leisure spaces ideologically dominated by hegemonic masculinity, such as gaming and traditional fandom, which are substantially more diverse in terms of race, ethnicity, class, and gender[26] and, thus, might offer better opportunities for interactions across different status groups. All in all, and although some participants may not even be aware of it, fantasy sports increase the social capital of those already privileged in such regard[27]—filling a needed niche for White, geographically mobile, professional men and women in a contemporary U.S. landscape in which brick-and-mortar third places and social capital–building clubs and activities are on the decline.

Men's Friendships in the Context of Fantasy Sports

So far, we have highlighted how fantasy sports foster social capital, contributing to relationships in largely similar ways for women and men. Yet, as is the case with most aspects of fantasy sports, the social side of participation is gendered as well. Although both men and women indicate bonding with friends through the hobby, male players do so with greater frequency.[28] Perhaps more striking is the critical role fantasy sports play in the maintenance of White, class-privileged men's friendships with other men. These men, unlike women, repeatedly and explicitly note that fantasy sports are a primary way to "keep in touch" with old friends from high school, college, and previous employment and that they very likely would not communicate with these individuals were it not for fantasy sports. For many men, fantasy sports are not just a way to interact with one another—they are *the* way. Typical of this, one male player reported that fantasy sports gave him "continued relationships with friends further away—some of which I wouldn't talk to anymore if not for the league." Dino, a married insurance agent who has been playing for twenty years, also referenced how fantasy sports keep him in touch with various others he has known since college, including his fraternity brothers, whom he otherwise "wouldn't talk to" were he "not in the league with them." In Dino's estimation, "the big thing with some of the leagues is they keep people together," something particularly needed "as people get older and get married and start to move away." Likewise, Brendan, who has also played for twenty years, told us:

> Really what I get out of it [playing fantasy sports] is the continued interactions and friendships with people that I knew—that I recognize I would not have maintained without it. That's the real reason that I started playing again after having taken a few years off without playing, because I missed that contact that I was having with people.

Some men also highlight that fantasy sports—despite being played through online platforms and thus without the requirement for face-to-face interaction—are the reason for seeing their friends, and without them, they would not do so. Fantasy sports are not unlike some forms of video gaming in this regard, as they also form the basis for in-person interaction among friends.[29] Exemplifying this idea is Charlie, a long-term player who works from home; in speaking of a handful of specific friends, he asserted that without fantasy sports,

> I would never see them, I would see them once a year . . . and it would be a much different friendship, and during the season we'll go out and spend a Sunday together and watch games, and maybe three of us will do that. So that's nice; I would never ever do that otherwise.

Bill, a hard-core player who has participated for twenty-five years, effectively argued that were it not for the opportunity to interact through the hobby with men in his friend group (specifically at their mandatory in-person draft), he would no longer continue his often-time-consuming fantasy sports participation. To that end, he explained what he gains from playing fantasy sports:

> The chance to interact with the fellows, really, especially the football league. I mean, some of these guys anymore, I only see them at the draft. It's just the way life goes—I have three kids and one's going to college next year and all that sort of stuff. There are so many more things to worry about than [your] fantasy team, but you also don't have time to get together. So that's one of the reasons we do it live [the draft], and you gotta go, [it] is so that you know everybody is kinda hanging out. So I'd say it really, it forces me to maintain contact with friends that I've had for twenty-five, thirty years. So I'd say that's probably the biggest reason why I still do it. . . . You say, "Well, I really don't want to quit, 'cause if I don't do it, I'll never see these guys." So I'd say that's probably the biggest driver.

As Bill suggests, for many men, but not women, fantasy league drafts in particular are pivotal points of in-person contact. These drafts are at least partly attractive because they exclude women (especially wives and girlfriends) and thus support the escapism embedded in jock statsculinity. For instance, one male player wrote that he played fantasy sports "mainly to stay in touch with my high school buddies and for our 'draft weekend' each year when no wives are allowed." Another likewise commented, "I particularly enjoy the drafts, which provide a social event outside my family [and which is] centered around something I love (sports)."

All of this reveals that fantasy sports participation increases the frequency of contact men have with other men in their friend groups—both in person and via new media—and, thus, strengthens these strong ties, adding to men's social capital. Yet strong ties involve an emotional component as well, and it is in this regard that men's relationships with other men are typically limited. The expanded version of masculinity that fantasy sports offer, however, may increase the likelihood of expressive connections among men for more men than real sports do—or, at least, for more White, middle- and upper-class men. Indeed, as men are more able to demonstrate appropriate masculinity through fantasy sports, emotional expression in their friendships with other men may become less intimidating. However, if and to the extent that jock statsculinity exists in a hierarchy within which hegemonic masculinity is ideal, emotionally close relationships with other men may threaten the seemingly tenuous grasp on legitimate masculinity that these men now have. As a result, men may downplay the level of intimacy they share or fail to invest in deep, personal ties with other men through fantasy sports.

These opposing potentials manifest themselves in men's comments, which are replete with contradictions and ambivalence as they variously embrace and deny—sometimes simultaneously—their emotional connections to other men. Men often use terms of endearment such as *buddies* or *the fellows* to refer to the friend group with whom they play fantasy sports, suggesting indirectly the realization of the expressive function of fantasy sports for social relationships. Some men are also explicit about emotional closeness resulting from their fantasy sports involvement, attributing deep connections to the sports talk and increased contact promoted in fantasy sports. For example, Ted, a five-year fantasy sports participant, revealed, "Some guys I talk to more because we used to be in a league together and now I know them better as a, I would say we got closer because of it." Likewise, Charlie, who plays in two leagues, discussed how fantasy sports allow him to foster and strengthen a relationship with a "good friend" of his, as they provide "a great connection."

Yet in discussing their getting close with other men through fantasy sports, men frequently and directly point out, as Jerome in the opening, that these friendships are often largely about talking and bonding over their love of sports and not about sharing in experiences and feelings that may draw them together, such as those they have as fathers, husbands, workers, aging adults, and so forth. These personal topics more typically form the foundation of expressive, emotional ties. Charlie, whom we quoted above, acknowledged about his "good friend," "[I] end up talking to him multiple times a week; we text. It's possible that our friendship is mostly about football, but that's OK." Or there is Drew who told us:

> Not only do you get to keep in touch, but you actually have something to talk about other than "Hey, how's the wife, how's the kids, how's work?" So you can kind of have less superficial, actually have some interesting conversations, for lack of a better way to describe it, some bonding experiences.

Another male player similarly discussed how conversations about fantasy sports supplant those about topics usually seen as more personal:

> I also play it [fantasy sport] as it gives me a reason to interact with friends that I might otherwise not interact with. Most guys in my leagues (and they are predominantly male), we'll go years without talking about life, relationship, but instead we'll have several conversations about the backup infielder for the St. Louis Cardinals.

Thus, on the whole, fantasy sports augment the emotional components of men's relationships with other men because they are able to touch base and engage in conversations with one another and, in their words, "bond" as they do so. But at the same time, the depth of these bonds is variable. And while it may be easy to dismiss these connections as superficial insofar as they stay largely grounded in the world of sports, the way these men talk about the bonds they forge with other men suggests that fantasy sports provide a means for developing elusive expressive ties among men.

In addition, in embracing the expressive elements of men's connections to other men through fantasy sports, some attempt to distance themselves from feminine ways of bonding and, accordingly, women. More specifically, some men fall back on popular stereotypes that rely on a biologically based binary and suggest women's close friendships are built on shared feelings, but men's are built on shared activities rather than conversations about more emotional topics such as relationships and family.[30] Although research suggests these stereotypes are not true nor are they biologically based—men's and women's same-gender friendships both include a combination of conversation and activity—men frequently underscore the importance of a shared activity, in this case fantasy sports, for their friendships. The argument goes something like this: fantasy sports (or sports in general) are something men, but not women, need, either because men otherwise would not connect at all or because men are more comfortable or skilled at connecting through activities, particularly sports, than they are through stand-alone conversations. Frank, a married twenty-seven-year-old who is expecting his first child, nicely explains this notion:

> I think just how we [men] are wired relationally and you get into really touchy subjects there, but for guys, relationships are so much easier if we are able to share an activity rather than just talk. . . . Whether that's inherently wired that way or whether that's how socially, we just societally we've constructed ourselves, you have this where it's much easier for women to interact and be friends and just have relationships for relationships' sake. I think men still have that same inherent need and need relationships and need friendship and connection and community, but it's just so much easier to do that around an activity. And so, maybe that's why it's more interesting for men, why we are more drawn to it [fantasy sport] because you have that.

Likewise, recall Jerome's words from the opening in the chapter:

> Society has drilled into our [men's] heads we bond by playing sports when we're growing up, and then when that's over, we bond by now—we

have this other thing we can do. . . . So maybe part of it [the attraction of fantasy sports] is just this societal thing of how we, how does one bond with their peer group and with other members? And you bond in a way you don't have to [delve deep]; there's not a lot of delving deep into [each other's lives].

Men, therefore, highlight how they bond and become closer with friends through fantasy sports but make clear that they do so in ways that differ from women and that any resulting closeness they may achieve may not go very "deep." In this way, they resolve the contradictions in performing manhood, even with expanding definitions of what that means, and being emotionally connected to other men.

An additional important and distinguishing feature of men's versus women's interactions and bonding in this space (and one that also helps resolve the competing mandates of masculinity and being close with others) revolves around the manner and content of men's conversations. As Chapter 3 documented, men, much more than women, take part in and value trash talk and gaining bragging rights over others. Such dominance talk, though, is not just something in which men engage—it is part of *how they connect*. Engaging in smack talk with others in one's league and reporting that gaining bragging rights is important are both positively associated with bonding with one's friends through fantasy sports and are also more common sentiments among male players.[31] In fact, men repeatedly suggest that they view the bonding and positive social interaction that occur among men as going hand in hand with competition, one-upmanship, and trash talking, all of which are also integral to the performance of jock statsculinity. Ted, who plays in three leagues that include only men, seemed to link friendship with competition as well as trash talking. He told us:

> I have a friend of mine whom I'm very close with and I told him this year that really the only reason I'm ever really interested in fantasy football is just to try to destroy his team. To just, if a wide receiver gets hurt and he's looking to pick up a new wide receiver, I'll pick up a wide receiver just so he doesn't get him. It's actually like a friend competition more than it is a sports, football competition. . . . [Trash talking is] kind of [showing an] interest in your friends as much as it's an interest in football things.

Similarly, other men note that through "talk[ing] trash with other league members . . . you get to know people a little more." This underscores how competitive discourse and one-upmanship more generally are central to both masculinity *and* men's bonding. While on the surface this emphasis on competition and smack talking may suggest that men are avoiding intimacy through fantasy sports, actually, they are using these appropriately masculine tools to seek out and gain intimacy with others—to, as Jerome told us, "show affection to each other"—even if they rarely talk about personal issues or their feelings.

Recall, as was the case with the in-person drafts celebrated above, women are often explicitly excluded from these contexts and methods of bonding. This further drives home a key point. Although jock statsculinity is potentially broader and more accessible than hegemonic masculinity, fantasy sports remain a domain dominated by men and masculinity. In fact, for men, but not for women, being in a league composed entirely or mostly of men increases their bonding through fantasy sports, as does the number of close connections who play fantasy sports.[32] In other words, fantasy sports are particularly effective in augmenting men's relationships with other men when they play alongside existing friends in leagues numerically dominated by men. This is reflected in the comments of Ted, who claimed, "In answering and going through the survey, I realized it's really more about the guys, my [men] friends that are in the league, another way to hang out with my friends." That some men find interactions in fantasy sports attractive specifically because women are generally excluded is simultaneously reflective of and a contributor to women's marginalization in this space. Tony, a single man who describes his relationship with fantasy football as "love-hate" and who quit playing this year, alludes to this draw for some men, when he noted about one of his friends that "he and his buddies go to Atlantic City and they'll get a hotel for the weekend and they'll party and then they'll do their draft. It's kind of just like a big drunken guys' weekend." Likewise, another male player reported that he loved "being able to get together with my buddies a couple nights a year without the wives being there."

In these ways, fantasy sports are a significant source of bonding social capital employed for expressive ends among men. They serve as additional or, perhaps, substitute venues for men's bonding and relationship building when time and/or distance make in-person connections infeasible and when men cannot play real sports (due to age, ability, and/or opportunity). They also do this in the context of a larger cultural environment in which other forms of connection between men are not socially acceptable and facilitated. Although jock statsculinity is potentially more accessible than traditional masculinity, it is no less potent and, in fact, is grounded in some of the same key elements—stoicism, rationality, competition, and dominance over women. As such, there are contradictions in the expressive potential of men's same-gender friendships in fantasy sports. Men report growing closer to and "bonding" with their "buddies," yet these relationships rarely stray from conversations about sports to a deeper knowledge of one's life. Furthermore, competitive, masculinized trash talking is central to this bonding. Although fantasy sports remove direct physical athletic participation and offer a new, more accessible form of masculinity, they still emphasize the importance of exhibiting dominance as a masculine activity and trait. And while sometimes not intentional, bonding through dominance talk excludes women as they are less apt to play for, value, and participate in such talk. Accordingly, and as Rosabeth Kanter's work on tokens suggests, trash talk may serve an additional function of effectively isolating women. Thus, men's bonding through fantasy sports—and the manner in which they do so—serves interactional purposes as men perform masculinity while also developing and cultivating relationships. At the same time, their bonding contributes and reflects an institutional context that privileges men and masculinity and marginalizes women.

Notably, men's higher investment in the hobby relative to women likely facilitates their use of fantasy sports for bonding. As gender is embedded and institutionalized in families in ways that lead women to devote more hours to household labor and carework than men and, therefore, to have less leisure time,[33] women likely do not have the time or energy to cultivate relationships through fantasy sports to the same extent as men. Substantial commitment to fantasy sports, in fact, may be necessary for relationship building to occur, as pursuing other interests at the expense of fantasy undermines the enjoyment of others in the league.[34] Since men spend more time and invest more energy into the hobby, they reap more gains in terms of building and maintaining bonding social capital in this space than women—and they often indicate that the hobby is not just *a* way to bond with the friends in their leagues but *the* way to do so. That their friends are like them in other ways—they are also likely to be White, highly educated, and in professional occupations—further contributes to the potential for bonding and the benefits men reap through fantasy sports participation.

Men as Kin Keepers through Fantasy Sports

Much of the bonding that men achieve through fantasy sports is among friends—and, notably, friends they have before their involvement in fantasy sports. But some men play fantasy sports, at least partly, to connect to family members. As such, fantasy sports provide a mechanism by which men may increase both the frequency and emotional tenor of their relationships with family members. Some reflect fondly on how they started playing because their fathers introduced them to the hobby, such as one male player who claimed, "My dad introduced it to me when I was a kid. I grew up 'helping' him run his teams. By the time I was a teenager, I had my own teams. We also [still] comanage a couple teams together." Others note that one motivation they currently have for playing fantasy sports is to gain more of a connection with their own children or other family members. One male player wrote that what he gains from fantasy sports is "common interest with my children," and another commented, "My son started playing this year, and it gives something else to bond together." Bill, a forty-eight-year-old married father of three, saw fantasy sports as a family activity, having one league that he does "for my family, too, with my kids and my wife. . . . It's just something for the kids to be able to talk about really." He continued, indicating that fantasy sports also allow him to provide his children important life lessons:

> As the dad, you try to set the example to win the right way. I don't know, maybe not a lot of dads think about it; I definitely do with my son. He and my little guy, the youngest, started talking trash after he won three [fantasy football] games. And I said, "Well, I don't know if I would go there; that's probably not where you want to be. You don't wanna be talking too much trash." . . . When you compete in anything with them [sons], you want to set the right example so that they learn how to be [a] good winner and a good loser.

Therefore, some men, like Bill, clearly move beyond fantasy sports as a shared interest and topic of conversation, alluding to the ways in which they allow deeper connections to family members (typically boys and men in their families) by opening up a window into their lives that they may not otherwise have. Cole, a forty-three-year-old married father of two, also reflects this point: "I don't live close to my brother, but it creates stronger social ties with my brother." And Frank provided this perspective as well when he explained:

> I'm in a league with my brothers and my older brother's friends and a couple of my friends are in it to fill out the league so when he [my brother] references stories of different people, it's like, "Oh, that's so-and-so; I know them from the league." And so it kind of augments our relationship because it's kind of part of our life that's shared and helps me to understand his life and vice versa.

While Frank and Cole focus on their brothers, Charlie, a married thirty-eight-year-old father who noted, "I think that at some point, playing with my son is going to be fun," extended a similar analysis to his in-laws, discussing how fantasy sports allow him to build relationships with his wife's family members, particularly the men. He offered:

> I knew I was accepted into the family [when I joined their league]. . . . My cousin, who again is my wife's cousin, but I like him very much and we have a great relationship with him, but a lot of our relation-

ship is based off of me playing in this league with him. . . . I think we have strong relationship in large part because of [my participation in the league].

Comments like these on the connective power of fantasy sports within families are best understood in light of research on gender in families more generally. Notably, a large body of research demonstrates that women play the role of "kin keeper," maintaining ties with and providing support to family members.[35] This is, in fact, simultaneously a source and outcome of women's typical advantage in strong, expressive ties and the bonding social capital they entail. Women's day-to-day activities, Marjorie DeVault argues, actually create home and family—and the social relations within. For example, "the work of 'feeding the family'" gathers various family members together, "cajoling them into some version of the activity that constitutes family."[36] For some men, though, fantasy sports participation presents a mechanism by which they, who are typically not kin keepers, can produce, maintain, and repair relationships within the family, augmenting their bonding social capital through these more expressive activities. Just as men use youth sports to achieve the emotional closeness[37] Nicholas Townsend argues is integral to modern fatherhood,[38] fantasy sports provide men an appropriately masculine space to teach their children lessons and father through sports, to get to know their family better, and to relate to them.

Given that fantasy sports transcend the temporal, geographic, and ability-based boundaries that exist in real sports, they magnify the scale on which such relationship building is possible. Fantasy sports, therefore, may further disrupt some traditional gender relations in the home and family as they offer men a mechanism through which they can take on more of the emotion work typically associated with femininity and women. Thus, men's efforts in this regard may actually be partly transformative. While quite different than the agency women exercise, men here use fantasy sports to contest gender beliefs (e.g., that women are responsible for carework). That this work is done through an appropriately masculine pursuit, however, may minimize the transformative effects of this gender transgression.

To be clear, these kin-keeping possibilities are not part of the fantasy sports experience for the majority of men. Even for those who do report this kind of familial bonding, it often occurs alongside using fantasy sports to escape family life and feminized spaces. Our data suggest that fantasy sport–enabled kin-keeping is of a specific variety: it is a way for men to develop a sense of inclusion, connection, and emotional closeness with particular family members—typically, other men (as with Charlie and his wife's cousin and Frank and his brothers) but sometimes also their own children. At the same time, men utilize fantasy sports to escape the institutionalized responsibilities of them as men—those associated with the demands of work and family.

This seemingly paradoxical relationship—that one might use fantasy sports to, for example, spend time with children and endow them with values such as good sportsmanship and respect for others while also using the hobby to escape more onerous carework typically associated with women—is not unlike the experiences of men who use their involvement in youth coaching to avoid other household responsibilities.[39]

There are other differences between those men who report using fantasy sports to bond with family members and romantic partners and those who express using them as escape. Escapers are on average a bit older than familial bonders and are more likely to be married and to have children. They are also more likely to have advanced degrees, whereas the majority of familial bonders have a bachelor's degree only.[40] These differences make sense, as escapers need something from which to escape, such as time-demanding work (often characteristic of jobs that require PhDs, MDs, and JDs) and wives and children.

Beyond this, familial bonders are more often casual or limited players and less likely to be hard-core ones. They also are less fully adherent to jock statsculinity and view fantasy sports as less connected to and less a reflection of their overall identities. More specifically, they are less likely to view themselves as aggressive competitors, die-hard sports experts, and fans who want to show this off. Accordingly, while there are exceptions, familial bonders seem to approach fantasy sports as a fun hobby that is much like other leisure pursuits that one can do with and thereby connect to family. Those using the hobby to escape are more invested and more serious players. It is not that they do not use the hobby to bond, but when doing so, they are connecting with their fellow competitive players or, sometimes, men family members outside of their nuclear family. Thus, familial bonders and escapers differ not only demographically and in terms of motivations, but they also differ in terms of the targets of their bonding and escaping—escapers use fantasy sports to get away from the responsibilities of work, wives, and/or children, while familial bonders utilize the hobby as an opportunity to connect primarily with men who are family members.

Gendered Bridging and Bonding Social Capital and Cultural Capital in Fantasy Sports

Fantasy sports can be a powerful tool for those White, class-privileged individuals who play to bond with one another, but an important point lurking under the surface of the preceding narratives is that men are largely the targets of this relationship building. This again makes sense given that men (and boys) use fantasy sports to relate to others, as they do real sports, and to achieve some level of intimacy that is otherwise often difficult to attain because of the dictates of masculinity in contemporary U.S. society. At the same time, research indicates that men exert a large influence on women's sports consumption, socializing women into sports fandom and habits.[41] As a result, some women may watch and attend sporting events (or play fantasy sports) to spend time with men in their lives, acquiescing "to the leisure demands of their husbands, boyfriends, and sons" and using their sport spectatorship to fulfill wifely and motherly expectations and to connect to men.[42]

The centrality of men in this space (and sports more generally) sets up different dynamics in terms of the social capital the hobby provides for those men and women who play. For men, it predominately fulfills a bonding function as they connect with men who are their buddies, coworkers, and family members. Involvement in the hobby also serves to elevate their status among men and as a means to accomplish masculinity (as Chapter 3 demonstrated), both of which foster inclusion in groups of similarly socially located men. One male player, for instance, noted rather articulately:

> Fantasy sports provide a social group, something to talk about with other people, knowledge of something that *men* have high esteem for, etc. It can provide status in a male social group if you know a lot about a sport. . . . I definitely have felt like some people are more interested in getting to know me because I can talk a lot about basketball.

Given this, men may be able to leverage their knowledge in this area to better their employment prospects—thus, indicating that fantasy sports also may serve more instrumental purposes for them. One male player revealed, for example, that fantasy sports provide "a subject matter to talk to with coworkers, so I believe it is good for my career." However, despite some instances in which men reveal that fantasy sports act as leverage social capital—the type of capital that provides access to better opportunities and aids in social mobility,[43] men's involvement in fantasy sports operates primarily in expressive and bonding ways.

For women, though, fantasy sports involve a larger bridging aspect—the kind of social capital that links people who are different from one another—in that they deploy their fantasy sports participation to increase the gender diversity of their networks and enhance and build ties to similarly socially located men. In some cases (often among more casual women players), this bridging element is apparent in the context of strong ties to family members and romantic partners and thus is largely expressive in function. Kate, a casual player, for instance, started playing about nine years ago to bond with her brother. She recounted:

My brother is like a super–sports fanatic, and he's been doing it since the [fantasy] sports really started . . . [so] it was a really good way for us to like have a common bond. He moved out, and I was still living at home, so we always had something to talk about [with my playing fantasy sports].

Likewise, Alyssa, who plays in one league and invests very little time in the hobby, noted how playing fantasy allows her to bond with her husband and other men in her family: "My husband and I talk about football more; I talk about football more with my dad and brother. So in a way, playing FF [fantasy football] has given us another connection and topics to talk about."

Some women discuss these connections extending to those in their part-ners' networks, reflecting how fantasy sports participation can convert weak ties into strong ties and provide a reason for interaction. Alyssa, whom we just quoted, also reported, "I have built a better friendship with my hus-band's coworkers due to playing." And Lynn, a thirty-eight-year-old hard-core player, recounted increased contact with her boyfriend's friends because of her fantasy sports involvement:

I've only met his best friend once, but I talk to his best friend all the time [now] because he plays fantasy football, and so he'll text me before the draft time, "What do you think of this guy?" He'll ask me, if he has Cardinals players, "What have you heard down there about this or that?" so I talk to his best friend more than he does, but it's football related.

Lynn's comments focus our attention on two key differences between men's and women's discussions of relationships and interactions forged through fantasy sports. First, women are more likely than men to mention fantasy sports as a means of creating new ties with strangers, acquaintances, and work colleagues. Furthermore, female players' reports of bonding with friends through fantasy sports decrease as the number of *other* social groups they belong to increases.[44] This relationship does not hold for male players, suggesting that women do not use fantasy sports to build ties with preexist-ing friends in the same way or to the same extent as men.

Second (and related to the above), women, much more so than men, frame their fantasy sports knowledge and participation as a resource that gives them not just access to but credibility in groups and spaces dominated by White middle- and upper-class men. In essence, though they do not often speak in these terms, women understand that their involvement in fantasy sports serves as a form of cultural as well as social capital. Sociologist Pierre Bourdieu coined the term *cultural capital* to refer to symbolic resources—for example, tastes, styles, preferences, attitudes, and mannerisms—that create a collective identity and can be key to group belonging.[45] He argues that holding and embodying the appropriate type of cultural capital can act as a sort of currency enabling one to gain entrée to and acceptance in high-status groups and entities. Thus, cultural capital can help one gain social capital as well.

For some women, the cultural capital fantasy sports provide helps them form ties with and establish credibility among men acquaintances and sports fans more generally. One female survey respondent summed this up when she noted that fantasy sports are "a big social lubricant in today's fantasy-obsessed society. It's an easy subject to discuss with other people because they probably play fantasy sports as well." She also noted gaining "confidence, social currency, and a way to find common ground with others" through playing. As is evident in this player's comments, key to this credibility is the knowledge gained through playing and the confidence that comes with that—knowledge is, as we argued earlier, central to legitimate (masculinized) fandom. Another female player similarly claimed that she now has the "ability to engage more confidently in sports-related conversations."

Claire, a married mother of two who began playing fantasy sports seventeen years ago, offered additional comments that are emblematic of how women forge connections and establish credibility with men through fantasy sports. She did so by comparing fantasy sports to other, more stereotypically feminine topics about which she is very knowledgeable but which provide little in the way of social esteem. She told us:

> I have always felt like I can talk about our home teams—I have always felt I could talk about the Flyers, the Phillies, the Eagles—but now I felt like I can talk about individual players that are on other teams and what their stats are. I do feel a little more knowledgeable in a social setting, especially with men, getting into that conversation. . . . I like to talk about other things besides the kids, now that they are older, and it gives me an outlet for people, and [to] not sound like a moron. . . . It is kinda nice, like, "Oh, that's a woman who knows all this stuff about sports."

Jennifer, a casual player who just started playing this year, told us that part of the attraction of being accepted as a legitimate fantasy sports participant is that it allows her entrée into groups and interactions from which women are typically excluded. She explained, "I love that when I went to those weddings, I was standing with the group of frat brothers, all talking about fantasy football while the rest of their wives are in another place." Mindy, a thirty-one-year-old document fulfillment manager who has been playing for three years, offered a related account:

> I like knowing things, and I like the fact that I can actually sit and talk with men and know what I'm talking about—there's two guys I work with and every week they ask me, "What do you think about this? Should I draft this player? Should I pick this person up? Who do you think I should start?" Like they actually valued my opinion on this stuff 'cause they knew I knew what I was talking about.

Thus, while both men and women use fantasy sports to connect to men and gain legitimacy among them, this is particularly noteworthy for women who, by virtue of their gender, are not given default standing and acceptance in men's circles but rather must earn such recognition.

Fantasy sports may be a particularly powerful tool for women in the workplace, as Mindy suggests above. Traditional associations of men with work and women with the home that arose in the mid-to-late 1800s in the United States result in workplaces being typed masculine. Workplaces are also raced and classed, as the "separate spheres" ideal from its inception ignored the paid labor of Black, Hispanic, and working-class women. Accordingly, traditional forms of water cooler talk, such as sports talk, invariably privilege the interests and pursuits of White, middle-, and upper-class men over those of women and other marginalized groups. As Williams and Dempsey argue, sports are then an "accepted form of professional small talk" while feminized subjects such as "children or shopping . . . are seen as a distraction from the real work at hand."[46]

Fantasy sports, though, offer women a way to contest at least one element of men's dominance by giving them a valued masculine pursuit in common with their colleagues—and one that does not involve physical competition and that is accepted as fodder for interaction in workplaces. Reflecting transformative agency, women are forming ties and interacting with men in ways that challenge gender beliefs and dynamics, using their fantasy sports participation to gain entrée into groups of men at their places of employment. One female player, for example, commented that playing gave her "knowledge of the sport; therefore, I can contribute to conversations that others, mainly the men in my office, have every week." Lindsey, a magazine editor and dedicated player, also alluded to fantasy sports' aiding in relationships with men at work when she claimed:

> I noticed that the year I didn't play fantasy sports, I just felt really out of touch with everything that was going on in the football NFL . . . and that makes working in an office with all men hard. I wanna know what happens on Sunday when people come in and talk about it . . . know what's going on when there's a scandal or a coach gets fired or something like that. It's nice to know about it and actually be able to contribute to a conversation.

Similarly, Annick, a former practicing lawyer, explained how fantasy sports offer a potential route to gender equity with men colleagues because they provide a "way to connect." She related that for her,

> it was kind of a social way to connect with the people in my group. I had been at the firm for just about a year; I was one of only a handful of women in a largely male-dominated group, so this was a way to sort of find that common bond and compete as equals.

In line with this, women are much more likely than men to discuss fantasy sports in the workplace in strategic ways. So, while women certainly use fantasy sports for expressive purposes to bond with friends, spouses, family, and even coworkers, they employ their involvement for instrumental aims as well, to network with and "impress" their colleagues. Brittany's comment on this point, which we quote in our chapter opening, warrants rementioning, as she explained:

> It's a good starter for conversation. While a lot of people may say that they [fantasy sports] are kind of stupid, it really does help you to get to meet a lot of, as much as I hate the word *networking*, it really is a good networking tool. . . . Professionally, even I have been able to open up my horizons and talk to people that I may not have spoken to before just 'cause of the sports knowledge that I have gained.

Jane, who currently is a sports writer, similarly linked playing fantasy sports with potential gains at work. She recalled, "I had this job, and there were some people I kind of wanted to impress at the job, and they decided to have a fantasy football league at work, and I figured I . . . might as well do it." Thus, for these women and others, fantasy sports promote entry into groups and environments dominated by men and subsequent standing in them through providing women with legitimate and valued nonwork-related knowledge and reasons for interactions. But, importantly, the vast majority of the women able to engage in and leverage these interactions are White and in middle- and upper-class professional contexts. Here again, we see that the potential for transformative agency for women in fantasy sports is limited to those who belong to otherwise privileged groups and are located in socially advantaged spaces.

Conclusion

This chapter highlights how fantasy sports serve as an important source of social capital, offering participants, who are largely White, geographically mobile, professional men and women, the opportunity to build and strengthen a range of connections—both weak and strong ties—in a period in which opportunities to do so may be dwindling. Using their knowledge of sports as cultural currency and through spending time and conversing with others around the hobby, participants forge and strengthen ties to family, friends, coworkers, acquaintances, and strangers—expanding their networks in the process. The results of these efforts are largely beneficial in expressive ways. They offer participants a sense of belonging and community, satisfaction and happiness, and emotional support and intimacy that once, perhaps, brick-and-mortar third places, civic organizations, local clubs, and sports leagues made possible. Accordingly, fantasy sports are a powerful source of bonding social capital, bringing together similar individuals who become closer to one another through their shared love and experience of the activity.

Gender is salient in these interactions to a greater and lesser extent. Both men and women discuss their fantasy sports participation as a means of strengthening relationships with spouses and friends with, on occasion, little or no explicit mention of the sex or gender of those with whom they are connecting. Yet more frequently, it is clear that men are the targets of this bonding and the interactions that support it, thus underscoring the primacy of men even in a mixed-gender sporting pursuit. In fact, it is striking how much of the social capital being built through fantasy sports is about men. Although exceptions exist, men and women discuss fantasy sports as a way to stay in touch with, get to know, and connect to men. Notably, across all of our data, there are only a handful of examples in which this is not the case. For men, these instances typically involve bonding with their wives or girlfriends. For women, they typically involve women's bonding with one another in response to their token status in environments otherwise dominated by men.

The ways in which this is a gender story do not end with the mere acknowledgment that the targets of bonding in fantasy sports are men. Men make greater use of and depend more fully on fantasy sports to "stay in touch" and bond with friends than do women. As masculinity in the U.S. context is tied to heterosexuality, intimate same-sex connections for men prove difficult.[47] Moreover, as attentiveness to and interest in intimate relationships are often characterized as feminine, women typically have an advantage in close ties to friends and family.[48] Accordingly, men need to rely more heavily than women on bolstering their relationships with others, particularly with other men, within the safe confines of appropriately masculine environments to avoid potential threats to their masculinity. That this is the case even as legitimate masculinity has expanded underscores a key element to the social construction of masculinity in contemporary U.S. society. Although it contains new elements, masculinity is an exclusively male domain built on antifemininity. Fantasy sport, like its real-life counterpart, being constructed as a masculine domain, can thus provide "a means of communication and connection" for men[49]—a safe vehicle through which they can both demonstrate masculinity and establish close bonds with one another.[50] Given men's high investment in the hobby, fantasy sports provide ample time and opporutnities for men to do this connecting. Some, typically less hard-core players, also take on some kin-keeping roles, albeit in an appropriately masculine environment and with boys and men in their families. Women, on the other hand, need not rely on fantasy sports to the same extent as men to "stay in touch" and "bond" with others. In fact, as discussed in the previous chapter, because sports are constructed as men's turf, men may view women's participation as deviant, disruptive, and a threat to their hegemony, resulting in women's less full or less inclusive interactions with others.

In addition and because of much of the above, intimacy in this space for men is contradictory. On the one hand, men describe how they have gotten to know friends and family members better and have become closer emotionally to them as a result of their fantasy sports play. On the other hand, their reliance on trash talking and dominance talk to set up masculine hierarchies and their acknowledgment that their conversations often fail to "delve deep" suggest that the intimacy achieved is fragile and potentially limited in scope. For women, such dynamics are less at play as they engage in and depend on such dominance talk among their close social ties to a much lesser extent than men (although some certainly do engage in bravado and one-upmanship after winning). Rather, women use the shared activity of fantasy sports as a way to honor or facilitate preexisting intimacies in a fun (rather than hierarchical) way.

Last, fantasy sports bridge women to men (both in their leagues and outside them), but they leave men's networks largely unchanged in this regard. Exploring the gender composition of the leagues in which our players participate helps demonstrate this point—our male players are significantly more likely than our female players to compete in leagues comprised entirely or mostly of men (94 percent of our male players did so compared to 69 percent of our female players). Given this, the fact that women are more likely than men to use their involvement in fantasy sports to leverage better interactions and opportunities among men, particularly in the workplace, and to make new ties to what were prior mere acquaintances makes sense.

Taken together, fantasy sports both counter and reinforce larger gender dynamics in regard to the social ties and capital they facilitate and create, and they do so in a context that is largely White and socioeconomically advantaged. They offer opportunities for White, class-privileged men and women to interact with others and develop social ties, albeit in ways that prioritize forming ties with and bridges to men, in a time when such opportunities may be dwindling. And given the typical profile of players, the ties and bridges fantasy sports facilitate contribute further to homosocial reproduction, failing to disrupt racialized and classed patterns of interaction. Finally, the import of the hobby for relationships varies considerably between men and women, with men relying on it to a greater extent than women as the way to bond with the "fellows," typically in settings and via masculine forms of exchange that exclude women. Women, however, leverage the hobby to a greater extent to extend their social ties and open up avenues of conversation and connection with men in both their personal relationships and workplaces, the latter of which may have tangible instrumental advantages. The flip side of all of this, however, is the potential for fantasy sports to invade work spaces, family life, and social interactions in less positive ways. It is to this we turn to last.

6

Going Overboard?

Time, Attention, and Emotional Absorption in Fantasy Sports

K els, a thirty-year-old, engaged-to-be-married, White woman, started participating in fantasy sports through a work-based fantasy hockey league. At the time, she was an intern in the "sports industry" and was motivated, in part, to get to know her fellow interns better. She explains:

> I was interning, and everybody in the group was around the same age—we were early twenties, and we thought it would be a good way to kind of get close and do something that involved a little competition. It was all good-natured fun and a way to get to know our co-workers a little better at that point.

Ten years later, Kels looks back at that original league as "bare bones, quite easy, minimal" and one in which "nobody seemed to really care too much." Accordingly, she spent little time on fantasy sports then, but now she estimates her immersion in the hobby has increased tenfold. Currently, Kels focuses these efforts on two fantasy National Hockey League (NHL) leagues in which she plays with "people with more in-depth desire and competitiveness to play." She devotes many hours to research before her fantasy hockey drafts each year, looking at the preseason rankings, gathering player information from various sources (sports websites, Twitter, hockey magazines), and carefully crafting her own player rankings based on her research. Furthermore, fantasy hockey requires a daily time investment after the draft—"on average fifteen to twenty minutes a day to set the lineup" and check on her players. To accomplish this, she "generally" carves out time during the earlier part of her workday. Despite this, Kels, who works in merchandising, does not view fantasy sports as impeding her work. While she "would like to say" she would be "doing other work" instead, Kels admits, "If I wasn't doing fantasy hockey, I would be looking at another website of some sort. I kind of use it as my downtime, my little break." Furthermore, Kels believes that her boss would "not at all" be annoyed if he knew she was spending worktime on fantasy hockey. She explains it this way:

> I get the impression in a world of an office like ours where everybody obviously has access to the Internet—and they encourage that and using it as a search tool—that maybe not everybody loves it, but they would expect that somebody is going to be checking their email at some point during the day, checking the weather, what's happening out in the world, and for a lot of us, it is playing a particular fantasy game depending on the season.

In fact, Kels believes the nature of her employment *enables* her to play fantasy sports, claiming she would not be as invested if she was in a different line of work. She asserts:

> I do not know if I would be playing fantasy sports as often if I was not in a situation where I was in front of a computer for the last ten years. . . . If I were working out in the field or working in construction or working in retail and you're not sitting in front of a computer, it does provide less of an opportunity [to play].

While Kels takes this time out of her workday to engage in fantasy sports, she is also clear that she tries "not to take it too seriously" and does not allow her fantasy sports involvement to become "a distraction for life" or "something unhealthy." Fantasy sports give her "a personal sense of pride" and a way "to personally challenge" herself and extend and exhibit her "passion" for sports. However, while sports are a "significant" part of her identity and fantasy hockey, in particular, encroaches on some of her worktime, Kels still maintains her other leisure activities. These include watching television, reading, gardening, and craftwork (such as crocheting and needlework). Moreover, while Kels acknowledges moments when she has "probably spent a little too much time . . . trying to analyze what was going on" to best manage her fantasy hockey team or has "spent a crazy amount of time trying to set that lineup," she is quick to note that these moments of overinvestment do not affect others. She explains, "I don't think that punished anybody except me, [I don't think it] takes away from other things. I don't think anybody else really noticed."

Kels also tries not to get too emotional about fantasy sports. She believes that fantasy hockey has "enhanced" her watching of games, but she is not one to be "screaming or hating or anything like that" while she observes the day's fantasy hockey events unfold. She reveals that "win or lose, I don't say anything" to other league members. This is not to say that Kels does not feel her losses (or victories for that matter) or that she experiences no fantasy-related stress. She is a fierce competitor and wants to win, but she does not get angry or lash out at others when things do not go her way. Rather, Kels tends to chastise herself for not making better decisions: "It's not that I'm disappointed when the other guy beats me; I'm more disappointed in myself. Like, 'Ugh, you could have gained three more points that week. You could have made that [better] decision.'" And while she recalls one instance when she "did kick myself for a little bit . . . [for about] a week" after missing placing in the top three "by literally one point," more typically, Kels moves on from these losses quickly. She summarizes how she feels when things do not work out as she hopes: "I'll just be like, 'Argh, you idiot' and I'll get annoyed . . . but I usually let it fade by the next morning and just move forwards 'cause, really, what could I do [at this point]?"

Kels's experience parallels that of other fantasy sports players but also differs in notable ways. Take, for example, CB, a White thirty-nine-year-old man with a degree in computer sciences from a junior college. Like Kels, CB began playing fantasy sports when he started a new job at which "all the guys in the office had an office fantasy football league, and it was pretty much expected that everybody in the office participate." With "no choice in the matter," CB joined this league in 2000. Since then, and to a greater extent than Kels, his involvement in fantasy sports has expanded. Currently, he plays in six fantasy football leagues. Some of these are free leagues with people he knows "mostly through the Internet"; others are money leagues with local friends. But regardless of the details, CB, who once had seventeen teams, admits fantasy football "has become more addictive every year."

CB invests much time on research and lineup setting. He, like Kels, estimates he spends, on average "at least two hours a week, maybe three" on these aspects of the hobby. He explains his typical routine as involving a couple of hours of roster-setting on Sunday mornings and then another hour or so of research or checking "to see if anybody has gotten hurt at practice or something like that" during the week. For CB, a cellular engineer doing "core network stuff," these non-Sunday time investments in fantasy sports "usually" occur "during the day at work," just as they do for Kels. However, CB also alludes to fantasy sports negatively impacting other aspects of his life. For instance, a self-described downside is fantasy football's encroachment on one of his favorite hobbies—deer hunting. He explains:

It's difficult to get up on Sunday morning [to go hunting] when I know that I need to get up and do research to set my fantasy teams. . . . I am sitting on a deer stand, and I am thinking, "Man, I really need to get back to the house so I can check the injuries so I can check to see who is playing and who is not playing."

Moreover, CB reveals that he expends "a lot of time a month before football season" preparing for and participating in his drafts. This married father of four children, ranging in age from eight to eighteen years old, describes what typically occurs during this month as "it is neglect wife, kids, job, everything like that." He also realizes that yard work gets "neglected on Sunday" during the season and that his wife finds it annoying that he "has to" get up each Sunday morning to figure out his lineups. To be sure, CB would invest *even more* in fantasy football if he did not have family or household responsibilities. He laments that fantasy football is "best if you are single and don't have kids because you can put more time into it. . . . Younger guys . . . when they come home, they just have to come home. They don't have to split time between family and other responsibilities." But even with his self-proclaimed willingness to split his time between family and fantasy football, CB expresses, "My wife hates fantasy football season."

CB's wife may not be alone in disliking aspects of his fantasy football involvement. CB is a self-described "antagonizer" who seeks to "encourage" smack talk in his leagues. He boasts, "I talk more smack than anybody. Every week I'm posting on the page, trying to call somebody out, my opponent out." Furthermore, CB's version of fun and "office camaraderie" is to "harass the other guys that you are sitting next to eight hours out of every day" by smack-talking them in person. Importantly, the dominance talk CB loves and uses as a "way to blow off some steam" is not without consequence. He reveals rather matter-of-factly and without any semblance of remorse that a "girl" he was "talking smack to" in one of his leagues "got offended" once, so he can no longer speak that way to her. He also freely and proudly admits to a "couple of situations" in which he has "talked smack and people have taken it personally, and there have been some hurt feelings." CB, in fact, seems to relish giving his fellow competitors, especially men whom he knows "well enough," a "hard time" in a way that "gets kinda personal" (e.g., by making fun of their appearance). What also separates CB from someone like Kels is his emotional reaction to losing, which is more intense and longer lasting. CB explains it this way: "I know that on Sunday night if I have had a horrible day and my teams aren't doing well, yeah, I'm grumpy. . . . I am just *pissed* my team didn't do well . . . until Tuesday morning." Therefore, while the boasting and bragging are part and parcel of CB's fantasy sports experience, so too are moments of anger and frustration, which may linger for days at a time.

Although fantasy sports have the potential to provide enjoyment, improve the sports viewing experience, and forge and strengthen relationships, Kels's and CB's accounts highlight how fantasy sports can encroach into various aspects of participants' lives and alter social interactions, with sometimes negative ramifications. Fantasy sports do so in ways that are fundamentally tied to the personalized, competitive fandom embedded in the hobby and reflective of the class and gender dynamics we have identified throughout this book. Fantasy sports participation takes time, and the simultaneously broader and more minute focus required of participants means that, on average, they spend more time consuming sports-related media than do traditional fans. Even for the most skilled of multitaskers, time spent on one activity impacts time spent on others. Players—often in professional occupations free from direct supervision, with schedule control, and with largely unfettered access to electronic devices—can research, trade, and update rosters anywhere they have access to the Internet and anytime they have windows of available time. These aspects combine to make workplaces and worktime prime sites for fantasy sports participation.

Fantasy sports, however, involve more than time investments. Here, success is about one's own knowledge and efforts, thus raising the stakes and, for at least some players, their emotional investments. The emotional aspect of participation plays out in ways that reflect fantasy sports' gendered elements. Insofar as men are presumed to be knowledgeable, competitive, and successful—indeed, jock statsculinity dictates that their claims to legitimate manhood in this space are contingent on this—many men, like CB, become deeply emotionally invested in their fantasy sports performance. Some do this to the detriment of their relationships with others, their wives, families, and the very men with whom the hobby allows them to connect.

Temporal and Emotional Investments in Fantasy Sports

As with any leisure pursuit and similar to traditional fandom, fantasy sports participation involves a commitment of time. With only twenty-four hours in the day, time is finite; time spent on one activity involves trade-offs with others. The unique attributes of fantasy sports fandom mean that participants invest substantial time—and more than traditional fans[1]—in consuming sports. Andrew Billings and Brody Ruihley, for example, find fantasy sports participants spend eighteen hours per week consuming sports media, a figure twice that of traditional fans.[2] Moreover, fantasy sports enthusiasts confront additional time binds, as they must monitor and manage their rosters and conduct research related to their fantasy sports squads.

These time investments must be understood in context. Fantasy sports occupy a unique niche that simultaneous changes in technology, media, and workplaces made possible. Because fantasy sports are in essence digital games that rely heavily on new media, participants can engage in the hobby anywhere they have access to the Internet, and that access has increased dramatically in recent years. According to the Pew Research Foundation, more than three-quarters of Americans own a smartphone, up from just 35 percent in 2011; ownership rates are highest among those under fifty, with a college degree, and in households earning $75,000 per year or more[3]—precisely the demographics among which fantasy sports participation is most common. Perhaps not surprisingly, the FSTA reports that 39 percent of fantasy sports participants "primarily use a mobile device" to manage their fantasy teams—up from 25 percent in 2012.[4] For the middle- and upper-class, connected men and women who play them, fantasy sports thus literally can go (nearly) anywhere and everywhere, increasing the potential for them to seep into and potentially distract from other activities.

Workplaces are a prime target for the infiltration of fantasy sports. The largely affluent, well-educated professionals who play fantasy sports work long hours[5] in precisely the types of occupations that facilitate combining work and this particular type of leisure pursuit. Like Kels, such workers are often free from direct daily supervision, possess flexibility and autonomy in shaping the contours of their workday, and spend large portions of the day already using a computer or other device. These conditions enable them to read up on their fantasy sports players or fiddle with their rosters while on hold with a client, between meetings or tasks, or during other workday lulls.

Beyond these more practical or technical matters, fantasy sports participation fits nicely into the changing culture of American professional careers and workplaces, unlike many other leisure pursuits. For the well-heeled professionals who are the core demographic of fantasy sports, clear boundaries between work and nonwork time have eroded. Employers ask their employees to be devoted fully to their work and, accordingly, require significant time both during normal work hours and after.[6] Digital technologies make it so that work may never end. One is "always" capable and, therefore, available to answer that work-related email or update that important work document, what Melissa Gregg refers to as *presence bleed*.[7] As a result, as is the case for Kels and CB whose fantasy sports participation began through a workplace league, employees are "incorporating their pastimes into their work day as a coping mechanism."[8] This, in turn, may require additional hours on work at home, multitasking work with family and leisure activities. Fantasy sports lend themselves well to this cycle. Individuals can be monitoring or researching their fantasy teams and pop in and out of work-related tasks at home or vice versa. The tech-savvy professionals who often participate in fantasy sports are particularly comfortable with digital multitasking; they are seemingly "always contactable, working, *and* consuming."[9]

Those in the sports and marketing industry know and facilitate this relationship between work and leisure. Film and media studies scholar Ethan Tussey details how sports leagues, in particular the MLB, provide digital sports services (e.g., MLB.TV) that encourage fans to "multitask" at work, allowing fans to check into sports content throughout the day on their computers or mobile devices. Digital sports products are examples of what Tussey calls "workspace media," "produced for, and consumed by, the workplace audience."[10] Fantasy sports players are particular targets and consumers of sports-related workspace media. After all, the type of fandom fantasy sports promotes makes them interested in the entire league and thus likely to consume digitally disseminated sports content regardless of the featured team. They are also the prime market for advertisers on these platforms, who target upper-class, tech-savvy young men "who, on account of their age, gender, and class status" can spend, move, and consume freely.[11] Some digital sports services (e.g., the National Collegiate Athletic Association men's basketball tournament streaming media player) understand this to be so prevalent that they come with "boss buttons." These allow the user to hide their activities with a keystroke, thereby quickly substituting the sports media they are watching with a more work-appropriate document.[12]

The encroachment of fantasy sports into participants' work lives is certainly tied to their privileged class position. Located in occupations that provide flexibility and control over time use, involve extended periods of time online, and increasingly require work to extend beyond the confines of the traditional workday, leisure and labor "bleed" into each other. These well-educated professionals multitask throughout their waking hours, a situation digital media companies keen on reaching this coveted target audience facilitate. But the extent and manner in which fantasy sports displace work time—or do not—is also deeply gendered. Men and masculinity dominate sports generally and fantasy sports in particular; men's presence in this space is assumed in ways that women's is not. Gender, furthermore, is institutionalized in families and workplaces—and, notably, in the intersection of these two institutions—in ways that produce largely divergent expectations and experiences for men and women.[13] The institutionalization of gender in sports, workplaces, and families has implications for individual time use. While time is finite for all, the constraints and opportunities shaping time allocation—to which activities we devote our time and to what extent we do so—are different for men and women.

Despite many gains in paid employment, sociologists such as Arlie Hochschild and Paula England remind us that the gender revolution has stalled.[14] Women have not made commensurate gains in the household, and the narrowing of gender gaps in time devoted to paid and unpaid labor has largely stagnated since the mid-1980s. Women still spend approximately twice the time men do on household labor and childcare, with particular responsibility for core tasks that must be performed routinely and with less flexibility.[15] Over the course of the past several decades, a gender gap in leisure has also emerged, with women having approximately 30 minutes less leisure time per day than men.[16] Sports consumption and fantasy sports data bear out these general trends. Women fantasy sports participants spend nearly half the time men spend on overall sports consumption (11.6 weekly hours versus men's 21.3 hours) and approximately three-quarters the time men spend on fantasy sports specifically (3.5 hours versus 4.7 hours).[17]

Men and women do not merely choose to spend their time differently. Cultural expectations for men and women, husbands and wives, and fathers and mothers dictate the appropriateness of their time use. That women spend more time on household labor and childcare (and often sacrifice self-care and leisure to do so) while still maintaining their commitments to paid labor is part and parcel of "doing gender."[18] For a woman to forgo household labor or carework to spend all day Sunday tracking her fantasy sports team would violate gender expectations and the very foundation on which her womanhood (and, if applicable, her status as a wife and/or mother) rests. Although the expectations for manhood generally and fatherhood more specifically have shifted to incorporate a greater breadth of activities,[19] it remains more acceptable for men to prioritize personal interests over those of their families and households. Indeed, we have demonstrated that although some men use fantasy sports to kin-keep, many participate to *escape* from family responsibilities. Accordingly, the time men and women invest in fantasy sports not only differs in amount but also cuts into different activities.

Fantasy sports also can be mentally and emotionally challenging. Co-creation in fantasy sports makes the rooting interests deeply personal; therefore, the highs and lows of fantasy sports can be greater than those of traditional fandom.[20] While traditional fans bask in the reflective glory (BIRG) of their favorite teams' successes and cut off the reflective failure (CORF) when they lose,[21] the glory and failure with fantasy sports are not merely reflected. Instead, team performance is a reflection on participants themselves, their knowledge, and their skills. As such, personal image and identity are at stake more so than in traditional fandom.[22]

Given the personalization of success and failure, making the "right" decisions and subsequently winning or losing become more salient issues for fantasy sports fans than traditional ones and have significant personal and interpersonal implications. The perceived control fantasy sports offer also contributes to heightened tension, anxiety, and "agonizing" over decision making in the hobby and when watching opponents' fantasy players on television.[23] Among fantasy football managers, anxiety actually increases as perceptions of control over fantasy outcomes increase.[24]

Personal well-being is at stake here as well as social relationships. Players who perceive themselves as being in control of their team's performance are more likely to avoid communication when their team loses (an element of CORFing) and to engage in communication when they win (an element of BIRGing).[25] Because fantasy sports players view themselves as having more control over their fantasy team's performance than that of their favorite teams, they are more likely to trash-talk after a fantasy win than after a favorite-team win.[26] Playing against one's friends, family, and coworkers in traditional season-long fantasy leagues heightens the pressure and anxiety to compete well—and the frustration when things go awry.[27] Because participants' choices and their outcomes are typically visible to known others, their reputation among close social ties is in jeopardy. This is something quite different than for traditional fans who are likely cheering alongside, rather than against, their friends and family and who are free from the perception that they are "responsible" for their team's performance. What is more, the possibilities for relationship strain are heightened among middle- and upper-class men and women whose friendships revolve around shared leisure much more so than their working-class counterparts.[28]

The emotional toll of fantasy sports and players' reactions to it are gendered as well. The dictates of jock statsculinity mean that men are expected to be, and attempt to demonstrate that they are, in control, statistically savvy, dedicated and knowledgeable sports fans, and competitive. Cognitive dissonance theory, which posits that increased stress and discomfort arise when individuals simultaneously hold two or more opposing ideas, behaviors, attitudes, values, or beliefs,[29] would predict that these sometimes contradictory expectations would lead to increased mental distress for men who play fantasy sports. Control may be difficult when one is experiencing or exhibiting the aggression associated with competition, particularly for men whose claim to legitimate masculinity necessitates proving and asserting dominance over others.[30] Furthermore, success requires mental and emotional energy, as does accounting for failure, particularly when that failure calls into question one's manhood. Finally, given that men use fantasy sports to bond with other men, often in leagues with only men, the potential for relationship strain is necessarily heightened. The trash talking that facilitates such bonding can just as easily produce conflict.

Women face a different set of pressures than men do. As Kanter's research on tokens suggests, women must prove themselves in a space in which they are outsiders under hyperscrutiny and expected to fail.[31] Socialized to respond to fear, disappointment, and uncertainty differently than men, women react to the pressures they face in gendered ways. Although men and women are more similar than different on a range of psychological measures, women and girls are more likely to exhibit internalizing behaviors such as depression, rumination, and anxiety than are men and boys.[32] Gender beliefs that position women as less knowledgeable, competitive, and legitimate also frame women who play fantasy sports. This may result in their worrying more about each roster move and ultimately blaming themselves for their mistakes. Moreover, in trying to not live up to negative stereotypes about women and sports, women's anxiety may increase and actually hinder their performance. Psychologist Claude Steele advanced the concept of stereotype threat to refer to the dynamics of performance when members of marginalized groups are "at risk of confirming, as self-characteristic, a negative stereotype about one's group."[33] When activated, whether directly or indirectly, stereotype threat results in underperformance in line with the negative stereotype. Indeed, researchers have found stereotype threat to be significant in creating racial and gender differences in education as well as sports.[34] Notably, Jeff Stone, Aina Chalabaev, and Keith Harrison find that being highly skilled, prepared, and invested in sports makes athletes more, not less, susceptible to stereotype threat.[35] This suggests that women may be particularly vulnerable to increased anxiety—and its detrimental effects—during their participation.

Ultimately, what we argue in this chapter is that the dynamics of fantasy sports fandom, gender, and class come together to impact participants' work, personal, and family lives.[36] The digital nature of fantasy sports and the privileged position of the typical participant enable both men and women to devote significant time to fantasy sports that otherwise would be spent on other leisure activities, household labor, civic engagement, and/or work-related tasks. Men, however, invest more time into the hobby and express that it invades "more important" activities than women do. Furthermore, women's emotional trials tied to fantasy sports are no less frequent than men's, but they are of lesser extent and duration and more self-directed. Men's experience of the emotional toll of fantasy sports is lengthier, more severe, and more likely to result in externalizing behavior, such as lashing out at family or friends. Interestingly, men often indicate they do not get "too emotional" about fantasy sports or take them "too seriously" even though they often reveal in their accounts that they do just that.

Our data ultimately point to several negative outcomes associated with the contradictions of jock statsculinity. For one, men are supposed to be in control and successful in sports—and in control of their emotions. Yet, precisely because they are supposed to be more knowledgeable and successful, they sometimes get overly emotional when the outcomes of their efforts do not align with their desires and expectations. In addition, the very same aspects of performing jock statsculinity that promote bonding among men—aggression, competitive banter—can also strain the same-gender friendships that fantasy sports purportedly strengthen. Accordingly, fantasy sports not only creep into men's and women's workplaces and households (and, at times, affect their productivity in these spheres), but they also introduce the possibility of relationship strain—particularly for men.

Fantasy Sports' Encroachment on Leisure, Civic, Household, and Work Activities

Like traditional fans, fantasy sports managers spend time researching, watching, monitoring, and socializing around "their" teams; however, the league-wide focus integral to fantasy sports fandom intensifies these time burdens relative to traditional fandom (see Chapter 2). Still, some, like Kate, a self-described not "typical fantasy sports person," spend "less than five minutes" a week on fantasy sports (in Kate's case, on fantasy football). Others invest much more time, like Archie, a married college professor, who acknowledged spending "close to twenty hours a week . . . maybe not quite [that high]; well, yeah, it's a lot" on fantasy football. Overall, though, our fantasy sports managers typically report investing anywhere from one to six hours a week on the hobby during the season, *excluding* the time they spend watching live sporting events.[37] Kate and Archie, although extremes, are indicative of a pattern—time expenditures are gendered. Men invest more time in fantasy sports than women—about an additional hour each week.

Furthermore, men are more likely to characterize, without specific prompting, their fantasy sports time expenditures as excessive or embarrassing. For instance, when asked the number of hours he spends on fantasy sports, Bob, a married father who plays in four leagues, quickly responded, "Too much. Probably more than I should." Likewise, David, a hard-core player, sheepishly admitted of the eight to ten hours a week he spends on fantasy baseball: "That's kind of embarrassing almost, how much time" it consumes. Roland, a Hispanic married man without children, also revealed, "The amount of time I dedicate to it is probably excessive. I realize that. And I could be doing, well, who knows what I could be doing with that time?"

As Roland indicates, participants are well aware they could employ the time they dedicate to fantasy sports elsewhere. Again, men seem more critical of their time usage, as they are twice as likely as women to state explicitly that fantasy sports lead to a reduction in time for "more productive" or "important" things. Men also repeatedly allude to fantasy sports as a "time suck," express that "there are probably better uses of my time," or note that "you 'waste' time looking at your respective teams when you could do something else that would be (arguably) more productive with your time." Others admit that fantasy sport "consumes a lot of time, and if there is something else important to do, I would still spend time playing fantasy, which could affect the other activity."

Many men, however, speak of fantasy sports' effects on those "more important" activities rather matter-of-factly—or even positively. As one male respondent wrote, "I suppose I could use the time and effort put into this [fantasy sports] in a more productive manner. But screw it! I like it!" This is perhaps not surprising given the dominance of men and masculinity in this space. Occupying a privileged position, men have less reason to question the legitimacy of their time use. But some, like Ted, who plays in three leagues and whose wife is pregnant, are more concerned about how the hobby invades participants', particularly men's, lives. He explained:

> I have friends who are obsessed with fantasy sports. I have a friend
> of mine [who] did not do good on his LSATs because of fantasy base-
> ball, right? And it's kind of like, "What are you doing with your life?"
> I understand that paying attention to the fantasy baseball thing is
> fun *if you have nothing to do* that night. But if you are studying for
> your LSATs, get your head out of your ass! You know what I mean?
> You have a life to live. I have a friend who is in seven football leagues.
> And he's, all day at work, he's managing, he's getting his teams in
> order at work all day. And it's like, you are going to get fired. Your
> boss is going to find out about this. . . . They are going to know. That's
> obsession, I think. That's where it's like, your career, your future are
> in jeopardy.

Likewise, but after some reflection, Frank, a married man who plays in eight leagues, questioned the time he has invested in fantasy sports. He noted:

> I pretty much sack out in front of the TV on Sunday. Once I get
> home from church, it's pretty much football. . . . When I pull back in
> a conversation like this and think, "Man, I've spent seven years of my
> life investing in this—for what?" And it's like, I think of how many
> hours I've spent on fantasy football, and it's like, "Man, there are lots
> of other things I could be doing with my life." . . . I think like, "Boy,
> in terms of life goals and long term, would I be better off investing
> that time in something more constructive than this sort of silly pride
> with my friends?"

A number of gender and class dynamics underlie men's greater expenditures of time and their greater likelihood of reporting that their or their friends' involvement in fantasy sports reduces time in and attention to more "productive" activities. The dominance of men and masculinity in sports generally and the dictates of jock statsculinity specifically presume men's involvement. Indeed, men are likely to be questioned more for their lack of involvement than for their overinvestment. Moreover, research on men's and women's time use more generally suggests that women are more likely than men to prioritize other tasks (e.g., caring for children, household labor) over their own leisure activities.[38] Thus, men are likely more willing to let the hobby interfere with productive activities. The use of a productivity metaphor to discuss even leisure time use is also tied to the class standing of our participants—middle- and upper-class professionals for whom work often bleeds into every aspect of life, including even the terminology they use to describe their time trade-offs.

These players recognize time is finite. As such, they often identify specific areas of their lives given less time and attention because of fantasy sports. Often, both men and women note that fantasy sports take away from other leisure activities, with men and women equally likely to forgo reading and watching television or films to participate. Women much more than men, though, claim that if they were not doing fantasy sports, they would be spending this time on the Internet or social media or, as Caroline, a married woman who plays in one league, noted, "something else equally as wasteful of my time." Men, in contrast, are more likely to skip gaming or other hobbies (e.g., golf, hunting) in favor of fantasy sports participation, something only one woman we interviewed noted. Thus, women seem to displace online time to another online activity, fantasy sports. A likely reason for this is that women have less leisure time in general and online activities can be fit sporadically into their middle- and upper-class lives. With more leisure time, men substitute a greater array of leisure activities for fantasy sports, with a substantial minority swapping out digital or tabletop games, both highly masculine activities.

A few players also allude to forgoing charity work or other community engagement for the sake of fantasy sports. At times, they refer to this jokingly, as when Jamie claimed that if he was not playing fantasy sports, "Well, I could solve world peace." Others, while still often placing it in hypothetical terms, acknowledge that time spent on fantasy sports might be better spent contributing to their communities. One male player, for instance, commented, "Fantasy sports is my main nonwork, nonfamily outlet. So in theory, I could be reading more, volunteering, helping society, becoming more enlightened. Instead, I could spend two hours in one night researching left-handed middle relievers." Jerome, a married father who plays in five leagues, similarly acknowledged that he could theoretically be more civically engaged but admitted it was unlikely: "So I could be doing something else [with that time]. . . . [But realistically,] it's not like I would be volunteering at a shelter in the hours that I would be doing this."

Our players' class and racial privilege is evident in their discussions of how fantasy sports fit into their leisure and civic pursuits. A number of the activities being reduced—reading, watching films, "becoming more enlightened"—are reflective of what Pierre Bourdieu would consider contributions to one's cultural capital, or symbolic resources (which include pastimes) that can support or promote social mobility.[39] In addition, references to "volunteering at a shelter" and "helping society" suggest that it is others, not the players with whom we spoke, who need such help. Finally, it may be that part of the class and racial privilege of fantasy sports participants is that they not only have the free time for such a leisure activity but that they also have the option to ignore larger social issues that might benefit from their civic engagement.[40]

Fantasy sports participants, like Kels and CB in our chapter opening, more frequently discuss how their involvement in the hobby detracts from "required" tasks, such as household labor or paid employment. Despite women's disproportionate responsibility for performing household labor, women and men are equally likely to report that household chores go undone or are delayed because of fantasy sports.[41] Rebecca, a married college professor without children, noted her "house might be dirtier" because of the time she spends on fantasy sports. Another female player similarly claimed, "Instead of getting things done around the house, I spend all day sitting in front of my TV and computer." Jamie, who comanages several teams with his wife, claimed, "Maybe there's that little housework or some chore that should get done or could get done, but instead you spent those extra hours watching sports."

Perhaps the most common story we heard, however, is that, like Kels and CB, the relatively well-to-do professionals who engage in the hobby often set their lineups, make trades or waiver moves, trash talk with others, or do research at their places of employment or during times when they could (and often should) be working. Thus, in line with what scholars like Ethan Tussey might expect, fantasy sports as a leisure activity bleed into the workplace or, at least, certain types of workplaces. Fantasy players engage in media snacking and fantasy sports–related tasks while on the job—an eventuality the largely unsupervised, professional occupations participants hold and the accessibility of digital technologies make possible.[42] For instance, one male player claimed, "[fantasy sports can] be distracting at work, as I spend most of my work day alone in my office on my computer—where all of my fantasy football information is easily accessible." A different male player likewise asserted that fantasy sports are "a bit of a time-suck, distraction from doing work," while Kate, who works in human resources, admitted that if she wasn't spending those minutes on fantasy sports, she would "be working."

Although a subject of disagreement, time spent on fantasy sports may have measurable impacts on workplace productivity, with estimates of the financial impact of fantasy football alone on employers hovering at approximately $1 billion per week during the football season.[43] Some players acknowledge this, with many reporting that a *downside* to fantasy sports is that they make players or others "less productive," as fantasy sports "get in the way" of work. Thraka, a single man who currently teaches college English, recalled, "When I did work nine to five and play fantasy football, it did seriously impact my productivity as a marketing assistant." Likewise, Jennifer, a single woman who works in public relations, told us that without fantasy sports,

> I'd probably be a little more productive. . . . Sometimes at work—if I get a text from my boyfriend [about fantasy sports] . . . my first inclination is to stop what I'm doing and look something up. So I definitely think that I would be far, [*pause*] slightly [more] productive [without fantasy sports]. . . . It definitely takes some time away from other [work-related] things. It's not like I only do it when I have downtime.

Still, many frame the time they spend on fantasy sports during the workday as unproblematic, and there are both practical and ideological reasons why this is the case. Fantasy sports participants typically hold privileged positions in careers and workplace settings that offer flexibility, autonomy, control, and pockets of time free from any or close supervision. Such employees have more of a say in when, where, and how much they work than do those in nonprofessional occupations such as service workers and manual laborers.[44] Moreover, employees in professional and technical occupations, such as engineers, account executives, and academics, spend significant portions of the day in front of a computer. These employment conditions more easily lend themselves to combining work and leisure throughout the day (and to do so without detection) than do rigidly scheduled service and manual labor occupations involving a high degree of oversight from supervisors. Additionally, this group's privileged position as White, middle- and upper-class men and women provides insulation from potential attacks on their industriousness—protection that others, in particular poor men of color and welfare recipients, do not have given larger damaging stereotypes regarding their work ethic.[45] Therefore, our players can more freely acknowledge "slacking off" at work without worrying about jeopardizing any claims to their being hard workers. Last, aspects of such careers—for instance, their mental intensity—may provide a justification for employees to engage in leisure activities while on the job, as they may believe that they "need" a "mental break" to work effectively.[46]

Fantasy sports players, like Kels in our opening, often recognize that the structure of their work allows them to "multitask" leisure and work activities and to use pockets of "free" time while at work to accomplish fantasy sports–related tasks and monitoring. Dino, a married man with a master's degree in risk management insurance and actuarial science, vacillated on whether he is less productive as a result but ultimately specified that his fantasy sports involvement is not a problem given the type of career he has. He explained:

> It's pretty bad. . . . I'm on the phone at work looking at someone's insurance policies and [have] the fantasy on my cell phone up, or even fantasy on the computer, and Gmail account, Gmailing all my friends as well—four things at once. . . . There's days where I feel like I've wasted more time on fantasy. So yeah, yes it does hinder it [work], but it doesn't hurt my work too much, no. I have a job where it's not just a nine to five, straightforward, you've got work in front of you, do it [kind of] day. It comes and goes, the level of the business that I have at work, so I have more free time.

Similarly, Anne, who is a paralegal and "in front of a computer all day for work," acknowledged that fantasy sports likely make her less productive. She claims, "I probably would be a little more productive at work [without fantasy sports] [*laughs*]. I usually, generally do it during the day. . . . I read ESPN all the time."

Others reveal that their devoting time to fantasy sports during the workday is a nonissue overall because they "make up" that lost time later. For example, Charlie, who plays in two leagues and works in sales, argued:

> Fantasy football costs productivity for companies—that's been written about. But for me, for sure it does. . . . I definitely am reading fantasy stuff during the day when I should be working. . . . It does take away [from work], but I think that for the most part, it just makes my day longer or just makes me have to work in the evening when I should have had some free time.

Accordingly, Charlie and other fantasy sports players like him frame the potential lack of work productivity as not personally problematic because the nature of their employment allows them to complete their work after normal work hours. Such time trade-offs are the province of the privileged—factory workers cannot bring machinery home with them. Charlie's strategy of working into the evening to facilitate his fantasy sports play, however, has the potential consequence of impacting time on other activities, such as leisure, housework, or relationships with others insofar as evenings might otherwise be family time for this married father. Regardless, we witness the blurring of work and leisure time and space for the professional class—the presence bleed of which Melissa Gregg writes—as fantasy sports encroach on worktime and work impinges on leisure time.

Notwithstanding their numerous assertions that it's "fine" for them to use worktime for fantasy sports–related purposes, many players readily admit their employers may not agree with their allocating time to the hobby during work hours. Randall, who works in the finance division of a "top-tier university," first noted that he "could be more productive if not doing fantasy-related stuff" but decided "as long as the work gets done, I'm fine." Yet, after additional reflection, this married father of two admitted, "Maybe it wouldn't be great if my boss knew that I am spending time doing fantasy while at work." Likewise, Frank, after revealing his use of university time for fantasy sports, implored, "Don't tell my boss I do it at work." Jerome, who is in the film industry, encapsulated the ambivalence of many fantasy sports players in this regard when he simultaneously celebrated his on-the-job fantasy sports accomplishments while acknowledging he would not allow such activities among his own employees. He told us:

> If I'm working on a [fantasy sport] trade, that doesn't wait until 5:30 [when I'm off work], that has to happen whenever it has to happen. . . . One of the moments I'm most proud of in fantasy sports, probably life, [is] this three-team trade involving like twelve people and future draft picks and minor league people, and I was definitely at work on my cell phone and my office phone [working on that]. It's awful. I totally understand, like a friend of ours who plays in that league, their office has, doesn't allow employees to go on ESPN.com, which I understand and would be in favor of if I were somebody who was in charge of that. I'd be like, "Man, this is a lot of time [being wasted on fantasy]," 'cause I totally know that I do do that.

Beyond the advantaged position their type of employment affords, the technology their work involves, and larger cultural understandings of White and class-privileged individuals' work ethic, the fact that both workplaces and fantasy sports are gendered masculine likely contributes to participants' ability to devote time to fantasy sports while suffering few reported ill effects. Given the privileging of men and masculinity in gendered organizations, both employers and employees are more likely to accept and value the bleeding of leisure activities into the workplace that are culturally typed masculine than those typed feminine.[47] Thus, the costs of directing one's worktime attention to fantasy sports, a masculine pursuit, are quite different than if one were to engage in a "feminine" activity, such as those related to the home or family. This may be particularly the case for women, as assumptions that the family acts as a workplace distraction negatively impacts employers' *interpretations* of women's suitability for work and productivity, which in turn affect hiring, promotion, and salary considerations.[48] Being engaged in and distracted by fantasy sports on the job does not, at least according to our players, represent a detriment to their careers and, particularly for women, may serve as an important marker of cultural capital that, as we have previously argued, provides them entrée into largely male-dominated and masculinized spaces. Moreover, fantasy sports' association with masculine traits such as rationality, control, tech- and statistical-savvy, and competitiveness likely make them leisure activities that complement rather than contradict the workplace environments and duties of the White, educated professionals who participate in them.

The Emotional Toll of Fantasy Sports Participation

Besides taking up time—time that might be spent on other activities—fantasy sports also take an emotional toll on some participants. Unlike the twenty-four-hour limit on one's daily time, emotional investment or absorption in the hobby is potentially limitless, which can have substantial consequences for personal and family well-being. Indeed, fantasy sports players admit that despite all the positives they see in playing, their participation in the hobby leads to their becoming frustrated, stressed, depressed, or angry. One male player summed up the overall sentiment of many when he said, "It's fun and frustrating at the same time," while others describe "the lows of losing" as "rough" or feeling "depression" or "pissed" when losing.

Various aspects of fantasy sports promote negative emotions and, for some, high levels of absorption. As Chapter 2 detailed, fantasy sports fandom increases sports consumption and personalizes the outcomes of player performances, "upping" the stakes of real games. The result is an enhanced and fuller engagement with live sporting events than what many players, like Kels, have experienced before—even as traditional sports fans. This engagement, however, can also result in a greater intensity in emotions, the "lows" of which many fantasy sports players interpret negatively. Dino recognized this, explaining that with fantasy sports, "you get *way too into* games. On a Monday night game, when you're waiting for something, then you're yelling at the TV or something like that." Jennifer, who plays in only one league, also described feeling "consumed" by fantasy sports "at times" and commented that "Sundays are no longer fun football days for me." She went on to highlight how fantasy football is not just time intensive (she devotes the whole day to her fantasy football preparation and watching football) but also that watching games is emotionally taxing and sometimes unrewarding. This is the case even when her favorite real team, the New York Giants, is doing well. She explained:

> Watching football now is just so much more stressful. . . . [Recently,] I ended up playing Eli Manning [New York Giants quarterback] over Matt Ryan [Atlanta Falcon quarterback], and this is the game that I needed to win for a playoff spot, and Eli was doing horribly, and I was watching my app and seeing Matt Ryan's points going up. . . . I

got so mad and so upset I went to my room and I started watching *Ally McBeal* on Netflix, because I just did not wanna watch football anymore because I was getting so pissed off at my fantasy players. It completely was like, [my boyfriend] was like, "You need to calm. Your team's winning. You should be happy." And I was like, "But my *fantasy team isn't winning*." . . . So I would say the downside is, it makes it more stressful.

This stress, like Jennifer experiences, can be so intense that the end of the fantasy sports season comes as a relief, a period of "freedom and relaxation" when players can finally watch games again for "pure enjoyment."

Both women and men experience emotional lows and mental stresses related to fantasy sports. There are notable differences, however, in the nature of men's and women's negative feelings and reactions to fantasy sports–related decisions and outcomes, as well as in their depth and duration. A higher proportion of women than men report feeling minor levels of stress over fantasy sports. Framed by definitions of legitimate fandom that emphasize the importance of knowledge and gendered expectations that presume they lack it, many of their feelings of stress, frustration, dejection, and anxiety revolve around their making a "wrong" fantasy sports decision and, thus, living up to negative stereotypes about women. For instance, one female player acknowledged, "I waste a lot of time and energy obsessing about roster moves and feel bad when I make the wrong decisions." Another explained, "I obsess over wrong managerial choices all the time." Still another claimed, "I get upset (at myself) if I feel I made a poor decision (benched the wrong guy, forgot to set my lineup), but I usually let it go pretty easily." What's critical here is that unlike men, women who play fantasy sports express internalizing their frustration and disappointment when their decisions do not pan out. Rather than lashing out at friends or family members—or perhaps the television or iPad screen—women more typically focus on *their* fantasy sports "mistakes" as a reflection of themselves and something about which they should "feel bad." Yet, because their legitimacy and very identities are not wrapped up in their fantasy sports success, they recover from even these internalized failures "pretty easily."

Men, like CB, report more durable, extreme, and externalizing negative feelings and reactions arising from their play. Specifically, when men talk about the lows of fantasy sports, they often explain that they let fantasy losses "ruin" their entire day, the day or two subsequent, or even the entire week. They also explain how they get angry, express their anger and frustrations visibly or direct them at others, or let their "bad moods" otherwise damage their interactions with others. In fact, comments from men are replete with statements such as "Sometimes I get overly emotional and have outbursts at the people I live with and the people I play with. It's a problem I have been working on" and "My wife hates when I ruin Sundays by getting mad at my team." One male respondent wrote that a downside to playing is the "frustration that sometimes affects those around me—particularly my children." Still another linked the effects of time and emotional investments when he commented, "My wife doesn't like it when I spend all day Sunday watching football. I can invest a lot emotionally in my team, so sometimes losses can take a toll on my emotional state."

Women also take note of men's inability to handle the lows of fantasy sports. Lynn, a hard-core player who participates in eight leagues, told us that in her experience, men get more worked up than women when things in their fantasy sports world go awry. She explained:

I think guys are more emotional about it than girls are, I really do, and I know that they will all deny it.... They're gonna be the ones cussing at the TV more often or cussing at their computer screen more often. If that [was a] one-point loss, they're gonna be bitching to the heavens and everybody on the message board. I think they just take it more, [are] more high strung about it. Yeah, I wanna win, but it's not gonna totally ruin my day if I don't, whereas I hear a guy say they're, some of them are cutting back on leagues because it's ruining [their days]— [that they are] so pissed off all the time when they lose and they don't want to be that emotionally invested, and I'm like, "Really?"

Accordingly, and as Lynn notes, some men—but almost no women with whom we talked—admit that they have had to force themselves to take fantasy sports less seriously, have considered quitting, or have quit because of the emotional lows associated with playing. Thraka, who currently plays in three leagues, is one of these men. He explained his situation as follows:

So there have been a couple of tense moments where I [think I] might need to stop doing this—if I can't keep my perspective straight. And so far, I've been OK, and obviously, I'm still playing, but it came pretty close once where I might just have to walk away from this.

Reflecting their greater propensity to fixate on winning or losing for longer periods, significantly more male players than female players also report losing sleep over fantasy sports.[49] Explicitly linking his loss of sleep to a problematic emotional absorption in fantasy sports, Charlie grappled with whether his time expenditures and lack of sleep means fantasy sports are an "obsession." He, like other men, reported:

At night, late at night, that's when I probably should not be doing it. I'm just, I wanna go to bed so much, but I can't stop just seeing what else is out there. So it's a little strange, but that's when I tend to, [I] do troll the Internet kinda late at night. . . . [But] I don't think about it as an obsession. [Yet] I hear myself and the amount of time it takes up, so it's gotta be to some extent.

These findings on the gendered nature of the mental and emotional trials of fantasy sports align well with what we know about gender more generally and in fantasy sports specifically. Women, unlike men, need to *prove* their worth and credibility in the highly masculinized and male-dominated space that is fantasy sports. Against a backdrop of gender beliefs that presume they are less knowledgeable and experienced, women exhibit less confidence in their own abilities. Women, though, are not immune to the stress and anxiety surrounding fantasy sports decisions (and express feeling this in higher proportions than men) and often attribute their losses to wrong decisions that were the result of their own ineptitude (and not, say, "bad luck"). This is exactly what the literatures on stereotype threat, tokens, and gender more generally would predict. Women know all too well that many men in their leagues will notice any unsuccessful choices they make and will use these instances as further evidence that women, on the whole, cannot compete. This, along with women's lesser confidence in themselves and their fantasy sports abilities, adds stress and anxiety to every decision—and may ultimately impede women's performance in fantasy sports.

Men, however, also face stress and frustration in the game, and here the dictates—and contradictions—of jock statsculinity shape the contours of men's emotional reactions. While the risk of making a poor decision for women is proving correct the stereotype that women cannot compete, for men, their very manhood might be questioned. Men, after all, should be inherently capable in fantasy sports, and as we demonstrated in Chapter 2, they feel more in control of their fantasy outcomes—something that previous studies have found contributes to higher levels of stress and anxiety.[50] As a response, men distance themselves more from their losses than women (e.g., they were "unlucky"), likely in part to resolve the cognitive dissonance involved in the combination of presumed competence and actual poor performance.[51] At the same time, due to the great importance of winning and bravado in the performance of jock statsculinity, men can and do express anger at losses, lash out at others, and ruminate at length about defeats. In short, anger is acceptable but admissions of personal weakness or fallibility are not, as the former reinforces masculinity while the latter jeopardizes it. Women, on the other hand, can be sad and self-questioning but, with less time to devote to leisure pursuits in general and less at stake in terms of their identities and legitimacy, cannot afford to fixate on it for days on end. As Claire, who returned recently to fantasy sports after a long layoff due to her needing to devote time to family responsibilities, noted, the lows (and highs) of fantasy sports last only "until the kid yells, 'MOM' ten minutes later."

Relationship Tension for Men in Fantasy Sports

The investments of time, energy, and emotion fantasy sports require also negatively impact relationships, and reports of fantasy sports' damaging or straining social interactions and relationships—even if only momentarily—characteristically involve men.[52] Fantasy sports thus occupy a contradictory place in men's lives. As Chapter 5 demonstrated, fantasy sports are a key way by which men attempt to bond with other men, particularly long-term friends and family members. At the same time, fantasy sports create tensions and difficulties for men's relationships with both women and other men.

Men describe a range of problems that fantasy sports introduce to their relationships, the consequences of which vary in severity. A number of men point generally to lost time with or attention to their friends who do not play or note that fantasy sports come to dominate group discussions and activities, leaving some in their social circles reportedly feeling annoyed or left out. Paul, whose wife also plays, rather unapologetically explained:

> [Fantasy sports take] time from friends who don't play, because instead of going out to dinner with friends on the weekend or something like that, we're like, "We'll go, but let's go here [somewhere broadcasting the games] instead." And then they don't want to go to the sports bar to watch the game around the corner or something like that.

Dino, who currently plays in four leagues, asserted that fantasy sport is "kind of exclusive when you're in it." He further explained, "When you're in a league, you usually just talk to people in the league, and people outside the league" do not find "really interesting" the conversations about fantasy sports. Ted similarly acknowledged that fantasy sports are annoying to his nonplaying friends, noting that this was more likely to be an aggravation for the "girls" than the "guys" in his friend group. He explained:

> We end up talking about football and our fantasy football league, and other people get annoyed with that. . . . It's kind of like [the nonplayers say], "Let's talk about something that everybody can talk about instead of about the stupid league." . . . A part of my friend group is people who don't do the fantasy football; a couple guys and all of the girls don't do it. So we were at a party once and they were saying, "Guys, stop talking about the draft. Just shut up about the draft. No more football talk."

Other players and nonplayers confirm Ted's sentiments. One nonplayer in reflecting on her close social ties whose "involvement in fantasy sports is at a very high level," complained that her friends' participation "can have a negative effect on communication, as discussion becomes slim during the time they are engaging in the activity and they become distracted by fantasy sports." Others note that the constant focus on and obsession with fantasy sports among men in their friendship circle is annoying or even unbearable to them—making hanging out with these men difficult. Anne, a dedicated player who currently is in one league, complained about a friend in the league:

> The first thing he brings up is something about our fantasy leagues. I don't know why, but that always rubs me the wrong way. I'm like, "You have nothing else to talk about besides fantasy football?" So stuff like that, for some reason that gets under my skin. . . . Every time he says something about fantasy sports, I wanna lose my mind.

Men's fantasy sports participation seems to uniquely strain their friendships with other men—precisely those relationships the hobby strengthens. Some men recount how tensions have culminated in arguments with other men in their leagues. Sometimes these are the result of disagreements over rules or protocol. Otto, a married man who has ten teams, recounted a time when "everything really blew up where a couple guys didn't pay their dues, so by partway through the season, a big argument broke out and things got ugly." Roland, a hard-core player in four leagues, lamented one of his close friends' being terrible to deal with regarding rules and trade negotiations. Specifically noting both his affection and frustration, he explained:

> I have a buddy in the league . . . who's one of my best friends and who was in my wedding. He's a pain in the ass to deal with in fantasy. . . . I love him as a real-life human being, but as a fantasy owner in my league, he drives me insane. . . . And I guess that bothers me 'cause I don't want to be aggravated at him because of a silly game. . . . He's such a great guy; I love him. But he's the worst kind of person to be in a fantasy league with.

In addition, although some men bond specifically over competitive banter, others admit that their self-reported "competitive nature" results in "stupid petty" and sometimes "serious arguments with others." Some merely complain about "being told that I suck," note that with trash talk comes the "potential to stick your foot in your mouth and hurt someone's feelings," or report rather unapologetically, like CB, instances of smack talk offending or wounding others. For others, the consequences are more severe. Dino, for example, told us that he enjoys commenting on the league's boards and sending "rivalry texts" to his opponents but also admits that he has "pushed one or two people over the ledge before in one league." He went on to explain that some people in this league "seem like easy targets, and sometimes I go over the line" but that "I like to poke at people." He further elaborated:

I had a person confront me last year. . . . I don't see these people that much, so I just write stuff over the message board, and I'm kind of a, I have kind of a big mouth. . . . I guess just throughout the years someone thought I was going a little too far. When I was at an event for my friend who runs the league, a charity event actually, he [the offended party] yelled at me and told me to get away from him, which was very serious. He was very serious, so I very calmly went up to him and apologized and told him I was [sorry], things were over the limit, and calmed him down, but he was a little ridiculous.

Other men recall being on the receiving end of trash talk that goes "too far" or is "too personal"—the latter made possible by the fact that many of these men know their fellow competitors and know them well. Such intimate knowledge gives players the ammunition to inflict significant damage with a mere comment or two. Jerome, for instance, acknowledged these problems with smack talk:

There are times again particularly in this one baseball league where there's more trash talking in general, where it crosses a line and it gets a little personal. . . . [One time, I was] poking fun at somebody's bad contract that they signed, and the person responded, "Excuse me if I don't take accounting advice from the guy who produced [name of movie]," which is a massive like budgetary failure. And I remember I was at work when I got that email, and I like shut my computer and just kind of did this [slumps shoulders and looks down dejectedly] for like two to three minutes and just was like "ugh," and also because we were fresh off of that movie, and it was such a like career disappointment for everybody involved. . . . And then when he [said that], he just nailed it.

For Jerome, who claimed that "in general" he likes trash talking "when it's just kind of the playful, which it for the most part is," a line was crossed when a competitor insulted another key component of his White, upper-class masculinity—his workplace success.

It's not just among friends or acquaintances that men's involvement in fantasy sports purportedly causes problems. When asked to reveal the downsides to playing, men frequently focus on how the hobby negatively impacts their families. They emphasize how fantasy sports take "time away from my family" and "distract" from their "spouse"—claims that are largely absent among women. Some men go so far as to invoke the familiar label of the "fantasy football widow" to describe their wives during the football season. One, for instance, claimed:

> My wife considers herself a "fantasy football widow." . . . She doesn't see me usually from noon until about seventy thirty on Sundays during football season, as I go to a sports bar to watch all the games. I also go watch the Thursday and Monday night games in the room with our second television.

Other men are clear that their loved ones, particularly their wives, actively dislike or are upset by their involvement in fantasy sports. In fact, male players report greater relationship tension in their families resulting from fantasy sports than do female players; they acknowledge more so than female players that they hear complaints from loved ones about their fantasy sports involvement.[53] One male player simply stated about fantasy sports, "My wife hates it," and another wrote, "It can sometimes alienate my wife and distract me from my family." When asked if there are any downsides to his participation, Ray, a married father who currently plays in two leagues, responded, "Oh, I'm sure if you ask my wife there is—the fact that I'm doing this interview right now and not downstairs watching a chick flick with her [*laughs*]." Exemplifying a more extreme case, one male player wrote that fantasy sports "probably contributed to my divorce."

For some, this is about their wives' (or other family members') frustration with their fantasy sports teams monitoring, including "at six thirty, exactly when we are out doing something" (Ted). Some female nonplayers note similar problems with men's investment in fantasy sports. One female nonplayer wrote:

> My brother plays fantasy sports. He is an extreme sports fan, and I think that his need to never miss a game or update/check his fantasy sports teams can negatively impact my family. It takes away from the quality time he could spend interacting with his family.

Another female nonplayer likewise commented, "My fiancé is involved in fantasy sports. . . . It does get annoying when he continuously checks his fantasy football team every Sunday and Monday." Still another claimed it's "annoying that he checks stats a lot."

The financial investment in the hobby poses problems for some men's spouses in particular—something that we did not hear from women who play fantasy sports. FSU, who spends $850 in league fees alone for his teams, claimed, "Now my wife always just says, she always wants to see me bringing home the money. I was like, not everybody can win, not gonna win every time . . . [but] if I don't win anything, then my wife is disappointed in that." Another male player wrote that a downside of playing fantasy sports is "my wife reminding me I always lose (therefore, we always lose money)," while another explained, "My wife dislikes it, thinks it [is] gambling, and so I have to hide it from her. That sucks."

Additionally, recall from the previous section that men express that sometimes their fantasy sports participation results in their moods being ruined, thus negatively affecting family time, or their lashing out at their wives and children. This clearly represents an additional reason for wives (and other loved ones) to complain about men's fantasy sports involvement. Thus, the resources that fantasy sports demand—and that are directed away from families—are temporal, emotional, and monetary. That some men persist despite their loved ones' complaints, particularly their wives, further underscores men's dominance and privilege. Furthermore, that men commonly discuss their fantasy sports participation as alienating, annoying, and frustrating their wives reveals that their use of fantasy sports as an escape may actually contribute to arguments with and additional demands from their loved ones—something from which they might turn to fantasy sports to escape. In such a way, a cyclical process of escape-complaint-escape may result.

And here we have one of the great paradoxes of fantasy sports participation. They do bring people together—and are especially important in doing so for men. But the nature of interactions in leagues; the competitive, monetary, and reputational stakes involved; the time investment; and the frustrations and anger that arise from negative outcomes all create the potential for men's social relationships to be strained—with not only nonplaying friends, family members, and particularly wives but also with the fellows who play alongside them. Thus, an activity that builds relationships for men can also weaken or destroy such ties.

Conclusion

Although fantasy sports have the potential to provide enjoyment, improve the sports viewing experience, and forge and strengthen relationships, they also come with some downsides, including forgoing other activities and social interactions, experiencing negative emotions, and changing the degree and nature of interactions with others in ways that may strain them. Indeed, with only twenty-four hours in the day and the ability to devote attention to only so many things at once, time and energy spent on fantasy sports must take time and attention away from other activities, such as other leisure pursuits, civic and volunteer engagement, and household labor. In addition, fantasy sports players' experiences provide a prime example of how presence bleed is multidirectional and self-reinforcing, as they frequently admit to doing fantasy sports–related tasks during work hours and at their places of employment and then doing work at home to compensate for this. The kind of work they do and careers they have—frequently professional occupations that provide temporal flexibility, computer access, and limited supervision—simultaneously enable and justify as unproblematic their engaging in fantasy sports–related tasks during work hours. That they are employing a masculine activity to slack off and are not by default subject to damaging stereotypes regarding their work ethic further permits their use of work time for fantasy purposes.

Fantasy sports participation does not merely tax one's time; it also exacts an emotional toll. Players acknowledge a range of issues, from minor or temporary disappointment and stress to longer lasting feelings of anger and frustration. It is here that men's and women's experiences diverge. While women are more likely than men to report minor stress, anxiety, or frustration as a downside of their participation, their fantasy sport–induced emotional lows and mental distress tend to be relatively minor and short lived. Assumed to lack the requisite experience and knowledge to succeed and aware of these stereotypes about their competency, women are more likely to stress over decision making, blame themselves when things go awry, and experience more anxiety with a loss. These same gendered expectations, however, allow women to move on more quickly from their mistakes.

Men's experiences are indicative of the contradictions embedded in jock statsculinity. While the idealized Western masculinity—and jock statsculinity—is about being rational and in control of one's emotions,[54] men are not immune to the emotional trials of fantasy sports. Instead, when faced with expectations that their knowledge and statistical acumen should offer them greater control over their (inevitable) success, men are more likely to admit that fantasy sports frustrations "ruin" entire days or longer and/or that the negative emotions they feel and exhibit are severe. They also describe letting these lows get the best of them, as they lash out at loved ones or have difficulty getting out of their "bad moods" to interact happily with others.

Fantasy sports thus have paradoxical effects on men's social ties. As we argued in Chapter 5, they allow men to build and maintain often elusive emotional ties by facilitating expressive bonds with other men and providing opportunities to engage in kin-keeping activities. Yet the aggression that is part and parcel of masculine athletic involvement and the competitive banter integral to men's bonding promote harsh and hurtful dominance talk that can lead to disagreements and strained relationships. Last, men's emotional absorption in fantasy sports and their ability to direct time and attention to them—both because they are typically in occupations that facilitate this and because, as men, their contributions to family life are framed as optional—creates tensions in the home and with their wives in particular.

7

Conclusion

Whose Game? Gender and Power in Fantasy Sports

We are frequently asked, "Why fantasy sports?"

More than ten years ago, I began playing fantasy football when I was asked to join (with my husband as a comanager) a league run by one of my brother's closest high school friends and populated largely by his former college and high school soccer teammates.[1] As a sports junkie, former athlete, and die-hard fan of Philadelphia-based professional sports teams, I was excited to dip my toes into a sports-related hobby about which I had begun to hear so much. Yet, despite being that "girl who knows sports," I was timid about the prospect of entering, learning, and successfully competing in this new arena, particularly in a league in which I was the only woman manager. Oddly, I felt my reputation as a sports fan was at stake.

My husband and I had fun in that first league—debating (and often stressing) over coffee on Sunday mornings at our favorite breakfast spot about which players to start, commenting on other managers' decisions, and projecting what we needed to do to make the playoffs. We enjoyed it so much that we soon joined fantasy baseball and golf leagues, created a football league for which we acted as co-commissioners, and even tried fantasy ice hockey for one year. What once spanned the autumn and early winter months now became a year-round activity.

Research and roster decisions crept into our workdays—especially for baseball, where we continually lamented that weekday afternoon Cubs games meant we would have to set our fantasy team roster before most Major

League Baseball teams released their daily lineups, something we never gave a thought to when just watching baseball as fans. As a college professor, popping in and out of the league page to set lineups or to see how we were doing that day was easy—and even became a source of pre- and post-class conversation with students. My similarly professionally employed friends, including my husband, were also making roster moves during the day and sharing with me (typically via email) their insights on league happenings.

Fantasy sports became a way to connect with those in my social circle. All the leagues in which my husband and I participated contained and were run by a combination of coworkers, friends, family, and friends and family of friends. Conversations at our weekly pub quiz turned to fantasy sports–related topics, and emails flew back and forth about who was playing whom that given week. My circle also expanded, albeit to still-similar others. I began to know, at least virtually, friends and relatives of my friends. And I found myself making small talk about fantasy sports with strangers or acquaintances at professional conferences, at the store, or around campus.

As I devoted more time and energy to the hobby, I saw my relationship to real sports shift. I became even more invested in them than I was before but invested differently—focusing more so on and rooting for individual outcomes and scenarios (e.g., a particular player to steal a base) than the game as a whole. I felt some personal validation (and stake) in making the "right" decisions and a rush when "my team" did something positive. Summer nights involved a Phillies game on the television, a laptop computer with the live fantasy baseball scoring on the ottoman visible for me to see, and often, another laptop on my lap so I could do some work. I was immersed fully into the hobby and wondered how I ever "just" kept up with the Philadelphia sports teams before.

As a sociologist, I could not help but notice the dynamics of inequality in fantasy sports. I interacted with more people because of fantasy sports but not a more diverse set of people. There have never been more than two other women in my leagues, something I gathered was quite common based on my media observations. I felt waves of anger upon seeing sexist comments on public message boards and observing the treatment of the few fantasy sports experts on television and social media who are women. Personally, I never felt maligned in my leagues because I am a woman, but I have felt my gender highly visible. Though my leagues are not overly hostile or aggressive, I have noticed even the mildest of smack talk—typically lobbed among the men in my leagues—discomforted me. And when I have won, I noticed an extra little boost—that as a woman, I bested a bunch of really smart, really competitive men.

—RJK

These experiences and perceptions birthed this book. What started from curiosity about women in the hobby and its popularity more generally uncovered larger dynamics of privilege and power. *Whose Game?* documents the views and experiences of everyday traditional fantasy sports league participants in the United States, detailing the contours of fandom and highlighting the gendered dimensions of this relatively new, electronically mediated space. What *Whose Game?* shows is that women are indeed "game" to participate but that men and masculinity rule the game. Men are numerically dominant, to be sure, but they also govern the interactional and institutional dynamics of fantasy sports. Masculine terms define legitimate fandom and participation, even as that masculinity—what we call jock statsculinity—is broader and thus potentially more accessible than traditional hegemonic ideals. Importantly, the space is not just gendered but also classed and racialized. Particular types of men—White, professional, highly educated—dominate the space, and the controlling form of masculinity reflects and reinforces their privilege. Those women who end up being invited to the game largely reproduce these power dynamics—as White, well-educated, affluent women, they are insiders in everything but their gender.

The Turf We Have Covered: Key Findings

We began our inquiry into fantasy sports by explaining how they offer a personalized, competitive fandom that gives participants, particularly men, some measure of control and a direct connection between their successes and those of the real-life athletes they virtually employ and manipulate. The sole accepted definition of success in fantasy sports is winning—a type of dominance fitting with traditional notions of hegemonic masculinity. Accordingly, participants generally frown upon letting one's heart govern fantasy sports decisions and rooting loyalties. Despite this, many participants do just that—taking into account their real-team affinities, allegations of athletes' criminal and/or immoral behavior, or athletes' positive character in devising their teams. In these ways, fantasy sports, more so than traditional sports fandom, offer opportunities for participants to customize and control their experiences. Yet, the process of co-creation is gendered. The stipulation that successful participants must focus on rational decision making and disregard emotional attachments establishes a masculinized standard for legitimate play and fandom, and men heed to this requirement to a greater degree than women.

We further argue that through fantasy sports, largely White, highly educated, professional men can achieve and perform an expanded yet legitimate variant of masculinity we call jock statsculinity. Like traditional sports fandom masculinity, jock statsculinity is more accessible than athletic mascu-

linity. Yet, by being active, affording participants control, and having measurable outcomes, jock statsculinity is more potent than traditional fandom
masculinity. It is also qualitatively different from traditional fandom masculinity in more fully incorporating the core elements of hegemonic masculinity and combining those with elements of nerd and boyhood masculinities.
Jock statsculinity contains elements of traditional, hegemonic, and sports-
based masculinities, as men utilize the hobby to exert control, compete, and
exercise dominance. This traditional masculinity combines with elements
of nerd masculinity insofar as competition and dominance in this space
center on testing and demonstrating intellectual acumen and knowledge of
statistics and sports. Jock statsculinity also involves a boyish element, as
men play, act juvenilely, and relive their childhood dreams of being involved
in professional sports. They use the hobby to escape from demanding aspects of modern masculinity as well, notably the expectation that they be
more involved parents and partners while also being committed to their frequently demanding professional careers. Yet here, too, gender intersects with
race and class. The majority of men in the space are White, highly educated
professionals. They stake a claim to legitimate masculinity through control,
dominance, a bit of nerdiness, and a desire to escape, even temporarily, the
demands of marriage, parenthood, and employment. This underscores their
gender, race, and class status. When men who do not enjoy similar race and
class privileges embrace this constellation of attributes, their performances
of manhood are likely to be denigrated rather than celebrated.

Accordingly, and despite women's increased participation, fantasy sports
are still decidedly framed in the abstract and experienced as "men's turf."
Fantasy sports participants promote abstract views of women and men that
reflect a larger gender frame establishing men and women as distinct and
highly differentiated from each other in their knowledge of and interest in
sports, competitive "nature," and capacity to be rational and statistically in-
clined. Demonstrating the strength of these larger gender beliefs, women
often experience fantasy sports as exclusionary and find themselves framed
as outsiders who are looked down on as inferior to men. Gender intersects
with sexuality here, as heterosexualized assumptions (e.g., that women's attraction to male athletes drive their play or that women require their male
partners' assistance) further marginalize women. Women respond in varied
and often contradictory ways—sometimes failing to counter their position
in the hobby, other times engaging in conflicted or mediated agency (e.g.,
by enlisting the help of men to better their experience), and still other times
pushing back against gendered understandings of them and women more
generally and the masculinized environment of fantasy sports.

Whose Game? also details how fantasy sports serve as an important
source of social capital, with participants using their knowledge of sports
as cultural currency, forging and strengthening ties to family, friends, co-

workers, acquaintances, and strangers. Fantasy sports fill a unique niche for the largely White, professional men and women who play them, as demanding occupations and geographic mobility make in-person connections more challenging. At the same time, although their ties may strengthen and expand, they diversify very little; and further underscoring their centrality in this space, men are the targets of most of this relationship building and strengthening. Men also make greater use of and depend more fully on fantasy sports to "stay in touch" and bond with, typically, the men in their friend groups. The intimacy they achieve, though, is contradictory. Men describe getting to know friends and family members better and becoming closer emotionally to them as a result of their fantasy sports play. Yet their reliance on trash talking and dominance talk to set up masculine hierarchies, particularly with their friends, and their acknowledgment that their conversations often fail to "delve deep" suggest that the intimacy realized, especially between men, is fragile and potentially limited in scope. Women who play fantasy sports do not generally engage in such hierarchical interactions and employ the hobby as one of many ways to connect with others. Nonetheless, women do leverage their fantasy sports involvement to extend their social ties and open avenues of conversation and connection with men in both their personal relationships and workplaces. In their largely professional workplaces, sports knowledge and fantasy sports participation serve as a form of cultural capital, producing tangible instrumental advantages for the White, class-privileged women in the position to access and leverage this capital.

Finally, because they can be temporally and emotionally absorbing, fantasy sports impact, often negatively, other aspects of participants' lives. Participants frequently use family time or work hours to research, adjust their rosters, watch games, or connect with other fantasy sports participants. That they can engage in fantasy sports while at work—and that they see doing so as largely unproblematic—is evidence of their privileged class position. The majority of participants are employed in professional occupations that provide the schedule control, freedom from supervision, and technological connectedness for the blending of work and leisure. Men, however, most acutely face the negative emotional and temporal impacts of fantasy sports participation. They, more frequently than women, report missing out on family time and experiencing tension at home. They also more often express getting overly emotional, lashing out at others, and finding their day or week "ruined" when the outcomes of their fantasy sports efforts do not align with their desires and expectations to win. To be sure, women experience stress and anxiety while playing, but they internalize their emotions and tend to move on quickly from their disappointments. Finally, the very same aspects of performing jock statsculinity that promote bonding among men—one-upmanship and competitive banter—sometimes strain precisely those relationships they help men to build and strengthen.

The Long Game: Major Conclusions and Next Steps

Fantasy sports are contested and sometimes contradictory terrain. They reflect and reinforce larger binary, gender frames. Numerically and ideologically, men dominate the space. Dominance and control are central to (masculine) definitions of success, and men interact with one another in ways that reward these traits, serving to establish and reproduce masculine hierarchies. Women have entered, yet individual men and the masculinized institutional climate and structures resist their presence and stake to legitimacy. The dominance of men and masculinity drives forward narratives of women as lesser, (re)defines appropriate fandom in fantasy sports and real sports in ways that privilege masculine meanings and priorities, and pushes women out of "turf" that belongs to men, both individually and collectively. Some women respond by retreating or reinforcing these gendered assumptions—understandable behaviors that nonetheless reproduce the status quo.

At the same time, there are opportunities for expansion, resistance, and transformation in fantasy sports. The dominant form of masculinity—jock statsculinity—is accessible to aging, injured, and nonathletic men who possess the rationality and statistical acumen deemed necessary for success. Men forge relationships with other men and, to a lesser extent, family members, thus to some extent challenging gender beliefs that men cannot form and/or do not crave close ties with others. Moreover, through their very presence, skill, and assertions of power, women push against notions of the space as built only for men. Many women indicate that fantasy sports empower them, allow them to express their sports fanaticism, and foster better interactions with men at work and in their social lives. And, importantly, many women actively assert their belonging in ways that potentially transform dominant gender frames.

The simultaneous reinforcement and challenging of gendered assumptions and structures occurs within classed and racialized boundaries. *Whose Game?* reveals that fantasy sports are predominately a game owned, controlled, about, and for White, class-privileged men. They engender a mindset focusing on skill and control and do so in ways that reflect and reproduce the gendered and racialized dynamics in sports more generally. Indeed, the very sense of being in control of one's success as a result of one's efforts, abilities, and choices is steeped in notions of White, class-privileged men as dominant, rational, and in charge of themselves and others. That these White, class-privileged men are symbolically manipulating—and thus exerting at least virtual control over—athletes who are largely men of color demonstrates that this power is racialized as much as it is gendered. Fantasy sports, thus, reflect and reinforce associations of Whiteness with power.

Moreover, women's agency—particularly that which is potentially transformative—must be understood within the context of race and class. As typically White, educated, professional women, these women occupy a privileged position that affords them some protection from the extreme and direct sexism women experience in other male- and masculine-dominated spaces as well as opportunities for inclusion and legitimacy. More generally, the ties that players—men and women alike—form and enhance through fantasy sports are generally to similar others, increasing but not diversifying their networks. Instead, the bridges fantasy sports facilitate contribute to homosocial reproduction, failing to disrupt racialized and classed patterns of interaction. Importantly, while fantasy sports participants recognize some instances of gender salience and inequality, they leave these other power dynamics essentially unacknowledged, even though they participate in a context that reifies the status and privileges of White, middle- and upper-class men.

Accordingly, fantasy sports are more than just an inconsequential leisure activity. *Whose Game?* provides an account of how subtle sexism, racism, classism, and heteronormativity—invisible but consequential interactions, dynamics, and structures that perpetuate the dominance of certain groups and identities and the marginalization of others—manifest in fantasy sports. Understandings of men and women as fundamentally different and women as inferior abound here, not only reflecting but also reproducing larger gender beliefs. Underlying assumptions of women's heterosexuality—that they play, for instance, to meet men and ogle male athletes and win only when their boyfriends help them—abound and frame women's experiences in this space. Moreover, interacting almost entirely among similarly positioned men affords an exclusive sphere in which men can and do perform jock statsculinity, shore up resource-rich social capital, and (re)assert their dominance—not just as men but as *White, class-privileged* men. Fantasy sport is a domain in which not only women are often absent but also men who are subordinated, such as poor or working-class and Black and Latino men. That Black and Latino men do not typically play fantasy sports is particularly striking given their high investment in real sports as fans and participants. Fantasy sports, therefore, not only reinscribe binary notions of gender but also status beliefs regarding race, class, and gender and their intersections.

So where do we go from here? We see reasons to be both optimistic about expanded opportunities for women and men, as well as considerable evidence of continued and perhaps enhanced gender, race, and class inequality. Individual women assert their belonging in the space, although largely in ways that frame them as exceptional. They also use fantasy sports to gain entrée into groups and spaces otherwise dominated by men, whether that be a group of men at a party or in the workplace. In both cases, progress is made at the individual level and, to the extent that women's presence changes group dynamics, in interactions. The expansion of legitimate masculine performances indicates further change in gender at the interactional level.

Jock statsculinity means men can gain masculine status by being smart as well as by being physically strong and are free to embrace or reject certain elements of the masculine gender project. But by and large, what we describe in this book is a gender project that mirrors standard hegemonic masculinity in its emphasis on one-upmanship, dominance, competition, rationality, and control. Furthermore, little has changed at the institutional level. An individual woman's acceptance is not synonymous with women's belonging. That the manhood acts on display in fantasy sports allow men to enact masculine dominance through nerdiness does not fundamentally disrupt gendered hierarchies that privilege men and masculinity.

Herein lies the overarching conclusion: at the institutional level, fantasy sports reflect and reinforce the dominance of men and masculinity. Beliefs in gender as a binary and as signifying and reflecting fundamental differences remain unquestioned. Even the most forceful in bucking gender beliefs do not stray from understanding men and women as different and gender as offering two, and only two, options for individual identity. Gender beliefs link men with athletics and success in ways that presume their legitimacy and belonging and question women's. The very definition of fandom—even as it changes into the personalized, competitive fandom available in fantasy sports—is built on a male and masculine model. Real fans know sports and are rational and calculating; emotions and allegiances to athletes do not govern them. Masculinity has broadened to include statistical acumen but not emotionality. The dominant version of masculinity in this space may include more men, but there is little space for women or femininity.

This is not unlike any number of other domains in which innovations meant to (or with the potential to) level the playing field in fact do not. Despite decades of laws and programs designed to address gender inequities in paid labor, occupational sex segregation, the gender wage gap, and workplace discrimination and harassment persist.[2] Title IX has not eliminated systemic inequities in sports—they remain largely segregated; men dominate as athletes, coaches, media commentators, managers, and commissioners; men's sports receive substantially more airtime; and male professional athletes earn staggeringly more than female professional athletes.[3] Tech arenas, too, are largely dominated by men and masculinity, and this is true for both careers and hobbies such as digital gaming.[4]

These seemingly disparate examples have one thing in common: they are all male-dominated and masculine arenas that over time have opened up to women. Inroads toward gender equity can indeed be made through such an approach. However, systematic change does not come from making it more acceptable for women to be like men and to enter spaces dominated by men and masculinity or for some men to be "real men" while veering from some hegemonic masculine practices. Systematic change comes when

institutionalized gender beliefs and structures shift, when the very boundaries between masculinity and femininity blur *because both ways of being are
more inclusive of attributes of the other* and, indeed, when underlying gendered hierarchies that place men and masculinity at the top are dismantled.

While fantasy sports allow for a broadened form of masculine performance and offer belonging for some women (importantly, those who most
closely adhere to the masculine norm), these underlying gender hierarchies remain firmly intact and, what's more, there is evidence of retrenchment. Some men create or at least implicitly condone hostile environments
in leagues or, more commonly, on public message boards, establishing the
space as men's and encouraging women to leave or not join in the first place.
Defining legitimate fandom to exclude newcomers and decrying the lost
"purity" of the hobby—neither of which involve the explicit invocation of
gender—reflect, at their base, a presumed bygone era in which fantasy sports
were the province of "real," longtime fans—also known as men. That the
percentage of fantasy sports players who are women has declined recently
suggests retrenchment may be working. The latest Fantasy Sports Trade Association data reveal that 29 percent of current participants are female; in
2015, this percentage stood at 34 percent after having climbed for several
years.[5] It appears that fantasy sports are not alone in this regard. Another
male-dominated and masculinized arena—digital gaming—seems to be experiencing a similar pattern. The percentage of serious female gamers is on
the decline, a decrease experts attribute at least partly to hostile environments, particularly in the wake of Gamergate.[6]

Modern, widespread fantasy sports emerged specifically at a time when
expectations and experiences of men and women in other realms—namely,
workplaces and families—became more similar.[7] As such, men's firm grasp
on and attraction to fantasy sports is likely partly related to a collective desire
to have and (re-)create spaces that are uniquely theirs amid these other gender revolutions. Modern masculinity, at least for the White, class-privileged
men who predominate in fantasy sports, increasingly requires that men be
committed and successful employees while also being emotionally and physically involved parents and loving, attentive partners. Men use fantasy sports
to retreat to a more traditionally masculinized domain and escape these institutional demands and the feminized spaces and activities they entail. And
certainly, one could view the rise of daily fantasy sports (DFS) as a way for
men to carve out a space *within* fantasy sports that is more decidedly theirs.
Men numerically dominate DFS, and the dynamics that underlie them are
highly masculinized. DFS are fundamentally about winning and making
money; connections—to the game itself and to its participants—are not the
focus. Taken together, all this retrenchment—openly hostile behavior, re-
definitions of fandom to exclude newcomers, lamenting the lost purity of the

hobby, creating and retreating into masculinized spaces—is not surprising. When masculinity is threatened, men avoid femininity and exaggerate their masculinity.[8]

Yet we must not forget that a particular version of masculinity dominates. The ideologies and structures permeating fantasy sports—definitions of fandom; jock statsculinity; the prioritizing of relationships with men and masculine discourse, hobbies, and workplace cultures; the virtual manipulation of largely men of color—all reflect and reinforce the dominance of White, class-privileged men and masculinity. Here, too, we see parallels to real sports in ways that help us understand not only women's underrepresentation but also the relative dearth of racial-ethnic minority participants in fantasy sports. Despite being the highest-paid female athlete in the world—and frequently the only woman among the world's one hundred highest paid athletes—Serena Williams consistently receives criticism that reflects stereotypes of the angry Black woman. Professional football has clearly had its own troubled relationship with the dynamics of race and gender. Confirmed perpetrators of violence against women routinely continue to play after the league or their teams only minimally punish them, while Colin Kaepernick remains sidelined after making political statements about systematic racial violence. The bodies of men of color (and those from lower socioeconomic backgrounds) continue to bear the brunt of fans' desire to be entertained by violent spectacle, sacrificed like "contemporary gladiators" so "that the elite may have a clear sense of where they stand in the pecking order of inter-male dominance."[9] And team names and fan practices in various sports persist at invoking racial slurs and creating misinformation about and commodifying Native Americans. That the largely White men in positions of power in professional sports perpetuate these structures further underscores the institutionalized dominance of particular versions of men and masculinity—precisely those who have the power to ignore violence against women and racial and class inequality. Yet all these dynamics create a climate that marginalizes women and racial-ethnic minorities.

What *Whose Game?* presents is an initial understanding of these and other related dynamics in the context of everyday players in traditional leagues. Surely, there is much more to learn. We have asserted the existence of an institutional culture that marginalizes women and largely excludes participants from nondominant races, ethnicities, and class positions. We are eager to see work that extends this argument by analyzing how nontypical players and those playing alternative traditional fantasy sports experience these dynamics. Understanding how DFS are or are not a response to the interactional and institutional climate we identify here and, importantly, how players experience and interpret their participation in that version of the game will enhance our understanding of fantasy sports as a whole and its place in modern sporting cultures and contemporary American society.

We have presented an in-depth analysis of one significant component of fantasy sports, taking a multifaceted look into a realm that offers some opportunities for change at the individual and interactional levels yet reflects and reinforces larger institutional gender arrangements. Others no doubt will and should take up the mantle of investigating fantasy sports among other groups of participants and in other contexts.

Fantasy sports are one piece of a larger constellation of changes in which networked fandom and gaming are on the rise, people are virtually connected more than ever, distinctions between and relations among men and women are being challenged and reshaped, and the worlds of work, family, and leisure are blurring. Fantasy sports highlight the pervasiveness of ideologies and interactions that associate masculinity with competitiveness and athletic success. They do so even in this arena in which the distinctions between real and virtual sports on the one hand and passive fans and active participants on the other hand are muted; the physiological differences typically used to justify men's dominance are irrelevant; and legitimate masculinity is expanded. So, ultimately, whose game is fantasy sports? The answer is White, class-privileged men.

Appendix

Additional Information on the Data and Method

This is a mixed and multimethod project that includes quantitative data collected via an online survey and qualitative data collected via several methods. This confluence of data provides insight into myriad aspects of fantasy sports from various fantasy sports constituents and contexts. Before any data collection commenced, Lafayette College's Institutional Review Board (IRB) reviewed and approved the project.

Our first set of data comes from an online survey, which the first author (Kissane) launched in October 2012 and closed January 2013. She recruited respondents for the survey primarily by "advertising" the study on fantasy sports–related message boards and websites, on Facebook, and on Twitter. A Philadelphia sports columnist, Rich Hofmann, wrote an article on the study and included a link to the survey, further publicizing it.[1]

All survey respondents were asked about their demographics, social networks, and interest in sports more generally, as well as questions related to masculinity, femininity, and gender ideologies. Fantasy sports players were asked about their motivations for playing and investment in fantasy sports. The majority of the survey questions were close ended, although there were several open-ended questions exploring why respondents play fantasy sports, what they get out of playing, the downsides to playing, and for female players, if and how they felt they are perceived or treated differently in fantasy sports because of their gender.

In all, 453 individuals completed the survey; 396 were self-identified current or former players and 57 were nonplayers. Our survey sample of players is predominantly male (81 percent), White (approximately 95 percent), employed (just under 90 percent), and well-educated (over 75 percent have at least a four-year college degree). In addition, they are rather affluent, with 61 percent reporting having annual household incomes at or over $100,000. Most (70 percent) were between twenty-five and forty-four years old and married at the time of the survey. Nearly all of our survey players (91 percent of the male players and 87 percent of the female players) had participated in fantasy football in the last year. No other sport was played by more than half of the survey sample, and there was only one significant sex difference—49 percent of male players and only 24 percent of the female players played baseball.

While our convenience sample may limit generalizability, it accords with the Fantasy Sports Trade Association (FSTA) demographic information on fantasy sports players nationwide at the time of our data collection. The FSTA reported that the average age of players was thirty-three, 65 percent had a bachelor's degree or higher, and the average player's household income was $92,750. Our sample slightly underrepresents married individuals (61 percent of our sample was married versus 73 percent nationally) and non-Whites (6 percent of our sample versus 12 percent nationally). A lower percentage of fantasy sports players nationwide played fantasy football than did in our sample (72 percent versus 91 percent).

To gain additional and more in-depth information about fantasy sports and players' experiences and views, Kissane conducted semi-structured, qualitative interviews between October 2012 and January 2013 with forty-seven fantasy sports players who had completed the survey. The majority of these (N = 37) occurred over the phone, but three were done by email, five in person, and two via Skype. The phone, Skype, and in-person interviews were tape-recorded and transcribed verbatim[2] and, on average, lasted fifty-seven minutes. These qualitative interviews produced more than one thousand pages of transcripts for analyses.

In the interviews, the respondents discussed their entrée into fantasy sports, their current involvement and experiences in the hobby, and their perceptions of the pros and cons of playing. Kissane also asked the respondents about their thoughts on the popularity of fantasy sports, success and failure in the hobby, their involvement in real sports as participants and fans, their consumption of sports media, and why some groups (e.g., women and low-income individuals) are underrepresented in the hobby.

Thirty interviewees are men and seventeen are women. Mirroring the survey sample, the majority are well educated (87 percent had a bachelor's degree or higher), employed (89 percent), between the ages of twenty-five and forty-four (81 percent), married (70 percent), and White (96 percent). The interview respondents, on average, had played fantasy sports for a little more

FACING PAGE: *All data are presented as N (%). The survey sample data include only those who self-identified as ever playing fantasy sports.

TABLE A.1. DEMOGRAPHIC CHARACTERISTICS OF SURVEY AND INTERVIEW SAMPLES*						
	Survey			Interview		
	All N = 396	Male N = 321	Female N = 74	All N = 47	Men N = 30	Women N = 17
Educational Attainment						
MD, PhD, JD	44 (11.1%)	32 (10.0%)	11 (14.9%)	5 (10.6%)	3 (10.0%)	2 (11.8%)
Master's degree	69 (17.4%)	57 (17.8%)	12 (16.2%)	11 (23.4%)	9 (30.0%)	2 (11.8%)
Bachelor's degree	167 (42.2%)	133 (41.4%)	34 (45.9%)	25 (53.2%)	13 (43.3%)	12 (70.6%)
Some college or associate degree	72 (18.2%)	57 (17.8%)	15 (20.3%)	4 (8.5%)	3 (10.0%)	1 (5.9%)
High school or less	16 (4.0%)	15 (4.7%)	1 (1.4%)	1 (2.1%)	1 (3.3%)	
No response	28 (7.1%)	27 (8.4%)	1 (1.4%)	1 (2.1%)	1 (3.3%)	
Age (years)						
16–24	41 (10.4%)	28 (8.7%)	13 (17.6%)			
25–34	145 (36.6%)	111 (34.6%)	34 (45.9%)	25 (53.2%)	13 (43.3%)	12 (70.6%)
35–44	132 (33.3%)	115 (35.8%)	17 (23.0%)	13 (27.7%)	9 (30%)	4 (23.5%)
45–54	58 (14.6%)	50 (15.6%)	8 (10.8%)	9 (19.1%)	8 (26.7%)	1 (3.3%)
55+	20 (5.1%)	17 (5.3%)	2 (2.7%)			
Employment Status						
Employed for wages	298 (75.3%)	241 (75.1%)	57 (77.0%)	42 (89.4%)	26 (86.7%)	16 (94.1%)
Self-employed	28 (7.1%)	21 (6.5%)	6 (8.1%)			
Student	22 (5.6%)	16 (5.0%)	6 (8.1%)	2 (4.3%)	1 (3.3%)	1 (5.9%)
Not employed	21 (5.3%)	17 (5.3%)	4 (5.4%)	3 (6.4%)	3 (10.0%)	
No response	27 (6.8%)	26 (8.1%)	1 (1.4%)			
Marital Status						
Married	224 (56.6%)	191 (59.5%)	32 (43.2%)	33 (70.2%)	25 (83.3%)	8 (47.1%)
Cohabiting	38 (9.6%)	28 (8.7%)	10 (13.5%)	3 (6.4%)	1 (3.3%)	2 (11.8%)
Single, in relationship	34 (8.6%)	21 (6.5%)	13 (17.6%)	4 (8.5%)	1 (3.3%)	3 (17.6%)
Single, no relationship	55 (13.9%)	43 (13.4%)	12 (16.2%)	5 (10.6%)	2 (6.7%)	3 (17.6%)
Divorced, separated, widowed	19 (4.8%)	13 (4.0%)	6 (8.1%)	2 (4.3%)	1 (3.3%)	1 (5.9%)
No response	26 (6.6%)	25 (7.8%)	1 (1.3%)			
Parental Status						
Children under 18	156 (39.4%)	142 (44.2%)	14 (18.9%)	20 (42.6%)	16 (53.3%)	4 (23.5%)
Children, none under 18	30 (7.6%)	24 (7.5%)	5 (6.8%)	1 (2.1%)	1 (3.3%)	
No children	182 (46.0%)	129 (40.2%)	53 (70.3%)	26 (55.3%)	13 (43.3%)	13 (76.5%)
No response	28 (7.1%)	26 (8.1%)	2 (2.7%)			
Race (self-identified)						
White	372 (93.9%)	301 (93.8%)	70 (94.6%)	45 (95.7%)	29 (96.7%)	16 (94.1%)
Other	22 (5.6%)	18 (5.6%)	4 (5.4%)	2 (4.3%)	1 (3.3%)	1 (5.9%)
No response	2 (0.5%)	2 (0.6%)				
Household Income						
Less than $50,000	37 (9.3%)	25 (7.8%)	12 (16.2%)			
$50,000–$99,999	124 (31.3%)	96 (29.9%)	28 (37.8%)			
$100,000–$149,999	117 (29.5%)	101 (31.5%)	16 (21.6%)			
$150,000+	83 (21.0%)	67 (20.9%)	15 (20.3%)			
No response	35 (8.8%)	32 (10.0%)	3 (4.1%)			

TABLE A.2. SURVEY RESPONDENTS' FANTASY SPORTS BEHAVIOR			
	All	Male	Female
Number of Current Leagues			
1	90 (22.7%)	59 (18.4%)	31 (41.9%)
2	87 (22.0%)	63 (19.6%)	23 (31.1%)
3	71 (17.9%)	64 (19.9%)	7 (9.5%)
4	46 (11.6%)	42 (13.1%)	4 (5.4%)
5	27 (6.8%)	26 (8.1%)	1 (1.4%)
6+	73 (18.4%)	66 (20.6%)	7 (9.5%)
No response	2 (0.5%)	1 (0.3%)	1 (1.4%)
Weekly Hours Spent (excluding watching sports)			
<1	56 (14.1%)	30 (9.3%)	26 (35.1%)
1–3	169 (42.7%)	141 (43.9%)	27 (36.5%)
4–6	98 (24.7%)	86 (26.8%)	12 (16.2%)
7–9	28 (7.1%)	25 (7.8%)	3 (4.1%)
10+	44 (11.1%)	39 (12.1%)	5 (6.8%)
No response	1 (0.3%)		1 (1.4%)
Years Played			
1 or less	20 (5.1%)	7 (2.2%)	13 (14.6%)
2–5	96 (24.2%)	57 (17.8%)	39 (52.7%)
6–10	129 (32.6%)	114 (35.5%)	14 (18.9%)
11–15	86 (21.7%)	80 (24.9%)	6 (8.1%)
16–20	37 (9.3%)	35 (10.9%)	2 (2.7%)
Over 20	28 (7.1%)	28 (8.7%)	
Sports Played			
Football	358 (90.4%)	293 (91.3%)	64 (86.5%)
Baseball	174 (43.9%)	156 (48.6%)	18 (24.3%)
Basketball	93 (23.5%)	76 (23.7%)	17 (23.0%)
Hockey	59 (14.9%)	50 (15.6%)	9 (12.2%)
Other	53 (13.4%)	40 (12.5%)	13 (17.6%)

than ten years; over half (58 percent) currently play in one to three fantasy sports leagues. Almost all (94 percent) had played in at least one fantasy football league, 53 percent in a baseball league, 26 percent in a basketball league, and 11 percent in an ice hockey league.

We classified the interview respondents into four categories of players based on their level of investment in fantasy sports: hard-core, dedicated, casual, and limited. We used four investment-related areas in making these classifications: (1) the number of years participating in fantasy sports, (2) the number of current fantasy sports leagues, (3) the amount of money spent annually on league fees, and (4) the number of hours spent weekly, aside from watching sporting events, on fantasy sports. *Hard-core* players are those who fall on the high end of investment for all four categories or are in the moderate range for one category but high for the others. Hard-core players on the high end for each category have played for more than six years, currently play in four or more leagues, spend more than $120 annually on league fees, and invest 4.5 hours or more weekly (excluding watching sports) on the hobby. *Dedicated* players are generally those in the high or moderate zone for all four investment categories. Dedicated players in the moderate range for all categories have played for 3.5 to 6 years, currently play in two or three leagues, spend $31 to $120 annually, and invest more than one hour through four hours weekly on fantasy sports. *Casual* players typically rated in the low and moderate categories for each of the investment areas. Last, *limited* players are those on the low end in all four investment categories. This means that they have played for three years or less, currently play in one league (or none if they just recently quit), spend $30 or less annually, and invest an hour or less weekly on fantasy sports. We classified the majority of our interview respondents as dedicated (49 percent) or hard-core (30 percent). Notably a higher percentage of men than women are in the hard-core category (37 percent versus 18 percent) and a lower percentage are in the casual category (10 percent versus 24 percent).

Our book also relies on findings from a content analysis of fantasy sports message boards and chat forums and ethnographic observations at the 2015 FSTA summer conference. The message/chat board data involve systematic analysis of posts in an "off topics" forum of a popular fantasy sports site as well as additional analyses of several other fantasy sports message and chat forums Kissane frequents.

The ethnographic data include observations and informal conversations at the June 2015 FSTA summer conference. The FSTA conference is a three-day event where power players in the industry and those seeking to create and expand their fantasy sports–related businesses hobnob with one another, pitch their ideas, and gain information on the current state of the industry. Both authors attended the conference events and presentations and took extensive field notes afterward, which comprise our data for this part of the study.

We administered the survey through Qualtrics. Winslow downloaded the quantitative survey data as an Excel file and converted it for analysis in SAS using Stat/Transfer. For attitudinal measures using Likert response scales, Winslow reverse-coded some measures such that higher scores indicated higher agreement or a greater frequency for all measures. She utilized prior research on fantasy sports to replicate existing multi-item scale measures (e.g., for schwabism and mavenism[3]) and used Cronbach's alpha to measure internal consistency for any additional scale measures created from

TABLE A.3. INTERVIEW RESPONDENTS' FANTASY SPORTS BEHAVIOR			
	All	Men	Women
Number of Current Leagues			
0	1 (2.1%)	1 (3.3%)	
1	14 (29.8%)	6 (20.0%)	8 (47.1%)
2	6 (12.8%)	3 (10.0%)	3 (17.6%)
3	7 (14.9%)	5 (16.7%)	2 (11.8%)
4	7 (14.9%)	6 (20.0%)	1 (5.9%)
5	5 (10.6%)	4 (13.3%)	1 (5.9%)
6+	7 (14.9%)	5 (16.7%)	2 (11.8%)
Weekly Hours Spent (excluding watching sports)			
Mean	3.86	4.27	3.14
Median	3	3.25	2.75
Years Played			
Mean	10.19	12.42	6.26
Median	8.5	12.5	5
Sports Played			
Football	44 (93.6%)	29 (96.7%)	15 (88.2%)
Baseball	25 (53.2%)	19 (63.3%)	6 (35.3%)
Basketball	12 (25.5%)	8 (26.7%)	4 (23.5%)
Hockey	5 (10.6%)	3 (10.0%)	2 (11.8%)
Other	13 (27.6%)	10 (33.3%)	3 (17.6%)
Player Category			
Limited	3 (6.4%)	1 (3.3%)	2 (11.8%)
Casual	7 (14.9%)	3 (10.0%)	4 (23.5%)
Dedicated	23 (48.9%)	15 (50.0%)	8 (47.1%)
Hard-Core	14 (29.8%)	11 (36.7%)	3 (17.6%)

survey items, using .8 as a threshold for good reliability. Following standard procedures in SAS, bivariate and cross-tabulation analyses utilized all respondents with valid data on the measures under consideration; regression analyses employed listwise deletion.

Kissane imported the answers to the open-ended survey questions, the interview transcripts, and message/chat forum data into NVivo10, a qualitative data analysis software that allows for an inductive approach characteristic of qualitative analyses. She then organized the data into inductively derived conceptual categories (or nodes), subcoding into smaller nodes as she progressed with the analyses and looking for patterns within and across categories and cases. Thus, the qualitative findings that we primarily report in this book emerge from the coding process itself, rather than from pre-determined hypotheses.

In reflecting on the data, an important consideration is the authors' positionality. As White, highly educated professionals, both share a common set of cultural competencies with the study participants. As such, the framework within which many players situate their participation—from the ability to combine work and leisure to their comfort with asserting power—is familiar to the authors. The authors are thus insiders in this regard.

Kissane is an insider in an additional way—she has played fantasy sports for more than ten years. Her position is particularly important given that she collected most of the data, including conducting all interviews. These insider dynamics played out such that she was able to access populations to interview and survey and, for the interview participants in particular, to gain rapport with her respondents. She and the participants shared a common language, and her knowledge of the hobby provided her at least a modicum of legitimacy and status.

Winslow's position provides a counterpoint to Kissane's insider status. As a nonplayer, her exposure to and experiences with fantasy sports come primarily from friends and partners who play, as well as from her knowledge of academic research on the topic. She has not experienced the interactional dynamics of fantasy sports participation firsthand and thus may have been more attuned to exchanges that are normative within fantasy sports subcultures but out of the ordinary for those who do not play. She often felt that this, combined with her academic background as a gender scholar, made her particularly attuned to the sexist (and racist, classist, and heterocentric) assumptions underlying the organizational structure and participant interactions in fantasy sports. Winslow's position as a nonplayer also helped ensure that we adequately clarified and made accessible our arguments to those not immersed in this world.

It is clear that being women doing this research presented certain challenges.[4] Kissane's position as a woman may have discouraged some types of individuals from participating in the study and framed how some responded to some questions. For instance, in recruiting the survey sample on fantasy sports message boards, users questioned Kissane's expertise and motives for conducting the research. Some interview respondents did likewise, frequently asking why she was doing the study and whether she was out to attack fantasy sports. She was often met with skepticism and surprise from men when she responded that she is an avid fantasy sports player and sports junkie who wanted to learn more about the hobby. Nonetheless, respondents who assumed she was trying to paint a negative portrait of fantasy sports and their players may have answered questions from a defensive stance. Others likely were hesitant to answer questions in socially undesirable ways (e.g., by offering sexist views) or to admit engaging in embarrassing behaviors to avoid being viewed unfavorably.

The authors' position as women, however, also proved beneficial in some ways. At the FSTA conference, conference goers sought us out because we stood out as women. In the interviews, women respondents likely felt more comfortable talking about their experiences with a woman who plays than they would have with a man. And we were sometimes able to intimately feel and relate to the emotions and experiences of the women to whom we spoke, thus giving us a connected sense of their worlds, which was no doubt heightened by our shared race and class statuses. For example, we acutely felt our visibility as women at the FSTA summer conference and were angered when we read comments on the public fantasy sports message boards that disparaged women. Here, Winslow's status as a lesbian woman likely further shapes her particular interpretations. She was keenly aware that stereotypes of women's attraction to players hinge on their presumed heterosexuality and, as a married parent, recognized that men's ability to dismiss family obligations reflected the intersection of gender and heterosexuality. Moreover, a key aspect of women's narratives is that they feel that they have to prove themselves to men in their leagues—to demonstrate their competence and to repeatedly do so. In rereading the interview transcripts, Kissane noticed that she was interjecting specific facts about sports, athletes, and fantasy sports throughout her interviews with men, clearly, but not consciously, trying to prove that she knew what she was talking about in terms of sports and fantasy sports in particular. Thus, even as a researcher in this space, she was reacting to the larger forces we detail in this book, trying to stake out legitimacy in this space.

Accordingly, as we analyzed our data, we were cognizant of the issues we detail above and continually asked ourselves, and each other, how our positionality might be affecting what we saw, argued, failed to explain adequately, and ignored. Kissane's rapport with the interview respondents, in part as related to her insider status as a White, educated, affluent fantasy sports participant, and her decades of experience as a qualitative researcher collecting data on sensitive and uncomfortable subjects help to mitigate the impact of respondents' reactions to her being a woman. Winslow's status as a nonplayer added the lens of an outsider to our analyses, although her class and race make her decidedly an insider in other ways. It is thus possible that we are underreporting the negative aspects—in particular, the amount of misogyny—in fantasy sports. Having multiple sources of data to cross-check findings provide additional confidence in the results we report in this book. Such self-interrogation and awareness are hallmarks of good social science research.

Notes

CHAPTER 1

1. A pseudonym for another team in the fantasy football league in which the author and her friend play.

2. All historical information on fantasy sports is based on material in Billings and Ruihley 2013a. See their book for additional details.

3. Throughout this book, we use the phrase *real sports* to refer to organized or casual competitive, physical activity that excludes digital gaming such as e-Sports. We do so only for short-hand and not as a commentary on the authenticity or relative ranking of sports.

4. FSTA n.d.(a).

5. FSTA 2012.

6. Ibid.

7. The FSTA announced in January 2019 that the organization was changing its name to the Fantasy Sports & Gaming Association (FSGA), effective spring 2019. We use the organization's original name throughout the book, as this is the name they used when we collected data and literature from the organization.

8. FSTA 2015.

9. FSTA n.d.(a).

10. Drayer and Dwyer 2013.

11. Sports management and leadership scholars have conducted much of this research, publishing results in sports marketing and management journals. Noted scholars include Brendan Dwyer (sport leadership, Virginia Commonwealth University), Joris Drayer (sport and recreation management, Temple University), Brody Ruihley (sports administration, University of Cincinnati), and Andrew Billings (sports communication, University of Alabama).

12. Billings and Ruihley 2013a, 2013b; Lee, Seo, and Green 2013; Ruihley and Billings 2013.

13. Billings and Ruihley 2013a; Drayer et al. 2010; Dwyer and LeCrom 2012.

14. Billings and Ruihley 2013a.

15. Weiner and Dwyer 2017.

16. Ibid.

17. Dwyer and Weiner 2017.

18. FSTA n.d.(b).

19. FSTA n.d.(a).

20. FSTA n.d.(c).

21. FSTA n.d.(a).

22. Perhaps further indicating a link to gambling, the FSTA (2018) reports that 89 percent of fantasy sports players support legalization of sports betting and 79 percent of participants who do not presently bet on sports will likely do so once it is legalized. Dwyer, Shapiro, and Drayer (2018) conclude that the risk of problematic gambling among DFS players is similar to those engaging in online gambling activities, such as online poker, horserace betting, and sports betting.

23. Kelley and Carchia 2013.

24. Reporting of Don Sabo's research in Kelley and Carchia 2013.

25. Jones 2015.

26. Van Riper 2011.

27. Title IX prohibits discrimination on the basis of sex in federally funded educational programs and activities, including athletics.

28. Kelley and Carchia 2013.

29. Cooky, Messner, and Hextrum 2013.

30. FSTA n.d.(a).

31. For summaries of both pop psychology views on this as well as findings from academic research, see Connell 2009 and Crawley, Foley, and Shehan 2008.

32. Lorber 1993.

33. Sapolsky 1997.

34. Connell 2009, 53.

35. See, for example, Butler 1990; Lorber 1993; West and Zimmerman 1987.

36. In this book, we reserve the terms male, female, and sex for the following situations: (1) when discussing biological or sex-based distinctions; (2) when referring exclusively to the results of surveys, including our own, in which respondents were asked to select their sex category; and (3) when citing the work of others who specifically employ those terms or when a sex-based term is conventionally used in the literature on a given topic (e.g., male-dominated occupations). Because the dynamics we focus on are social and cultural, we utilize gender terminology—man, woman, masculinity, femininity—in all other instances. This includes employing man/men and woman/women as adjectives, as is common among feminist and gender scholars.

37. Connell 1987; Connell and Messerschmidt 2005.

38. Connell and Messerschmidt 2005.

39. Pascoe and Bridges 2016.

40. Bridges and Pascoe 2014, 246.

41. Messerschmidt 2016; West and Zimmerman 1987.

42. Messerschmidt 2016.

43. Ezzell 2016, 192.

44. Ridgeway 2011.

45. Correll, Benard, and Paik 2007.
46. McDonagh and Pappano 2008; Messner 2009.
47. Camporesi 2017.
48. Connell 1987; Crawley, Foley, and Shehan 2008.
49. Crawley, Foley, and Shehan 2008.
50. Messner 1990b.
51. Crawley, Foley, and Shehan 2008.
52. Ibid., 134.
53. DiSalvo 2016; Kocurek 2015.
54. Messner 1990a.
55. Connell 1987; Messner 2014.
56. Farrell, Fink, and Fields 2011, 196.
57. Howie and Campbell 2015; Messner 1987.
58. Messner 1987.
59. Pfister, Lenneis, and Mintert 2013, 862.
60. For an example, see Olive, McCuaig, and Phillips's (2013) research on surfers.
61. See, for example, Laurendeau and Sharara (2008) on snowboarders, Wachs (2005) on women playing in co-ed softball leagues, and Messner (2009) on youth coaches.
62. Cooky, Messner, and Hextrum 2013; Heywood and Dworkin 2003; Kian, Vincent, and Mondello 2008; Kian, Bernstein, and McGuire 2013.
63. Cooky, Dycus, and Dworkin 2013; Cooky et al. 2010.
64. Paaßen, Morgenroth, and Stratemeyer 2017.
65. Gray, Buyukozturk, and Hill 2017.
66. Gamergate refers to a widespread harassment campaign targeting both specific women and the position and status of women, feminism, and progressivism in digital game culture.
67. Gray, Buyukozturk, and Hill 2017.
68. Esmonde, Cooky, and Andrews 2015, 41. See also Toffoletti 2017.
69. Jones 2008.
70. Esmonde, Cooky, and Andrews 2015; Jones 2008; Klugman 2012; Pope and Williams 2011.
71. Farrell, Fink, and Fields 2011, 195.
72. Farrell, Fink, and Fields 2011.
73. Jones 2008; Esmonde, Cooky, and Andrews 2015; Pope 2013.
74. Laurendeau and Sharara 2008.
75. Heywood and Dworkin 2003.
76. Carlson 2010.
77. Heywood and Dworkin 2003.
78. Messner 2009.
79. Ruihley and Billings 2013.
80. Ibid.
81. Ibid.
82. Davis and Duncan 2006, 251.
83. Davis and Duncan 2006.
84. Howie and Campbell 2013, 236.
85. Crawley, Foley, and Shehan 2008; Messner 2009.
86. Crenshaw 1989.

87. Ibid., 140.

88. Coltrane and Messineo 2000.

89. Bridges and Pascoe 2014.

90. Drayer and Dwyer 2013.

91. Kimmel 2014.

CHAPTER 2

1. We use participant-selected pseudonyms when quoting interview respondents. Quotations not associated with pseudonyms are from survey respondents. All quotations from respondents, unless otherwise specified, are from those who identified as having played fantasy sports.

2. Keeper leagues allow managers to retain a small and limited number of players on their team ("keepers") each year before the draft.

3. Rowe 2014.

4. Gantz and Lewis 2014.

5. Ibid.

6. Ibid.; Tussey 2018.

7. Rowe 2014.

8. Gantz and Lewis 2014, 763.

9. Gantz and Lewis 2014; Rowe 2014; Tussey 2018.

10. Drayer et al. 2010; Karg and McDonald 2011.

11. Drayer et al. 2010, 134; see also Karg and McDonald 2011.

12. DelVecchio 2011.

13. Spyridakos 2011.

14. Dwyer 2011.

15. Dwyer and LeCrom 2012.

16. DelVecchio 2011.

17. Halverson and Halverson 2008; Spyridakos 2011.

18. Halverson and Halverson 2008.

19. FSTA n.d.(b).

20. Drayer et al. 2010; see also Dwyer and LeCrom 2012.

21. Yuksel et al. 2017.

22. Halverson and Halverson 2008.

23. Yuksel et al. 2017, 202.

24. Halverson and Halverson 2008, 292.

25. Dwyer and LeCrom 2012.

26. Halverson and Halverson 2008.

27. Cialdini et al. 1976.

28. Snyder, Lassegard, and Ford 1986.

29. Dwyer, Achen, and Lupinek 2016.

30. Yuksel et al. 2017.

31. Dwyer et al. 2016, 160.

32. Markovits and Albertson 2012.

33. Toffoletti 2017, 23.

34. Markovits and Albertson 2012.

35. Pope 2013; Toffoletti 2017.

36. Markovits and Albertson 2012, 235–236.
37. Markovits and Albertson 2012.
38. Toffoletti 2017.
39. Esmonde, Cooky, and Andrews 2015.
40. Pope and Williams 2011.
41. Toffoletti 2017.
42. Markovits and Albertson 2012.
43. Toffoletti 2017.
44. Esmonde, Cooky, and Andrews 2015.
45. Leonard 2003.
46. Ibid., 6.
47. Ibid.
48. Oates 2009, 31.
49. See Stabile 2006 for original usage.
50. Davis and Duncan 2006, 261.
51. Oates 2009.
52. Engber 2017.
53. Hill 2010, 3.
54. Throughout the book, we distinguish interview respondents by their current investment in fantasy sports (i.e., the number of leagues in which they play and time and money they spend on them) and the duration of their participation (i.e., number of years they have played). Accordingly, we categorize players, in descending order of investment and length of participation, as "hard-core," "dedicated," "casual," or "limited" players. See the Appendix for additional coding details.
55. Yuksel et al. 2017.
56. Our remaining respondents claim luck is a bigger factor or that outcomes are 50 percent luck and 50 percent within one's control.
57. Unless otherwise specified, any mention in this book of hours the respondents invest in fantasy sport *excludes* watching live sporting events.
58. Wachs 2005.
59. About three-quarters of the women we interviewed indicate letting assessments of the character of athletes affect their roster decisions (at least somewhat, sometimes) compared to slightly less than half of the men interviewed. Women who take such factors into account also do so more extensively. The quantitative survey data also show sex differences in this regard. Female participants are more likely to consider whether the athlete is a good person, and male participants are more likely to indicate that those drafting based on team loyalty or nonperformance factors are "suckers."
60. Participants are no more or less likely to elevate or denigrate athletes of particular racial-ethnic groups. Note that our data were collected before recent controversies over kneeling during the national anthem to protest racial injustices.
61. Connell 1987.
62. Our FSTA conference fieldwork revealed that the upper ranks of the fantasy sports industry are almost exclusively men. Moreover, more than 80 percent of the current members of the FSTA board of directors (and nearly 90 percent of voting members) are men.
63. Toffoletti 2017.
64. For an exception of a fantasy sports expert explicitly discussing violence against women as something worthy of taking into account when drafting, see Melissa

Jacob's "Do Not Draft: Fantasy Players to Avoid for a Family-Friendly Roster," created at the request of fantasy football players on social media. Notably, Jacobs herself drafted Joe Mixon, who punched and knocked out a woman while a college student, despite being "somewhat queasy" about it. She explains, "My approach to fantasy is admittedly narrow-minded. Compartmentalize the toxicity and win" (Jacobs 2017).

65. Burt 1980.

66. For example, Brock Turner, a White swimmer at Stanford, received a lenient sentence for what is widely regarded as a horrific sexual assault. The judge explained that "a prison sentence would have a severe impact on him" (Fantz 2016).

67. Luther 2016.

68. This is across both the interviews and survey.

69. Others have similarly found that women underestimate and are less confident in their abilities in math and science and, in the real sports world, in coaching—even when they have demonstrated that they are quite knowledgeable, skilled, and experienced in these areas. See, for example, Correll (2001) and Messner (2009).

70. Our survey indicates that female participants have played fantasy sports for fewer years than their male counterparts. Insofar as our data indicate participants become more focused on fantasy sports fandom over traditional fandom the longer they are involved, it is possible that women may look more like men over time in this regard.

71. One presenter noted that the biggest topic at his network's weekly sales meetings is fantasy sports and that they are "running out of ideas" to meet the demand for fantasy segments.

72. Bonesteel 2017.

CHAPTER 3

1. Schrock and Schwalbe 2009.

2. Schrock and Schwalbe 2009, 284.

3. Jones 2008.

4. See Kimmel 2005 and Messner 1990b for documentation of the arguments that we present in the following paragraphs. See also Ring 2009.

5. Ring 2009.

6. Ibid., 382.

7. Kocurek 2015.

8. See Kocurek's (2015) examination into arcade gaming and how it was gendered.

9. Kocurek 2015.

10. Ibid.

11. Ibid., 191.

12. Paaßen, Morgenroth, and Stratemeyer (2017) note that the popularity of digital gaming is eroding the stereotype of the gamer as a "nerd."

13. Almog and Kaplan 2017, 30. See also DiSalvo 2016.

14. Almog and Kaplan 2017.

15. Ibid., 30.

16. Green and Van Oort 2013, 713.

17. Crawley, Foley, and Shehan 2008.

18. Halverson and Halverson 2008.

19. Crawford 2005.

20. Pascoe 2003; Howie and Campbell 2013.

21. Davis and Duncan 2006; Eitzen 1996; Friedman 2013; Gottzén and Kremer-Sadlik 2012.

22. Women also mention the importance of winning, as we discuss in Chapter 4. However, what is distinct about men's discussion of winning is that it is a central lens through which they think about fantasy sports, their place within it, and their status among other men.

23. Davis and Duncan 2006, 252.

24. Of our survey respondents, 48 percent report playing in leagues in which the other managers are "all" or "mostly" their friends, and 38 percent report playing in leagues split between friends and acquaintances or strangers.

25. DiSalvo 2016.

26. Rainey 2012. Trash talk in real sports often involves "getting ugly" (swearing at opponents or calling them names) and disparaging the athletic skill or ability of the opposing player (Rainey 2012; Rainey and Granito 2010).

27. Cote 2017. Some male digital gamers see trash talk as too aggressive, and therefore, some contexts involve little of it (DiSalvo 2016).

28. For additional evidence of trash talk's importance in fantasy sports for men, see Howie and Campbell 2013, 2015.

29. If men were actively participating in or condoning misogynistic and homophobic smack talk, they might be uncomfortable revealing it to Kissane, a woman. Bedric alludes to this idea when he claimed, "There is a lot of smack talk . . . poking fun at each other, but I am trying to think of specific examples that I would be comfortable saying [to you]. Unfortunately, I am not the dirty one in the group [*laughs awkwardly*]."

30. Cote 2017; Gray 2012.

31. Gray 2012.

32. Howie and Campbell (2013) in their analysis of fantasy sports team and league names (in a nonanonymous league setting) find that both are reflective of hegemonic masculinity in that they often are misogynistic and heteronormative (e.g., many focus on female body parts and heterosexual sex) and/or reference popular culture (e.g., film characters and titles) that are "manly" (i.e., that focus on male power and dominance over others). Interestingly, they also find that in trash talking, men often glorified the male body, often in ways that included joking about sexuality. They argue that fantasy sports are one of the few arenas where men can openly admire the male bodies of other men without having their sexuality called into question.

33. DiSalvo 2016, 111.

34. Ruihley and Billings 2013.

35. Men who play sports-related digital games are also somewhat removed from the nerd stereotype associated with digital gaming as a whole. Scholars find that interest in digital sports games leads to greater engagement with real sports and vice versa (Crawford 2005; Crawford and Gosling 2005).

36. Pascoe 2003.

37. Overwhelmingly, those in positions of power in professional sports are White men. In 2017, for example, 75 percent of NFL head coaches, 100 percent of CEO/presidents, 90 percent of vice presidents, and 81 percent of general managers/directors of player personnel were White (Lapchick 2017).

38. Brooks 2008; Sage and Eitzen 2015.

39. Kimmel 2008, 73.

40. Ibid.

41. Bench et al. 2015.

42. Messner 1990a.

43. Kimmel 2008.

44. Martin et al. 2015.

45. As quoted in Kimmel 2008, 135.

46. Townsend 2002.

47. Gerson 2010.

48. Ibid., 160.

49. Bianchi et al. 2012.

50. Nelson 1994, 7 and 55.

51. Burrill 2008 as summarized in DiSalvo 2016.

52. For an equivalent experience and argument within a fantasy sports–like digital game, see Crawford 2006.

53. Crocket 2013.

54. Kanter 1977b.

55. Hynes and Cook 2013.

56. DiSalvo 2016.

57. Pope 2013; Jones 2008; Esmonde, Cooky, and Andrews 2015.

58. Markovits and Albertson 2012.

59. Kimmel 2008, 129 and 130, respectively.

CHAPTER 4

1. Kanter 1977b.

2. In our survey, 69 percent of the female players participate in leagues in which the other managers are all or mostly men; 19 percent play in leagues that are split in terms of gender composition; and 11 percent play in leagues with only women. The remainder do not know the gender of their fellow players. Male players are even more likely to be playing in leagues with all- or mostly men, with 94 percent indicating this on the survey. Only 2 percent of male players are in leagues split in terms of gender composition (the remainder responded in the survey that they do not know the gender breakdown of the league).

3. We present data, concepts, and arguments in this chapter that also appear in Kissane and Winslow 2016b.

4. Hays 1994.

5. We are aware of no national data providing information on fantasy sports participants' sexuality or gender identity. Our interview data contain this information.

6. Messner 2009.

7. Kanter 1977b.

8. Williams 1992.

9. Wingfield 2009.

10. Ridgeway 2009.

11. Ibid., 151.

12. Esmonde, Cooky, and Andrews 2015; Jones 2008; Markovits and Albertson 2012; Messner 2009; Pope 2013; Pope and Williams 2011.

13. Messner 2009.

14. Martin et al. 2015.

15. Hays 1994.

16. Ibid., 64.

17. Ibid.

18. Beavis and Charles 2007.

19. Ibid.

20. Gray 2012.

21. Cote 2017.

22. Ibid., 137.

23. See, for instance, Esmonde, Cooky, and Andrews 2015; Ezzell 2009; Jones 2008; Pope 2013; Toffoletti 2017.

24. Jones 2008; Pope 2013; Toffoletti 2017.

25. Laurendeau and Sharara 2008.

26. Wachs 2005.

27. See, for instance, George 2005.

28. See Laurendeau and Sharara (2008) for evidence of this regarding snowboarders; see Beavis and Charles (2007) and Cote (2017) for examples in digital gaming.

29. See, for instance, Cote 2017, 147.

30. Jones 2008; Toffoletti 2017.

31. Toffoletti 2017, 41.

32. Ibid.

33. McDonagh and Pappano 2008.

34. Our respondents, particularly the men, indicated some discomfort in discussing women's underrepresentation in fantasy sports, often prefacing their remarks with "I'm not sexist" or "not to be chauvinist" or phrasing their responses as questions or as if they were jokes. As an example, Ted, when suggesting that gossiping was a hobby for women, claimed, "I was going to say something that was very sexist, but I won't say it. . . . I was going to say, if there was a way, like if there was a fantasy football thing where you could talk behind other players' backs, maybe that would be it [a way to get women involved in fantasy sports]. All right, I'm kidding. I know that's a girly thing."

35. Kimmel 2008, 73.

36. Dunning 1986; Hargreaves 1994.

37. See Kissane 2018 and the Appendix for more details on the researchers' insider/outsider status.

38. Those few women who play in leagues with strangers expressed that other managers by default assumed they are men. One female player in this circumstance, for instance, wrote, "I kept getting called man, dude, etc., and it took them half the season to realize I was a 'chick.'" This may be partly why the one female survey participant who did not know the gender composition of her league reported that she was not treated differently because she was a woman—it is likely that her competitors did not know she was a woman and thus assumed she was a man.

39. We do not know how many women had registered for the conference, but at the start of the first full day, we counted 7 women in a sea of about 240 men—the vast majority of whom were also White. We were not the only ones to take notice. In talking with one of the few other women at the conference, she quickly (and without our prompting) noted, "There are no women at the conference."

40. On the first morning, for instance, this woman, wearing a V-neck T-shirt with black skinny pants and high pumps, was seated a few rows in front of us and left the room after the introductory presentations. Her departure was duly noted, as five sets of men's eyes (those seated between us and her) followed her movements intently, and some looked knowingly at each other for acknowledgment of the attractive woman they just observed.

41. Glick and Fiske 1996, 491.

42. Williams and Dempsey 2014, 23.

43. Lorber 1993, 578.

44. Wachs 2005.

45. Markovits and Albertson 2012, 209.

46. Blinde and Taub 1992.

47. Williams and Dempsey 2014, 181.

48. Ezzell 2009, 116.

49. Ezzell 2009.

50. Toffoletti 2017.

51. Carlson 2010; Pfister, Lenneis, and Mintert 2013.

52. Collins 2000.

53. See, for example, Associated Press 2018; Grant 2018.

54. Williams and Dempsey 2014, 41.

55. Gray 2012.

CHAPTER 5

1. We present data, concepts, and arguments in this chapter that also appear in Kissane and Winslow 2016a.

2. Walker 1995.

3. Putnam 2000.

4. For more definitions, see Lin (1999, 35), Putnam (1995, 67), and Bourdieu (1986, 248).

5. Bui and Miller 2015; Ladinsky 1967.

6. Bui and Miller 2015.

7. Jacobs and Gerson 2004.

8. Oldenburg 1999.

9. See Steinkuehler and Williams (2006) for more on this argument.

10. Steinkuehler and Williams 2006.

11. Some virtual, digital gaming worlds may also connect people who already know one another. For instance, Nick Yee's research not only counters notions that MMO players are "solitary hermits" but also that they play with only strangers. He finds that about 80 percent of MMO players play with someone they know in real life, with 25 percent playing with a real-life romantic partner (though, female players are much more likely to be playing with a romantic partner than male players). See Yee n.d.

12. McPherson and Smith-Lovin 1982.

13. Briggs 1998; Putnam 2000; Warren, Thompson, and Saegert 2001.

14. Kim and Rhee 2010, 481.

15. Lin 1999.

16. Schafer and Vargas 2016, 1797.

17. Connell 1987; Messner 2014.

18. Messner 1987.

19. Walker 1994.

20. Domhoff 2002.

21. See, for instance, Kanter 1977a and Elliott and Smith 2004.

22. See Steinkuehler and Williams (2006) for details on the characteristics of third places and how they apply to MMOs, another type of virtual setting and means of interaction.

23. Lenhart et al. 2015; Steinkuehler and Williams 2006.

24. For more on the strength of weak ties, see Granovetter 1973.

25. In the survey, of those who knew the race of the other members of their leagues, 86 percent said that the other league managers are mostly or entirely members of their same racial group. Of those who knew the economic class of the other league members, 59 percent claim to be playing in leagues where the majority or all of the other managers are of their same economic class as the respondent (38 percent claimed that their leagues are "split among different economic classes"). These patterns are similar for male and female players.

26. Drayer and Dwyer 2013; Duggan 2015.

27. A large body of research demonstrates that Whites and those of high socioeconomic status have access to more advantageous social capital than other groups. See Horvat, Weininger, and Lareau 2003; MacLeod 2009; O'Brien 2012; Shapiro 2005.

28. In the survey, two-thirds of male respondents indicated that fantasy sports help them bond with their friends "most of the time" or "always" compared to less than half of female respondents (who were more likely to say that it "sometimes" helped them bond with friends).

29. Of those who play multiplayer games, about half of their time is spent playing with others in person (Entertainment Software Association 2018). Furthermore, about 42 percent of all teen boys ages thirteen to seventeen play video games in person with friends on a daily, near-daily, or weekly basis (Lenhart et al. 2015).

30. Walker 1994.

31. Since the importance of both of these interactional practices is higher among men, this explains the overall differences we found in the survey data between male and female players in bonding with friends through fantasy sports. In simpler terms, male players' greater likelihood of reporting bonding with friends through fantasy sports appears to hinge on exchanging competitive discourse during league play.

32. Findings based on our analyses of the survey data.

33. Bianchi 2000; Sayer 2005.

34. Howie and Campbell 2015.

35. Rosenthal 1985.

36. DeVault 1991, 91.

37. Gottzén and Kremer-Sadlik 2012; Kay 2006, 2009; Messner 2009.

38. Townsend 2002.

39. Messner 2009.

40. These represent differences in the interview sample of players.

41. Markovits and Albertson 2012.

42. Farrell, Fink, and Fields 2011, 199.

43. Briggs 1998.

44. These findings are based off our survey data.

45. Bourdieu 1977, 1986.

46. Williams and Dempsey 2014, 38.

47. Connell 1987; Messner 2014.

48. Marsden 1987; McPherson, Smith-Lovin, and Brashears 2006.

49. Farrell, Fink, and Fields 2011, 196.

50. Howie and Campbell 2015; Messner 1987, 2014.

CHAPTER 6

1. Billings and Ruihley 2013a.

2. Billings and Ruihley 2013b.

3. Perrin 2017.

4. FSTA n.d.(a).

5. Jacobs and Gerson 2004.

6. Blair-Loy 2003; Gregg 2011; Schor 1991.

7. Gregg 2011.

8. Tussey 2013, 38.

9. Ibid., 49.

10. Ibid., 41.

11. Dawson 2007, 233 as cited in Tussey 2013, 39.

12. Workers can find numerous articles online with strategies for slacking off during the workday without garnering the attention of their bosses (e.g., Strohmeyer 2014). Thus, workers can media snack on how to successfully snack.

13. Acker 1990; Risman 2004.

14. England 2010; Hochschild 1989.

15. Sayer 2016.

16. Ibid.

17. Billings and Ruihley 2013a.

18. West and Zimmerman 1987.

19. Townsend 2002.

20. Engber 2017.

21. Cialdini et al. 1976; Snyder, Lassegard, and Ford 1986.

22. Dwyer, Achen, and Lupinek 2016.

23. See, for instance, Dwyer and Weiner 2017 and Dwyer and LeCrom 2012.

24. Dwyer and Weiner 2017.

25. Dwyer, Achen, and Lupinek 2016.

26. Ibid.; Dwyer and LeCrom 2012.

27. Dwyer and Weiner 2017 also posit this relationship.

28. Walker 1995.

29. Festinger 1957.

30. Connell 1987.

31. Kanter 1977b.

32. Hyde 2014.

33. Steele and Aronson 1995.

34. Ibid.; Stone, Chalabaev, and Harrison 2012.

35. Stone, Chalabaev, and Harrison 2012.

36. Some results and arguments presented in this chapter also appear in Kissane and Winslow 2016a.

37. See Appendix Tables A.2 and A.3 for complete information on participants' time investments.

38. Sayer 2016.

39. Bourdieu 1986.

40. McIntosh 1988.

41. The lack of gender difference here may relate to the demographics of our players. Our sample of women are less likely to be married and/or have children than are the men, suggesting women with the greatest household responsibilities are forgoing fantasy sports participation entirely, perhaps in part because of the time binds they face.

42. Howie and Campbell (2015) also find in their research on a fantasy NBA league in Australia that league members engage in fantasy sports while at work.

43. Challenger, Gray, and Christmas 2015. Others (see Tussey 2018 for literature) argue that the time spent on fantasy sports and other media may not hurt productivity since such breaks may allow workers to be more productive during the workday.

44. Matos and Galinsky 2011.

45. Kirschenman and Neckerman 1991.

46. See Tussey 2018 for literature.

47. Acker 1990.

48. Correll, Benard, and Paik 2007.

49. Our survey data indicate that male players are significantly more likely to indicate that fantasy sports keep them awake at night.

50. Dwyer and Weiner 2017.

51. Festinger 1957.

52. Men are twice as likely as women to identity as a downside of fantasy sports their negative effects on social ties and interactions.

53. Relationship tension is a scale measure created from two survey items: "Fantasy sports create tension in my relationship with my spouse or partner" and "My family complains that I spend too much time on fantasy sports." More than two-thirds of our female players report that fantasy sports *never* create tensions in their relationships with their spouse or partner compared to a little less than half of male players.

54. See DiSalvo's (2016) discussion of Seidler (2003).

CHAPTER 7

1. This narrative focuses on Kissane's involvement in fantasy sports. See the Appendix for more on Winslow's positionality.

2. Correll, Benard, and Paik 2007; England 2010.

3. Cooky, Messner, and Hextrum 2013; Hargreaves 1994; McDonagh and Pappano 2008.

4. Crawford and Gosling 2005; National Center for Women in Information Technology n.d.; Paaßen, Morgenroth, and Stratemeyer 2017.

5. FSTA 2015, n.d.(a).

6. Lofgren 2017.

7. Gerson 2010.

8. Cheryan et al. 2015; Nelson 1994.

9. Messner 1990b, 214.

APPENDIX

1. Hofmann 2012.

2. Throughout the book, when quoting respondents directly, we edited their words for readability, removing filler words and phrases such as *um, you know,* and *like* and revising punctuation and capitalization in written survey responses.

3. Ruihley and Billings 2013.

4. For more in-depth detail on the advantages and disadvantages of Kissane's insider-outsider status and specific examples, see Kissane 2018.

References

Acker, Joan. 1990. "Hierarchies, Jobs, Bodies: A Theory of Gendered Organizations." *Gender & Society* 4:139–158.

Almog, Ran, and Danny Kaplan. 2017. "The Nerd and His Discontent: The Seduction Community and the Logic of the Game as a Geeky Solution to the Challenges of Young Masculinity." *Men and Masculinities* 20 (1): 27–48.

Associated Press. 2018. "Serena's Treatment Resonates among Black Women." *Sport24*, September 11. Accessed January 18, 2019. https://www.sport24.co.za/Tennis/USOpen /serenas-treatment-resonates-among-black-women-20180911.

Beavis, Catherine, and Claire Charles. 2007. "Would the 'Real' Girl Gamer Please Stand Up? Gender, LAN Cafés and the Reformulation of the 'Girl' Gamer." *Gender and Education* 19 (6): 691–705.

Bench, Shane W., Heather C. Lench, Jeffrey Liew, Kathi Miner, and Sarah A. Flores. 2015. "Gender Gaps in Overestimation of Math Performance." *Sex Roles* 72 (11–12): 536–546.

Bianchi, Suzanne M. 2000. "Maternal Employment and Time with Children: Dramatic Change or Surprising Continuity?" *Demography* 37 (4): 401–414.

Bianchi, Suzanne M., Liana C. Sayer, Melissa A. Milkie, and John P. Robinson. 2012. "Housework: Who Did, Does or Will Do It, and How Much Does It Matter?" *Social Forces* 91 (1): 55–63.

Billings, Andrew C., and Brody J. Ruihley. 2013a. *The Fantasy Sports Industry: Games within Games*. London: Routledge.

———. 2013b. "Why We Watch, Why We Play: The Relationship between Fantasy Sport and Fanship Motivations." *Mass Communication and Society* 16 (1): 5–25.

Blair-Loy, Mary. 2003. *Competing Devotions: Career and Family among Executive Women*. Cambridge, MA: Harvard University Press.

Blinde, Elaine M., and Diane E. Taub. 1992. "Women Athletes as Falsely Accused Deviants: Managing the Lesbian Stigma." *Sociological Quarterly* 33 (4): 521–534.

Bonesteel, Matt. 2017. "NFL Players Don't Care about Your Fantasy Football Teams, Just like Everyone Else." *Washington Post*, September 19. Accessed January 17, 2019. https://www.washingtonpost.com/news/early-lead/wp/2017/09/19/nfl-players-dont-care-about-your-fantasy-football-teams-just-like-everyone-else/?noredirect=on&utm_term=.a67959409f84.

Bourdieu, Pierre. 1977. "Cultural Reproduction and Social Reproduction." In *Power and Ideology in Education*, edited by Jerome Karabel and A. H. Halsey, 487–511. New York: Oxford University Press.

———. 1986. "The Forms of Capital." In *Handbook of Theory and Research for the Sociology of Education*, edited by John G. Richardson, 241–258. New York: Greenwood.

Bridges, Tristan, and C. J. Pascoe. 2014. "Hybrid Masculinities: New Directions in the Sociology of Men and Masculinities." *Sociology Compass* 8 (3): 246–258.

Briggs, Xavier de Souza. 1998. "Brown Kids in White Suburbs: Housing Mobility and the Many Faces of Social Capital." *Housing Policy Debate* 9:177–212.

Brooks, Scott N. 2008. "Fighting like a Basketball Player: Basketball as a Strategy against Social Disorganization." In *Against the Wall: Poor, Young, Black, and Male*, edited by Elijah Anderson, 147–164. Philadelphia: University of Pennsylvania Press.

Bui, Quoctrung, and Claire Cain Miller. 2015. "The Typical American Lives Only 18 Miles from Mom." *New York Times: The Upshot*, December 23. Accessed March 22, 2019. https://www.nytimes.com/interactive/2015/12/24/upshot/24up-family.html.

Burrill, Derek. 2008. *Die Tryin': Videogames, Masculinity, Culture*. New York: Peter Lang.

Burt, Martha R. 1980. "Cultural Myths and Supports for Rape." *Journal of Personality and Social Psychology* 38 (2): 217–230.

Butler, Judith. 1990. *Gender Trouble: Feminism and the Subversion of Identity*. New York: Routledge and Kegan Paul.

Camporesi, Silvia. 2017. "Who Is a Sportswoman?" *Aeon*, February 27. Accessed January 17, 2019. https://aeon.co/essays/sports-culture-binds-us-to-gender-binaries-this-is-unfair.

Carlson, Jennifer. 2010. "The Female Significant in All-Women's Amateur Roller Derby." *Sociology of Sport Journal* 27:428–440.

Challenger, Gray, and Christmas Inc. 2015. "Fantasy Football Sacks Productivity: Annual Distraction Could Cost Employers Nearly $16 Billion, but That's No Reason to Shut It Down." Accessed August 4, 2015. https://www.challengergray.com/download/file/fid/252/.

Cheryan, Sapna, Jessica Schwartz Cameron, Zach Katagiri, and Benoît Monin. 2015. "Manning Up Threatened Men Compensate by Disavowing Feminine Preferences and Embracing Masculine Attributes." *Social Psychology* 46:218–227.

Cialdini, Robert B., Richard J. Borden, Avril Thorne, Marcus Randall Walker, Stephen Freeman, and Lloyd Reynolds Sloan. 1976. "Basking in Reflected Glory: Three (Football) Studies." *Journal of Personality and Social Psychology* 34:366–375.

Collins, Patricia Hill. 2000. *Black Feminist Thought*. New York: Routledge.

Coltrane, Scott, and Melinda Messineo. 2000. "The Perpetuation of Subtle Prejudice: Race and Gender Imagery in 1990s Television Advertising." *Sex Roles* 42 (5–6): 363–389.

Connell, Raewyn W. 1987. *Gender and Power: Society, the Person and Sexual Politics.* Cambridge, UK: Polity.

———. 2009. *Gender: In World Perspective,* 2nd ed. Cambridge, UK: Polity.

Connell, Raewyn W., and James W. Messerschmidt. 2005. "Hegemonic Masculinity: Rethinking the Concept." *Gender & Society* 19 (6): 829–859.

Cooky, Cheryl, Ranissa Dycus, and Shari L. Dworkin. 2013. "'What Makes a Woman a Woman?' versus 'Our First Lady of Sport': A Comparative Analysis of the United States and the South African Media Coverage of Caster Semenya." *Journal of Sport and Social Issues* 37 (1): 31–56.

Cooky, Cheryl, Michael A. Messner, and Robin H. Hextrum. 2013. "Women Play Sport, but Not on TV: A Longitudinal Study of Televised News Media." *Communication & Sport* 1 (3): 203–230.

Cooky, Cheryl, Faye L. Wachs, Michael Messner, and Shari L. Dworkin. 2010. "It's Not about the Game: Don Imus, Race, Class, Gender and Sexuality in Contemporary Media." *Sociology of Sport Journal* 27:139–159.

Correll, Shelley J. 2001. "Gender and the Career Choice Process: The Role of Biased Self-Assessments." *American Journal of Sociology* 106:1691–1730.

Correll, Shelley J., Stephen Benard, and In Paik. 2007. "Getting a Job: Is There a Motherhood Penalty?" *American Journal of Sociology* 112 (5): 1297–1339.

Cote, Amanda C. 2017. "'I Can Defend Myself': Women's Strategies for Coping with Harassment while Gaming Online." *Games and Culture* 12 (2): 136–155.

Crawford, Garry. 2005. "Digital Gaming, Sport and Gender." *Leisure Studies* 24 (3): 259–270.

———. 2006. "The Cult of Champ Man: The Culture and Pleasures of Championship Manager/Football Manager Gamers." *Information, Communication and Society* 9 (4): 496–514.

Crawford, Garry, and Victoria Gosling. 2005. "Toys for Boys? Women's Marginalization and Participation as Digital Gamers." *Sociological Research Online* 10:1–16.

Crawley, Sara L., Lara J. Foley, and Constance L. Shehan. 2008. *Gendering Bodies.* Lanham, MD: Rowman & Littlefield.

Crenshaw, Kimberlé. 1989. "Demarginalizing the Intersection of Race and Sex: A Black Feminist Critique of Antidiscrimination Doctrine, Feminist Theory and Antiracist Politics." *University of Chicago Legal Forum* 1989 (1): 139–167.

Crocket, Hamish. 2013. "This Is *Men's* Ultimate: Recreating Multiple Masculinities in Elite Open Frisbee." *International Review for the Sociology of Sport* 48 (3): 318–333.

Davis, Nickolas W., and Margaret Carlisle Duncan. 2006. "Sports Knowledge Is Power Reinforcing Masculine Privilege through Fantasy Sport League Participation." *Journal of Sport and Social Issues* 30 (3): 244–264.

Dawson, Max. 2007. "Little Players, Big Shows: Format, Narration, and Style on Television's New Smaller Screens." *Convergence: The International Journal of Research into New Media Technologies* 13 (2): 231–250.

DelVecchio, Steve. 2011. "NFL Orders Teams to Show Fantasy Football Stats on Scoreboards at Stadiums." *Larry Brown Sports.* Accessed July 29, 2018. http://larrybrown sports.com/fantasy/nfl-orders-teams-to-show-fantasy-football-stats-on-scoreboards -at-stadiums/86105.

DeVault, Marjorie. 1991. *Feeding the Family: The Social Organization of Caring as Gendered Work.* Chicago: University of Chicago Press.

DiSalvo, Betsy. 2016. "Gaming Masculinity: Constructing Masculinity with Video Games." In *Diversifying Barbie and Mortal Kombat: Intersectional Perspectives and Inclusive Designs in Gaming*, edited by Yasmin B. Kafai, Brendesha M. Tynes, and Gabriela T. Richard, 105–117. Pittsburgh, PA: Carnegie Mellon ETC Press.

Domhoff, G. William. 2002. *Who Rules America? Power and Politics*. Boston: McGraw Hill.

Drayer, Joris, and Brendan Dwyer. 2013. "Perception of Fantasy Is Not Always the Reality: An Exploratory Examination into Blacks' Lack of Participation in Fantasy Sports." *International Journal of Sport Management* 14 (1): 81–102.

Drayer, Joris, Stephen L. Shapiro, Brendan Dwyer, Alan L. Morse, and Joel White. 2010. "The Effects of Fantasy Football Participation on NFL Consumption: A Qualitative Analysis." *Sport Management Review* 13:129–141.

Duggan, Maeve. 2015. "Gaming and Gamers." *Pew Research Center*. Accessed November 14, 2018. http://www.pewinternet.org/2015/12/15/gaming-and-gamers/.

Dunning, Eric. 1986. "Sport as a Male Preserve: Notes on the Social Sources of Masculine Identity and Its Transformations." *Theory, Culture, & Society* 3 (1): 79–90.

Dwyer, Brendan. 2011. "Divided Loyalty? An Analysis of Fantasy Football Involvement and Fan Loyalty to Individual National Football League (NFL) Teams." *Journal of Sport Management* 25 (5): 445–457.

———. 2013. "The Impact of Game Outcomes on Fantasy Football Participation and National Football League Media Consumption." *Sport Marketing Quarterly* 22 (1): 33–47.

Dwyer, Brendan, Rebecca M. Achen, and Joshua M. Lupinek. 2016. "Fantasy vs. Reality: Exploring the BIRGing and CORFing Behavior of Fantasy Football Participants." *Sport Marketing Quarterly* 25 (3): 152–165.

Dwyer, Brendan, and Carrie W. LeCrom. 2012. "Is Fantasy Trumping Reality? The Redefined National Football League Experience of Novice Fantasy Football Participants." *Journal of Contemporary Athletics* 7 (3): 120–139.

Dwyer, Brendan, Stephen L. Shapiro, and Joris Drayer. 2018. "Daily Fantasy Football and Self-Reported Problem Behavior in the United States." *Journal of Gambling Studies* 34 (3): 689–707.

Dwyer, Brendan, and James Weiner. 2017. "Daily Grind: A Comparison of Causality Orientations, Emotions, and Fantasy Sport Participation." *Journal of Gambling Studies* 33:1–20.

Eitzen, D. Stanley. 1996. "Ethical Dilemmas in American Sport: The Dark Side of Competition." *Vital Speeches of the Day* 62 (6): 182–185.

Elliott, James R., and Ryan A. Smith. 2004. "Race, Gender, and Workplace Power." *American Sociological Review* 69:365–386.

Engber, Daniel. 2017. "Does Fantasy Football Ruin Football Fandom?" *Slate*. Accessed January 17, 2019. https://slate.com/culture/2017/08/does-fantasy-football-ruin-football-fandom.html.

England, Paula. 2010. "The Gender Revolution: Uneven and Stalled." *Gender & Society* 24:149–166.

Entertainment Software Association (ESA). 2018. "Essential Facts about the Computer and Video Game Industry." Accessed November 13, 2018. http://www.theesa.com/about-esa/essential-facts-computer-video-game-industry/.

Esmonde, Katelyn, Cheryl Cooky, and David L. Andrews. 2015. "'It's Supposed to be about the Love of the Game, Not the Love of Aaron Rodgers' Eyes': Challenging the Exclusions of Women's Sports Fans." *Sociology of Sport Journal* 32:22–48.

Ezzell, Matthew B. 2009. "'Barbie Dolls' on the Pitch: Identity Work, Defensive Other-ing, and Inequality in Women's Rugby." *Social Problems* 56 (1): 111–131.

———. 2016. "Healthy for Whom?—Males, Men, and Masculinity: A Reflection on the Doing (and Study) of Dominance." In *Exploring Masculinities: Identity, Inequality, Continuity, and Change*, edited by C. J. Pascoe and Tristan Bridges, 188–197. New York: Oxford University Press.

Fantasy Sports Trade Association (FSTA). 2012. "Industry Demographics." Accessed October 18, 2012. https://fsta.org/industry_demographics.

———. 2015. "The Wide World of Fantasy Sports: Examining Trends in Participation, Spending, and Mobile." Presentation at the Fantasy Sports Trade Association (FSTA) Summer Conference, June 23, 2015 by Jason Allsopp, Ipsos Reid.

———. 2018. "Fantasy Sports Industry Releases First-Ever Study Highlighting Signifi-cant Crossover between Fantasy Sports Players and Sports Wagerers." Accessed July 27, 2018. https://fsta.org/press-release-fantasy-sports-industry-releases-first-ever-study-highlighting-significant-crossover-between-fantasy-sports-players-and-sports-wagerers/.

———. n.d.(a). Fantasy Sports Demographic Information." Accessed July 27, 2018. https://fsta.org/research/industry-demographics/.

———. n.d.(b). "Press Release: Fantasy Sports Now a $7 Billion Industry." Accessed July 27, 2018. https://fsta.org/press-release-fantasy-sports-now-a-7-billion-industry/.

———. n.d.(c). "Why Fantasy Sports Is Not Gambling: Understanding a Game of Skill." Accessed July 27, 2018. https://fsta.org/research/why-fantasy-sports-is-not-gambling/.

Fantz, Ashley. 2016. "Outrage over 6-Month Sentence for Brock Turner in Stanford Rape Case." *CNN*, June 6. Accessed August 11, 2018. https://www.cnn.com/2016/06/06/us/sexual-assault-brock-turner-stanford/index.html.

Farrell, Annemarie, Janet S. Fink, and Sarah Fields. 2011. "Women's Sport Spectator-ship: An Exploration of Men's Influence." *Journal of Sport Management* 25:190–201.

Festinger, Leon. 1957. *A Theory of Cognitive Dissonance*. Stanford: Stanford University Press.

Friedman, Hilary Levey. 2013. *Playing to Win: Raising Children in a Competitive Culture*. Berkeley: University of California Press.

Gantz, Walter, and Nicky Lewis. 2014. "Sports on Traditional and Newer Digital Media: Is There Really a Fight for Fans?" *Television & New Media* 15 (8): 760–768.

George, Molly. 2005. "Making Sense of Muscle: The Body Experiences of Collegiate Women Athletes." *Sociological Inquiry* 75 (3): 317–345.

Gerson, Kathleen. 2010. *The Unfinished Revolution: Coming of Age in a New Era of Gen-der, Work, and Family*. New York: Oxford University Press.

Glick, Peter, and Susan T. Fiske. 1996. "The Ambivalent Sexism Inventory: Differentiat-ing Hostile and Benevolent Sexism." *Journal of Personality and Social Psychology* 70:491–512.

Gottzén, Lucas, and Tamar Kremer-Sadlik. 2012. "Fatherhood and Youth Sports: A Balancing Act between Care and Expectations." *Gender & Society* 26 (4): 639–664.

Granovetter, Mark. 1973. "The Strength of Weak Ties." *American Journal of Sociology* 78 (6): 1360–1380.

Grant, Teddy. "Serena Williams and the Burdens of Being a Black Woman." *Ebony*. Accessed January 17, 2019. https://www.ebony.com/entertainment-culture/serena-williams-and-the-burdens-of-being-a-black-woman.

Gray, Kishonna L. 2012. "Intersecting Oppressions and Online Communities: Examining the Experiences of Women of Color in Xbox Live." *Information, Communication, & Society* 15 (3): 411–428.

Gray, Kishonna L., Bertan Buyukozturk, and Zachary G. Hill. 2017. "Blurring the Boundaries: Using Gamergate to Examine 'Real' and Symbolic Violence against Women in Contemporary Gaming Culture." *Sociology Compass* 11:1–8.

Green, Kyle, and Madison Van Oort. 2013. "'We Wear No Pants': Selling the Crisis of Masculinity in the 2010 Super Bowl Commercials." *Signs: Journal of Women in Culture and Society* 38 (31): 695–719.

Gregg, Melissa. 2011. *Work's Intimacy*. Malden, MA: Polity.

Halverson, Erica Rosenfeld, and Richard Halverson. 2008. "Fantasy Baseball: The Case for Competitive Fandom." *Games and Culture* 3 (3–4): 286–308.

Hargreaves, Jennifer. 1994. *Sporting Females: Critical Issues in the History and Sociology of Women's Sports*. London: Routledge.

Hays, Sharon. 1994. "Structure and Agency and the Sticky Problem of Culture." *Sociological Theory* 12 (1): 57–72.

Heywood, Leslie, and Shari L. Dworkin. 2003. "Bodies, Babes and the WNBA." In *Built to Win: The Female Athlete as Cultural Icon*, edited by Leslie Heywood and Shari L. Dworkin, 76–99. Minneapolis: University of Minnesota.

Hill, Stephanie Rene. 2010. "Using Critical Race Theory to Read Fantasy Football." PhD diss., University of Tennessee.

Hochschild, Arlie R., with Anne Machung. 1989. *The Second Shift: Working Parents and the Revolution at Home*. New York: Metropolitan.

Hofmann, Rich. 2012. "Our Fantasy Connection." *Philadelphia Daily News*. Accessed January 8, 2012. http://articles.philly.com/2012-10-26/sports/34730994_1_fantasy -eagles-foles.

Horvat, Erin McNamara, Elliot B. Weininger, and Annette Lareau. 2003. "From Social Ties to Social Capital: Class Differences in the Relations between Schools and Parent Networks." *American Educational Research Journal* 40 (2): 319–351.

Howie, Luke, and Perri Campbell. 2013. "Privileged Men and Masculinities: Gender and Fantasy Sports Leagues." In *Digital Media Sport: Technology, Power and Culture in the Network Society*, edited by Brett Hutchins and David Rowe, 235–238. New York: Routledge.

———. 2015. "Fantasy Sports: Socialization and Gender Relations." *Journal of Sport and Social Issues* 39 (1): 61–77.

Hyde, Janet Shibley. 2014. "Gender Similarities and Differences." *Annual Review of Psychology* 65:373–398.

Hynes, Deirdre, and Ann-Marie Cook. 2013. "Online Belongings: Female Fan Experiences in Online Soccer Forums." In *Digital Media Sport: Technology, Power and Culture in the Network Society*, edited by Brett Hutchins and David Rowe, 97–110. New York: Routledge.

Jacobs, Jerry A., and Kathleen Gerson. 2004. *The Time Divide: Work, Family, and Gender Inequality*. Cambridge, MA: Harvard University Press.

Jacobs, Melissa. 2017. "Do Not Draft: Fantasy Players to Avoid for a Family-Friendly Roster." *The Football Girl*. Accessed January 18, 2019. http://thefootballgirl.com/do -not-draft-joe-mixon/.

Jones, Jeffrey M. 2015. "As Industry Grows, Percentage of U.S. Sports Fans Steady." *Gallup*. Accessed January 18, 2019. http://www.gallup.com/poll/183689/industry-grows-percentage-sports-fans-steady.aspx?version=print.

Jones, Katharine W. 2008. "Female Fandom: Identity, Sexism, and Men's Professional Football in England." *Sociology of Sport Journal* 25:516–537.

Kanter, Rosabeth Moss. 1977a. *Men and Women of the Corporation*. New York: Basic Books.

———. 1977b. "Some Effects of Proportions on Group Life: Skewed Sex Ratios and Responses to Token Women." *American Journal of Sociology* 82 (5): 965–990.

Karg, Adam J., and Heath McDonald. 2011. "Fantasy Sport Participation as a Complement to Traditional Sport Consumption." *Sport Management Review* 14 (4): 327–346.

Kay, Tess. 2006. "Where's Dad? Fatherhood in Leisure Studies." *Leisure Studies* 25 (2): 133–152.

———. 2009. *Fathering through Sport and Leisure*. New York: Taylor and Francis.

Kelley, Bruce, and Carl Carchia. 2013. "Hey, Data Data—Swing!" *ESPN*. Accessed January 18, 2019. http://www.espn.com/espn/story/_/id/9469252/hidden-demographics-youth-sports-espn-magazine.

Kian, Edward, Alina Bernstein, and John McGuire. 2013. "A Major Boost for Gender Equality or More of the Same?" *Journal of Popular Television* 1 (1): 143–149.

Kian, Edward, John Vincent, and Michael Mondello. 2008. "Masculine Hegemonic Hoops: An Analysis of Media Coverage of March Madness." *Sociology of Sport Journal* 25:223–242.

Kim, Young-Choon, and Mooweon Rhee. 2010. "The Contingent Effect of Social Networks on Organizational Commitment: A Comparison of Instrumental and Expressive Ties in a Multinational High-Technology Company." *Sociological Perspectives* 53 (4): 479–502.

Kimmel, Michael S. 2005. *History of Men: Essays on the History of American and British Masculinities*. New York: State University of New York Press.

———. 2008. *Guyland: The Perilous World Where Boys Become Men*. New York: Harper.

———. 2014. "Toward a Sociology of the Superordinate." In *Privilege: A Reader*, 3rd ed., edited by Michael S. Kimmel and Abby L. Ferber, 1–12. Boulder: Westview.

Kirschenman, Joleen, and Kathryn M. Neckerman. 1991. "'We'd Love to Hire Them, But . . .': The Meaning of Race for Employers." In *The Urban Underclass*, edited by Christopher Jencks and Paul E. Peterson, 203–232. Washington, DC: Brookings Institution.

Kissane, Rebecca Joyce. 2018. "Researching Fantasy Sports Using Mixed and Multi-Methods." *SAGE Research Methods Cases*. doi: 10.4135/9781526446244.

Kissane, Rebecca Joyce, and Sarah Winslow. 2016a. "Bonding and Abandoning: Gender, Social Interaction, and Relationships in Fantasy Sports." *Social Currents* 3 (3): 256–272.

———. 2016b. "'You're Underestimating Me and You Shouldn't': Women's Agency in Fantasy Sports." *Gender & Society* 30 (5): 819–841.

Klugman, Matthew. 2012. "Gendered Pleasures, Power, Limits, and Suspicions: Exploring the Subjectivities of Female Supporters of Australian Rules Football." *Journal of Sport History* 39 (3): 415–429.

Kocurek, Carly A. 2015. *Coin-Operated Americans: Rebooting Boyhood at the Video Game Arcade*. Minneapolis: University of Minnesota Press.

Ladinsky, Jack. 1967. "Sources of Geographic Mobility among Professional Workers: A Multivariate Analysis." *Demography* 4:293–230.

Lapchick, Richard E. 2017. "The 2017 Racial and Gender Report Card: National Football League." *TIDES: The Institute for Diversity and Ethics in Sport*. Accessed October 18, 2018. https://www.tidesport.org/racial-gender-report-card.

Laurendeau, Jason, and Nancy Shahara. 2008. "Women Could Be Every Bit as Good as Men': Reproductive and Resistant Agency in Two 'Action' Sports." *Journal of Sport and Social Issues* 32 (1): 24–47.

Lee, Seunghwan, Won Jae Seo, and B. Christine Green. 2013. "Understanding Why People Play Fantasy Sport: Development of the Fantasy Sport Motivation Inventory (FanSMI)." *European Sport Management Quarterly* 13 (2): 166–199.

Lenhart, Amanda, Aaron Smith, Monica Anderson, Maeve Duggan and Andrew Perrin. 2015. "Teens, Technology and Friendships." *Pew Research Center*. Accessed November 23, 2018. http://www.pewinternet.org/2015/08/06/teens-technology-and-friendships/.

Leonard, David. 2003. "'Live in Your World, Play in Ours': Race, Video Games, and Consuming the Other." *Studies in Media & Information Literacy Education* 3 (4): 1–9.

Lin, Nan. 1999. "Building a Network Theory of Social Capital." *Connections* 22 (1): 28–51.

Lofgren, Krista. 2017. "2017 Video Game Trends and Statistics—Who's Playing What and Why?" *Big Fish*. Accessed November 23, 2018. https://www.bigfishgames.com/blog/2017-video-game-trends-and-statistics-whos-playing-what-and-why/.

Lorber, Judith. 1993. "Believing Is Seeing: Biology as Ideology." *Gender & Society* 7 (4): 568–581.

Luther, Jessica. 2016. *Unsportsmanlike Conduct: College Football and the Politics of Rape*. New York: Akashic Books.

MacLeod, Jay. 2009. *Ain't No Makin' It: Aspirations and Attainment in a Low-Income Neighborhood*, 3rd ed. Boulder: Westview.

Markovits, Andrei S., and Emily K. Albertson. 2012. *Sportista: Female Fandom in the United States*. Philadelphia: Temple University Press.

Marsden, Peter V. 1987. "Core Discussion Networks of Americans." *American Sociological Review* 52 (1): 122–131.

Martin, James S., Christian A. Vaccaro, D. Alex Heckert, and Robert Heasley. 2015. "Epic Glory and Manhood Acts in Fantasy Role-Playing: Dagorhir as a Case Study." *Journal of Men's Studies* 23 (3): 293–314.

Matos, Kenneth, and Ellen Galinsky. 2011. "Workplace Flexibility among Professional Employees." *Families and Work Institute*. Accessed August 4, 2016. http://familiesandwork.org/site/research/reports/WorkFlexAndProfessionals.pdf.

McDonagh, Eileen, and Laura Pappano. 2008. *Playing with the Boys: Why Separate Is Not Equal in Sports*. New York: Oxford University Press.

McIntosh, Peggy. 1988. "White Privilege and Male Privilege: A Personal Account of Coming to See Correspondences through Work in Women's Studies." Working paper, Center for Research on Women, Wellesley College.

McPherson, J. Miller, and Lynn Smith-Lovin. 1982. "Women and Weak Ties: Differences by Sex in the Size of Voluntary Organizations." *American Journal of Sociology* 87 (4): 883–904.

McPherson, J. Miller, Lynn Smith-Lovin, and Matthew E. Brashears. 2006. "Social Isolation in America: Changes in Core Discussion Networks over Two Decades." *American Sociological Review* 71 (3): 353–375.

Messerschmidt, James W. 2016. "Masculinities as Structured Action." In *Exploring Masculinities: Identity, Inequality, Continuity, and Change*, edited by C. J. Pascoe and Tristan Bridges, 207–219. New York: Oxford University Press.

Messner, Michael A. 1987. "The Meaning of Success: The Athletic Experience and the Development of Male Identity." In *The Making of Masculinities: The New Men's Studies*, edited by Harry Brod, 193–209. Boston: Allen and Unwin.

———. 1990a. "Boyhood, Organized Sports, and the Construction of Masculinities." *Journal of Contemporary Ethnography* 18 (4): 416–444.

———. 1990b. "When Bodies Are Weapons: Masculinity and Violence in Sport." *International Review for the Sociology of Sport* 25 (3): 203–220.

———. 2009. *It's All for the Kids: Gender, Families, and Youth Sports*. Berkeley: University of California Press.

———. 2014. "Becoming 100 Percent Straight." In *Privilege: A Reader*, edited by Michael S. Kimmel and Abby L. Ferber, 73–80. Boulder: Westview.

National Center for Women and Information Technology. n.d. "Women and Information Technology by the Numbers." Accessed January 4, 2018. https://www.ncwit .org/sites/default/files/resources/btn_04042018_web.pdf.

Nelson, Mariah Burton. 1994. *The Stronger Women Get, the More Men Love Football: Sexism and the American Culture of Sports*. New York: Harcourt Brace.

Oates, Thomas Patrick. 2009. "New Media and the Repackaging of NFL Fandom." *Sociology of Sport Journal* 26:31–49.

O'Brien, Rourke L. 2012. "Depleting Capital? Race, Wealth and Informal Financial Assistance." *Social Forces* 91 (2): 375–396.

Oldenburg, Ray. 1999. *The Great Good Place: Cafes, Coffee Shops, Community Centers, Beauty Parlors, General Stores, Bars, Hangouts, and How They Get You through the Day*. New York: Marlowe.

Olive, Rebecca, Louise McCuaig, and Murray G. Phillips. 2013. "Women's Recreational Surfing: A Patronising Experience." *Sport, Education and Society* 20 (2): 258–276.

Paaßen, Benjamin, Thekla Morgenroth, and Michelle Stratemeyer. 2017. "What Is a True Gamer? The Male Gamer Stereotype and the Marginalization of Women in Video Game Culture." *Sex Roles* 76:421–435.

Pascoe, C. J. 2003. "Multiple Masculinities? Teenage Boys Talk about Jocks and Gender." *American Behavioral Scientist* 46 (10): 1423–1438.

Pascoe, C. J., and Tristan Bridges. 2016. "Multiplying Masculinities: An Introduction." In *Exploring Masculinities: Identity, Inequality, Continuity, and Change*, edited by C. J. Pascoe and Tristan Bridges, 123–135. New York: Oxford University Press.

Perrin, Andrew. 2017. "10 Facts about Smartphones as the iPhone Turns 10." *Pew Research Center*. Accessed July 20, 2018. http://www.pewresearch.org/fact-tank/2017 /06/28/10-facts-about-smartphones/.

Pfister, Gertrud, Verena Lenneis, and Svenja Mintert. 2013. "Female Fans of Men's Football: A Case Study in Denmark." *Soccer & Society* 14 (6): 850–871.

Pope, Stacey. 2013. "'The Love of My Life': The Meaning and Importance of Sport for Female Fans." *Journal of Sport and Social Issues* 37 (2): 176–195.

Pope, Stacey, and John Williams. 2011. "Beyond Irrationality and the Ultras: Some Notes on Female English Rugby Union Fans and the 'Feminised' Sports Crowd." *Leisure Studies* 30 (3): 293–308.

Putnam, Robert D. 1995. "Bowling Alone: America's Declining Social Capital." *Journal of Democracy* 6 (1): 65–78.

———. 2000. *Bowling Alone: The Collapse and Revival of American Community*. New York: Simon and & Schuster.

Rainey, David W. 2012. "Sport's Official's Reports of Hearing Trash Talk and Their Responses to Trash Talk." *Journal of Sport Behavior* 35 (1): 78–93.

Rainey, David W., and Vincent Granito. 2010. "Normative Rules for Trash Talk among College Athletes: An Exploratory Study." *Journal of Sport Behavior* 33 (3): 276–294.

Ridgeway, Cecilia L. 2009. "Framed before We Know It: How Gender Shapes Social Relations." *Gender & Society* 23 (2): 145–160.

———. 2011. *Framed by Gender: How Gender Inequality Persists in the Modern World.* New York: Oxford University Press.

Ring, Jennifer. 2009. "America's Baseball Underground." *Journal of Sport and Social Issues* 33 (4): 373–389.

Risman, Barbara J. 2004. "Gender as a Social Structure: Theory Wrestling with Activism." *Gender & Society* 18 (4): 429–450.

Rosenthal, Carolyn J. 1985. "Kinkeeping in the Familial Division of Labor." *Journal of Marriage and Family* 47 (4): 965–974.

Rowe, David. 2014. "New Screen Action and Its Memories: The 'Live' Performance of Mediated Sport Fandom." *Television & New Media* 15 (8): 752–759.

Ruihley, Brody J., and Andrew C. Billings. 2013. "Infiltrating the Boys' Club: Motivations for Women's Fantasy Sport Participation." *International Review for the Sociology of Sport* 48 (4): 435–452.

Sage, George H., and D. Stanley Eitzen. 2015. "Is Sport a Mobility Escalator?" In *Sport in Contemporary Society: An Anthology*, 10th ed., edited by D. Stanley Eitzen, 188–198. New York: Oxford University Press.

Sapolsky, Robert M. 1997. "Testosterone Rules." *Discover.* Accessed January 17, 2019. http://discovermagazine.com/1997/mar/testosteronerule1077.

Sayer, Andrew. 2005. "Class, Moral Worth and Recognition." *Sociology* 39 (5): 947–963.

Sayer, Liana C. 2016. "Trends in Women's and Men's Time Use, 1965–2012: Back to the Future?" In *Gender and Couple Relationships*, edited by Susan M. McHale, Valerie King, Jennifer Van Hook, and Alan Booth, 43–78. New York: Springer.

Schafer, Markus H., and Nicholas Vargas. 2016. "The Dynamics of Social Support Inequality: Maintenance Gaps by Socioeconomic Status and Race?" *Social Forces* 94 (4): 1795–1822.

Schor, Juliet. 1991. *The Overworked American: The Unexpected Decline of Leisure.* New York: Basic Books.

Schrock, Douglas, and Michael Schwalbe. 2009. "Men, Masculinity, and Manhood Acts." *Annual Review of Sociology* 35:277–295.

Seidler, Victor J. 2003. *Rediscovering Masculinity: Reason, Language and Sexuality.* New York: Routledge.

Shapiro, Thomas M. 2005. *The Hidden Cost of Being African American.* Oxford: Oxford University Press.

Snyder, C. R., MaryAnn Lassegard, and Carol E. Ford 1986. "Distancing after Group Success and Failure: Basking in Reflected Glory and Cutting off Reflected Failure." *Journal of Personality and Social Psychology* 51:382–388.

Spyridakos, Basil. 2011. "Fantasy Football: 3 Ways It Has Ruined the NFL Experience." *Bleacher Report.* Accessed July 29, 2018. https://bleacherreport.com/articles/805138 -3-ways-fantasy-football-has-ruined-the-nfl-experience#slide0.

Stabile, Carol. 2006. *White Victims, Black Villains: Gender, Race, and Crime News in US Culture.* New York: Routledge.

Steele, Claude M., and Joshua Aronson. 1995. "Stereotype Threat and the Intellectual Test Performance of African Americans." *Journal of Personality and Social Psychology* 69 (5): 797–811.

Steinkuehler, Constance A., and Dmitri Williams. 2006. "Where Everybody Knows Your (Screen) Name: Online Games as 'Third Places.'" *Journal of Computer-Mediated Communication* 11:885–909.

Stone, Jeff, Aina Chalabaev, and C. Keith Harrison. 2012. "The Impact of Stereotype Threat on Performance in Sports." In *Stereotype Threat: Theory, Process, and Application*, edited by Michael Inzlicht and Toni Schmader, 217–230. New York: Oxford University Press.

Strohmeyer, Robert. 2014. "10 Tools for Stealthily Slacking Off at Work." *PCWorld.* Accessed August 1, 2019. https://www.pcworld.com/article/2158204/10-tools-for -stealthily-slacking-off-at-work.html.

Toffoletti, Kim. 2017. *Women Sport Fans: Identification, Participation, Representation.* London: Routledge.

Townsend, Nicholas W. 2002. *The Package Deal: Marriage, Work, and Fatherhood in Men's Lives.* Philadelphia: Temple University Press.

Tussey, Ethan. 2013. "Desktop Day Games: Workspace Media, Multitasking and the Digital Baseball Fan." In *Digital Media Sport: Technology, Power, and Culture in the Network Society*, edited by Brett Hutchins and David Rowe, 37–51. London: Routledge.

———. 2018. *The Procrastination Economy: The Big Business of Downtime.* New York: New York University Press.

Van Riper, Tom. 2011. "The Sports Women Watch." *Forbes*, September 30. Accessed February 23, 2017. http://www.forbes.com/sites/tomvanriper/2011/09/30/the-sports-women -watch/#76fdde106098.

Wachs, Faye Linda. 2005. "The Boundaries of Difference: Negotiating Gender in Recreational Sport." *Sociological Inquiry* 75 (4): 527–547.

Walker, Karen. 1994. "Women, Men, and Friendship: What They Say, What They Do." *Gender & Society* 8 (2): 246–265.

———. 1995. "'Always There for Me': Friendship Patterns and Expectations among Middle- and Working-Class Men and Women." *Sociological Forum* 10 (2): 273–296.

Warren, Mark R., J. Phillip Thompson, and Susan Saegert. 2001. "The Role of Social Capital in Combating Poverty." In *Social Capital and Poor Communities*, edited by Susan Saegert, J. Phillip Thompson, and Mark R. Warren, 1–30. New York: Russell Sage Foundation.

Weiner, James F., and Brendan Dwyer. 2017. "'A New Player in the Game': Examining Differences in Motives and Consumption between Traditional, Hybrid, and Daily Fantasy Sport Users." *Sport Marketing Quarterly* 26 (3): 140–152.

West, Candace, and Don Zimmerman. 1987. "Doing Gender." *Gender & Society* 1 (2): 125–151.

Williams, Christine L. 1992. "The Glass Escalator: Hidden Advantages for Men in the 'Female' Professions." *Social Problems* 39 (3): 253–267.

Williams, Joan C., and Rachel Dempsey. 2014. *What Works for Women at Work: Four Patterns Working Women Need to Know.* New York: New York University Press.

Wingfield, Adia Harvey. 2009. "Racializing the Glass Escalator: Reconsidering Men's Experiences with Women's Work." *Gender & Society* 23 (1): 5–26.

Yee, Nick. n.d. "Playing with Someone." *Daedalus Project*. Accessed January 18, 2018. http://www.nickyee.com/daedalus/archives/001468.php.

Yuksel, Mujde, Mark A. McDonald, George R. Milne, and Aron Darmody. 2017. "The Paradoxical Relationship between Fantasy Football and NFL Consumption: Conflict Development and Consumer Coping Mechanisms." *Sport Management Review* 20 (2): 198–210.

Index

Accessibility of fantasy sports, 54, 74–79; criticism of, 46; masculinity and, 74–79
Accomplishment, sense of, 15, 31, 32–36
Accomplishment of gender, 61, 74, 80–81
Achen, Rebecca, 24
Age: aging socioeconomic White men, 16; average age of players, 190; demographic characteristic of samples, 191tab.A.1; fantasy sports participation and, 119, 126; real sports participation and, 6, 74, 126, 137; sports media platforms and, 156; technological savvy and, 56; vicarious masculinity and, 10
Aggression: bonding and, 141, 159, 176; competition and, 158, 176; control and, 26, 158; familial bonding and, 140–141; gender and, 7; hegemonic masculinity and, 16, 21, 53; jock statsculinity and, 58, 159; masculinity and, 9, 53, 55; race and, 13, 26–27, 115; trash talking and, 62, 66, 76–77, 101, 105, 176, 178, 203n27; women and, 11–12, 91, 99, 100–101, 105, 109, 115
Albertson, Emily, 25–26, 80–81
Almog, Ran, 56
Andrews, David, 26
Athleticism: femininity and, 11; hegemonic masculinity and, 16, 53, 55, 75; jock statsculinity and, 53, 75; shifting, 52, 75

Attachments: impartial selection and, 38; as individualistic and personal, 37; to real-life players, 23, 35–36; to teams, 18, 35–36
Attention: overview, 20–23, 29, 48, 154; to fantasy sports, 161–162, 166, 175–176; investments in fantasy sports and, 160–167; loss of, 171; relationship tension for men in fantasy sports, 171–175, 181, 209nn52–53; to statistics, 94; to women participants, 100; women's demand for, 72, 81

Barmack, Erik, 71–72
Baseball Seminar, 2–3
Bask in reflected glory (BIRG), 24, 30–31, 34, 157, 158
Beavis, Catherine, 90
Benard, Stephen, 9
Bennett, Martellus, 49
Berry, Matthew, 47
Billings, Andrew, 12, 154, 198n11
BIRGing (basking in reflected glory), 24, 30–31, 34, 157, 158
Bonding: aggression and, 141, 159, 176; competition and, 207n31; cultural capital and, 141–146; familial bonding, 140–141; friendship and, 126, 128, 132,

Rebecca Joyce Kissane is an Associate Professor of Sociology at Lafayette College.

Sarah Winslow is Senior Associate Director of the Honors College, Director of the National Scholars Program, and Associate Professor of Sociology at Clemson University, and co-editor of *Gender in the Twenty-First Century: The Stalled Revolution and the Road to Equality.*